'The recent emphasis on police health and well-being is brought to a well thought out synopsis in this book. The book approaches this important topic from a holistic point of view to include not only the structural and societal impact of policing but also the human dimension. It is well worth reading for police practitioners as well as mental health professionals.'

John M. Violanti, *Research Professor of Epidemiology and Environmental Health, University at Buffalo School of Public Health and Health Professions*

'Setting aside the extraordinary content within, I am thoroughly impressed by the names of those who submitted their material for this book. You would be hard pressed to find a better example of having so many of the best of the best between two book covers.'

Sylvio (Syd) A. Gravel, *M.O.M., O.O.O., Staff Sergeant (ret'd)*

'*Wellbeing in Policing* is an essential read for those interested in the nexus between organisational psychology and operational policing. It neatly brigades views from across academia and practical policing contexts and makes a valuable contribution for those interested in the pursuit of evidence-based practice in this critical area of applied research.'

Nick Caveney, *Assistant Chief Constable Hertfordshire Constabulary, and Chair of the Open University Centre for Policing Research & Learning*

'*Wellbeing in Policing* offers a comprehensive and timely exploration of the psychological health challenges faced by police officers. With evidence-informed strategies and practical insights, this book is an essential resource for fostering resilience, reducing trauma, and advancing organisational wellness in policing.'

Katy Kamkar, *CPsych, Clinical Psychologist and Fellow, Global Law Enforcement and Public Health Association (GLEPHA)*

'The well-being of police officers has only recently appeared on the radar of administrators and executives. Fortunately, well-being is now vital to police management, so this splendid volume arrives at an ideal time. Ian Hesketh has compiled a well-structured volume of the key topics, authored by leading figures in the business. It will be an essential reference work.'

Jerry H. Ratcliffe, *Professor of Practice, University of Pennsylvania, and Scientific Advisor to the International Association of Chiefs of Police (IACP)*

WELLBEING IN POLICING

Health and wellbeing at work is now a strategic issue for police organisations not just in the UK but across the developed world. This book provides insight into the issues that police organisations need to consider within this strategy.

The purpose of this book is to collate current thinking from experts in the field of wellbeing in policing. In doing this, the book aims to be the go-to resource for all those involved with wellbeing in policing, whether they are studying this fascinating of professions, are considering embarking on a career in policing or both. This book reflects the burgeoning interest in wellbeing as a subject of study and brings together expert commentary, advice and guidance on all aspects that are known to impact policing. It contains the latest evidence of what works (politics and finance aside) and will provide readers with references to the very latest studies in the UK. Unlike other books in the field, this is written from multiple dimensions.

This is key reading for Professional Policing degree students, as well as all those engaged in professional wellbeing, police culture, management and leadership. It also serves aspiring police officers and current personnel seeking evidence-based strategies to improve organisational health and operational effectiveness.

Ian Hesketh is Honorary Research Fellow at Alliance Manchester Business School, University of Manchester, Honorary Fellow of Durham University Business School, Honorary Researcher at Lancaster University and Visiting Fellow at the Open University. He is Chartered Manager, Fellow of the Chartered Management Institute, Fellow of the Royal Society of Arts and a Member of the Society for Education and Training.

Routledge Advances in Police Practice and Knowledge

Series Editors
Dr Tom Cockcroft, Leeds Beckett University, UK, and Dr Martin Wright, Canterbury Centre for Policing Research, UK

Routledge Advances in Police Practice and Knowledge is a new series of books which brings together established academics and authors in the field of police studies to provide themed textbooks that will support students engaging with professional police studies within higher education. The focus of the series is to provide academically rigorous accounts of research and knowledge and to contextualise them in the practical and applied context of policework. In doing so, the books that make up the series will provide an invaluable resource to students studying policing through a variety of academic and vocational routes.

The Editors, Dr Tom Cockcroft and Dr Martin Wright dedicate this series to the memory of Professor PAJ (Tank) Waddington who believed policing to be an honourable profession, and whose career's work embodied the values that inform the direction of the series.

Policing Structures
Colin Rogers

Improving Intelligence Analysis in Policing
Stuart Kirby and Scott Keay

Criminology for the Police
Craig Paterson and Ed Pollock

Policing Domestic Abuse
Risk, Policy and Practice
Katy Barrow-Grint, Jacqueline Sebire, Jackie Turton and Ruth Weir

Policing Ethically
Clive Harfield and Allyson Macvean

Wellbeing in Policing
Edited by Ian Hesketh

WELLBEING IN POLICING

Edited by Ian Hesketh

Routledge
Taylor & Francis Group
LONDON AND NEW YORK

Designed cover image: Shutterstock

First published 2026
by Routledge
4 Park Square, Milton Park, Abingdon, Oxon OX14 4RN

and by Routledge
605 Third Avenue, New York, NY 10158

Routledge is an imprint of the Taylor & Francis Group, an informa business

British Library Cataloguing-in-Publication Data
A catalogue record for this book is available from the British Library

ISBN: 978-1-032-85586-8 (hbk)
ISBN: 978-1-032-85585-1 (pbk)
ISBN: 978-1-003-51886-0 (ebk)

DOI: 10.4324/9781003518860

Typeset in Sabon
by Deanta Global Publishing Services, Chennai, India

CONTENTS

FIGURES

TABLES

CONTRIBUTORS

Garry Bottrill served in the Royal Navy before becoming a Police Officer, serving for almost 30 years. He co-developed a Police mental health app called Backup Buddy, which is now used in many forces in the UK and internationally. Garry won a Churchill Fellowship and travelled extensively to research PTSD assistance dogs. He then set up Service Dogs UK, a successful assistance dog charity for veterans of the armed forces and emergency services with PTSD, gaining accreditation from Assistance Dogs International. He is a trustee and volunteer Operations Director for the charity he founded and a trustee for Assistance Dogs UK. He serves on the Access and Advocacy Panel of Assistance Dogs International (ADI) and hosts the Shelter/Rescue dog group within ADI. In 2022, he joined the National Police Wellbeing Service, where he initiated and leads nationally with the award-winning Oscar Kilo OK9 Wellbeing and Trauma Support Dogs.

Dave Brewster is a former Chief Inspector with the Metropolitan Police Service, with 30 years' operational and leadership experience across a broad spectrum of challenging policing environments. Dave has always maintained a strong focus on staff wellbeing and meaningful leadership, and in the latter part of his career was responsible for developing the national strategy to improve the response to officer and staff assaults for the College of Policing – National Police Wellbeing Service, known as Operation Hampshire.

Samantha K Brooks is a research psychologist with interests in trauma, the impact of disasters and emergencies on mental health, and mental health in the workplace.

Natalie Brown is a researcher at Durham University Business School (DUBS) and holds a Master's by Research degree in work psychology. In 2015, she joined the Policing Research Unit at DUBS and has since conducted over 50 collaborative research projects with local and international police forces on themes including leadership, motivation, wellbeing, workplace stressors and proactive behaviour. In 2019, she was awarded a Chief Constable's Certificate of Commendation for her contributions to policing.

Carol Cox is Head of the Liverpool Centre for Advanced Policing Studies at Liverpool John Moores University; an ex-police officer, she has worked in the field of policing and academia for over 31 years. Her research interests are police culture, police wellbeing and police education. She is passionate about the wellbeing of police officers and works closely with Oscar Kilo and police forces nationally to research innovative ideas that support the work environment for serving police personnel. She is also a trained person-centred/trauma counsellor.

Liam Scott Curran is Lecturer in Policing at The University of Huddersfield and Member of the Crime and Policing Research Centre. Dr Curran completed his PhD in 2023, exploring the organisational and operational stressors and their impacts on the wellbeing of Senior Investigating Officers. Liam's previously published works include research on understanding stress and wellbeing in undercover police officers and the impact of the COVID-19 pandemic on police officer and staff wellbeing. Dr Curran is currently researching the impact of a Police Education Framework for personal, social, health and economic (PSHE) education sessions in England.

Zoe Davenport is a trauma therapist who has worked in policing for nearly 15 years. With a background in working with VAWG agencies before joining the Metropolitan Police Service, she developed a national wellbeing programme for specialist roles, before moving to the College of Policing, where she leads on Psychological Risk. Zoe is currently undertaking a doctoral research programme looking at the impacts and protective factors of voluntary policing roles.

Liz Eades trained at St Bartholomew's Hospital, London (Barts) and has over 35 years of experience in occupational health in a variety of workplace settings including utility, retail and NHS. She was Head of Occupational Health Services at Surrey and Sussex Police until 2018. She is currently the OH Practice and Standards Programme Lead at NPWS (College of Policing) and Director of EGR Associates Ltd, an OH specialist consultancy.

Jenna Flanagan is a communications leader with over 18 years of experience across policing, government and the charity sector. She has developed strategic communications for UK-wide programmes, built nationally recognised brands, delivered major digital and multi-agency projects and managed high-profile media engagement at local, national and international levels. As founder of Honest Engagement, Jenna now helps organisations communicate with clarity, purpose and impact—particularly in high-pressure, people-centred sectors. She is a regular speaker at national conferences on strategic communication and public service engagement and is passionate about creating honest, human-centred communication that builds trust from the inside out.

Jim Foley is a retired Detective Superintendent from the Metropolitan Police, with over 30 years of service in policing. A nationally accredited PIP3 and PIP4 Senior Investigating Officer (SIO), he has extensive experience in all aspects of major crime investigation, with a particular specialism in public protection—specifically rape, child abuse and domestic abuse. During his tenure in the Met's rape and child abuse command, Dr Foley became increasingly aware of the apparent psychological toll such investigations were taking on officers. This prompted a deeper inquiry into the impact of trauma and led him to undertake a PhD exploring how officers cope with the demands of investigating sexual and child abuse in London. Dr Foley currently serves as a sessional lecturer at Canterbury Christ Church University and as Co-Editor of *The Police Journal: Theory, Practice and Principles*.

Neil Greenberg is a clinical and academic psychiatrist based at King's College London, UK, and is the current President of the Society of Occupational Medicine. He is a specialist in adult, occupational and forensic psychiatry.

Charlotte E Hall is a behavioural scientist at the UK Health Security Agency, with a focus on mental health in the workplace, emergency preparedness and the impact of disasters and emergencies on mental health.

John Harrison is National Police Chief Medical Officer for England and Wales based in the College of Policing. Between 2014 and 2021, he was Chief Medical Officer for Devon and Cornwall Police and strategic health and wellbeing lead for the Alliance with Dorset Police. He was Clinical Director of Organisational Health and Wellbeing at Imperial College Healthcare NHS Trust (2003–2014) and Senior Lecturer in Occupational Medicine/Consultant Occupational Physician at the University of Newcastle-Upon-Tyne (1990–2003). He has held positions as Director of NHS Plus, Advisor to the Health and Work team of the Department of Health and Head of the National School for Occupational Health of England and Wales. He is Associate Professor at Brunel University, London, England. in clinical organisational development. Previously, he was Academic Dean of the Faculty of Occupational Medicine, a board member of ICOH and a past Chairman of EASOM.

Ceri Jones is Chartered Psychologist, Director of Wellworks Ltd and the Police Leavers Partnership and Tutor on the Doctorate in Occupational Psychology at Birkbeck, University of London. With over 20 years of experience in applied psychology across academia, NHS and Policing, her research and practice focus on public sector careers, retirement, resettlement, leadership development and employee wellbeing. She has been lead or co-investigator on projects that have generated over £10 million in funding. Her work has been published widely and has informed national public sector policy and practice.

Sarah-Jane Lennie is Associate Professor at the Centre of Excellence for Equity in Uniformed Public Services and a social and organisational psychologist chartered through the British Psychological Society. She is Subject Matter Expert for the College of Policing on mental health and wellbeing in leadership, where over the last six years, she has delivered educational workshops to ranks up to and including senior command (Assistant Chief Constable) on wellbeing and leadership in policing. Her research focus is on mental health and wellbeing within organisations, focusing on policing and police families, but also wider emergency services and industries. Her research has led to policy change at a national and local level within the police service. Outside of academia, SJ is currently training to be a psychotherapist with the Prince's Trust.

Claire Long is currently contracted to the National Police Wellbeing Service at the College of Policing as the Families and Leavers lead. Claire is also the managing director of her own consultancy and has spent over 20 years working with the police, leading on several key wellbeing programmes. Claire knows first-hand the challenges the police face. She has been a close friend of Dr Hesketh for almost 15 years and together they developed and introduced the very first Police Wellbeing Toolkit, published by Police Mutual Foundation in 2014.

Jess Miller is a neuropsychologist and Principal Investigator at The University of Cambridge, Director of Cambridge Resilient Research Ltd, and Non-Executive Director of Surfwell and has worked with the police for 20 years. Jess also brings an understanding of the brain to other frontline services (such as the RNLI) and the military and continues to consult with The Royal Foundation of the Prince and Princess of Wales on supporting the Emergency Response Sector. She is also author of *The Policing Mind: Developing Trauma Resilience for a New Era* and the forthcoming book Mindful Soldier: Building Resilience to Overcome Life's Challenges.

Stuart Noble is a former senior police officer and now Director of the Police Leavers Partnership. During his policing career, he held a number of challenging and high-responsibility roles. However, it was as he approached retirement that he came to fully appreciate the personal and professional challenges faced by officers preparing to leave the service. Driven by a passion for helping officers and staff transition successfully, Stuart, together with Dr Ceri Jones, has developed and delivered a range of initiatives and programmes designed to provide the support, skills, and tools needed to leave policing with confidence and purpose. Working closely with key strategic stakeholders and staff associations, their work is increasingly recognised and applied as national best practice.

Tony Parnell, CPsychol, CSci, RAPPS, AFBPsS, is Chartered Psychologist (BPS) and HCPC-Registered Practitioner Psychologist specialising in Trauma and PTSD. He is also Registered Applied Psychology Practice Supervisor (RAPPS) with the BPS. Tony has worked for Lancashire Constabulary since December 2017 in his role as Force Psychologist and Clinical Lead for Psychological Services within the Occupational Health and Wellbeing department. He carries a clinical case load as well as being responsible for the strategic development and management of psychological services. Tony leads a team of 3 full-time and 2 part-time in-house psychological therapists and 25 part time external associate therapists, which offer individual and group therapy services for all officers and staff. He also offers psychological assessments, high-risk role support, critical incident psychological group support along with bespoke group psychoeducation inputs.

Andy Rhodes, QPM, OBE, is the former Chief Constable of Lancashire Police, and together with Dr Ian Hesketh, founded the National Police Wellbeing Service (NPWS), Oscar Kilo, in 2015. Oscar Kilo is now a government-funded service supporting over 200,000 police personnel, and Andy has recently been appointed as the Service Director.

Jason Roach is Professor of Psychology and Policing and Director of the Crime and Policing Research Centre at the University of Huddersfield. He is also Editor-in-Chief for the Police Journal, Visiting Professor at the Centre for Police Research and Learning, at the Open University and a member of numerous UK Home Office and UK College of Policing advisory groups relating to problem solving, crime prevention and investigative decision-making. To date, Jason has written/co-written five books, including *Self-Selection Policing*, with Professor Ken Pease OBE, and has published over 40 research papers and edited book chapters on a range of different crime and policing related topics including child homicide, criminal investigation, using the nudge approach to reducing crime, police and criminal decision-making and cold case investigation. His most recent book, *Practical Psychology for Policing*, was published in January 2023.

Gareth Stubbs is Assistant Professor of Policing and Security at Rabdan Academy, Abu Dhabi. A former Chief Inspector and trained hostage negotiator, his career spans frontline policing, leadership development and academic instruction across the UK and UAE. He holds a PhD in Policing from Canterbury Christ Church University, where his research explored the influence of social networks on police recruitment. Dr Stubbs is Honorary Research Fellow at Kingston University and has published widely on recruitment, positive action and predictive modelling in policing. He regularly speaks at international conferences and serves as a peer reviewer for leading criminology journals.

PC Lee Taylor is Police Constable with Lancashire Constabulary, serving as the Peer Support Lead for Oscar Kilo, the National Police Wellbeing Service. His policing career commenced in 2004 with Hampshire Constabulary, initially as Special Constable and subsequently as a full-time officer from 2007. Lee transferred to Lancashire Constabulary in 2015, continuing his service in Roads Policing and as a Family Liaison Officer. In 2016, PC Taylor contributed to the establishment of the "Wellbeing Buddies" peer support network within Lancashire Constabulary. Recognising its success, he was invited to join Oscar Kilo in early 2019, initially as a delivery officer, and subsequently assuming the role of Peer Support Lead. In this capacity, he has been instrumental in developing an internationally recognised, evidence-based peer support training program for UK policing. PC Taylor established a national peer support network for UK policing, providing comprehensive training to new peer supporters and coordinators, while also offering ongoing support and assistance.

Yvonne Taylor is a police inspector with over 29 years' service across two police forces and in a national role. She has had a varied career across many roles, including patrol, roads policing, neighbourhoods, staff officer, partnerships and custody policy and safety. With a particular interest in driver and performance impairment, along with overall employee wellbeing, Yvonne completed her doctorate entitled "Shift Workers, Fatigued Driving and the Impact on Road Safety – An Investigation Involving Police Service Employees" with the Institute for Transport Studies at the University of Leeds. In addition, she holds an MSc in Biomedical Engineering Science from the University of Dundee, and a Bachelor of Engineering in Energy Engineering from Napier University, Edinburgh.

Noreen Tehrani represents the British Psychological Society on the Crisis, Disaster and Trauma Standing Committee of the European Federation of Psychological Associations. Dr Tehrani has supported first responders and victims of a wide range of traumatic incidents, including child abuse, murders, rapes, fatal accidents and road crashes. She works with policing to help reduce the incidence of primary and secondary trauma in police officers and staff.

Dale Weston is a principal behavioural scientist at the UK Health Security Agency, with a focus on public health, emergency preparedness, risk communication and infectious disease response.

Emma Williams joined Anglia Ruskin University in 2024 after serving as Academic Director at the Open University. Her career includes roles at the Metropolitan Police, Ministry of Justice and Canterbury Christ Church University. She has led significant research on policing, particularly in investigating rape and officer wellbeing.

FOREWORD – A HEALTHY POLICE SERVICE

Health and wellbeing at work is now a strategic issue for many organisations in the public and private sectors, not just in the UK but across the developed world. In the UK last year, 52% of all long-term sickness absence was due to the common mental disorders of anxiety, depression and stress, with 2.9 million people off with long-term sickness. The cost to organisations is enormous, not only in terms of sickness absence but also in terms of talent retention and lost productive value. Policing is one of the most vulnerable sectors (and occupations) to stress and lack of mental wellbeing, with the cutbacks in manpower and the increasing demands by society on the police service; that is, the increasing challenges of security, social media, cyber-crime, political instability, new technology and many more.

This book provides a comprehensive view of the issues confronting policing in the 21st century and what "good looks like" in terms of health and wellbeing today and into the future. There are 19 chapters covering topics like psychological risk assessments, peer support, sleep and fatigue, the impact of police assaults, the police and their families, social support and many more topics important for dealing with the increasing demands on policing, based on hard evidence and the experience of leading academics and practitioners to ensure that policing into the future will effectively meet the challenges ahead to support the police, their health, wellbeing and their families. As Mark Twain once wrote: "if you always do what you always did, you'll always get what you always got"! We're in a new era of societal demands which requires new approaches to policing our society, to adapting new technologies, to recruit new and different talent and, most importantly, to "change with the times".

We need a healthy police service, which creates the right supportive culture of support, caring and embracing change. As John Ruskin wrote at the beginning of the Industrial Revolution in 1851: "In order that people may be happy in their work, these three things are needed: they must be fit for it, they must not do too much of it, and they must have a sense of success in it". This particularly applies to those who look after our wellbeing and sense of security in society, the police! This book is a must-read for those who want to support the "guardians of our safety".

Sir Cary Cooper, CBE, 50th Anniversary Professor of Organizational Psychology & Health at the ALLIANCE Manchester Business School, University of Manchester and Chair of the National Forum for Health and Wellbeing at Work

PREFACE

During my time studying wellbeing and bringing it into the policing realm, including the creation of the National Police Wellbeing Service (NPWS), I have been driven to document the many examples of great practice and the professionals who have nudged this subject on from obscurity to a mainline part of the policing sphere in just the last ten years. After studying under Professor Sir Cary Cooper, I was inspired to try to make life better for all involved in the policing effort as they wrestle with a quickly changing world, new challenges and a dynamic workplace. The purpose of this book is to collate current thinking from experts in the field of wellbeing in policing. In doing this, the book aims to be the go-to resource for all those involved with wellbeing in policing – whether they are studying this fascinating of professions, are considering embarking on a career in policing; or both. This book reflects the burgeoning interest in wellbeing as a subject of study and brings together expert commentary, advice and guidance on all aspects that are known to impact on policing. The book does not enter into the complexities of political and financial gymnastics, but as in many other areas of policing, wellbeing is exposed to these. However, this book does contain the latest evidence of what works (politics and finance aside) and will provide readers with references to the very latest studies in the UK. Unlike other books in the field, this is written from multiple dimensions: Experienced academics, very experienced police officers and police staff, and everyone in between who is related to wellbeing in policing. This gives readers an opportunity to explore police wellbeing from multiple perspectives. The style employed by each contributor has been largely left to them, to explain their viewpoints in their own professional style, making this a broad and fascinating view of police wellbeing. The common denominator is that all have worked with the National Police Wellbeing Service at the UK College of Policing, as a member of the core team, as a contributor to specialist areas, or as a subject matter expert working on discrete work packages. It is hoped these accounts provide valuable insight into the key elements of a police wellbeing programme and some essential cues on how to organise the areas – the very reason for this book.

Dr Ian Hesketh

ACKNOWLEDGEMENTS

I would first like to thank my dear friend, Professor Sir Cary Cooper, without whose wisdom and guidance it would simply not be possible to take on such a critical publication for policing. I am also extremely grateful to all who have contributed to this wonderful publication and for the hard work and dedication each of them has given to this field. Finally, to my wife Sara, and our dear Yasmin and George. Thanks once again for your patience and understanding.

ABBREVIATIONS

APP	Authorised Professional Practice
ASD	Acute stress disorder
DUBS	Durham University Business School
EAP	Employee assistance programme
EBP	Evidence-based practice
ESTIM	Emergency Service Trauma Intervention Meeting
FLO	Family liaison officer
FLR	Front line review (of UK policing)
HMICFRS	His Majesty's Inspectorate of Constabularies and Fire & Rescue Services
IOPC	Independent Office for Police Complaints
LOC	Locus of control
MBA	Master of Business Administration
MPS	Metropolitan Police Service
MSc	Master of Science
NPCC	National Police Chiefs' Council
NPWS	National Police Wellbeing Service
OBE	Order of the British Empire
OCAT	Online Child Abuse Teams
OK	Oscar Kilo (brand name for the NPWS)
ONS	Office for National Statistics
OSCE	Organisation for Security and Co-operation in Europe
PACE	Police and Criminal Evidence Act
PC	Police constable
PFEW	Police Federation of England and Wales
PhD	Doctor of Philosophy

PIP	Professionalising Investigations Programme
PRM	Psychological risk management
PTSD	Post-traumatic stress disorder
QPM	Queen's Police Medal
SIO	Senior investigating officer
SOIT	Sexual Offences Investigation Team
SRO	Senior responsible owner
STRICT	Stress- and trauma-informed care and treatment
TRiM	Trauma Incident Management
UN	United Nations
VAWG	Violence against women and girls
VPS	Victim personal statement

ABOUT THE EDITOR

Ian Hesketh is an Organisational Psychologist and is the former Senior Responsible Owner (SRO) for the National Police Wellbeing Service (NPWS) – Oscar Kilo (OK). Dr Hesketh was the co-founder (with the then Chief Constable Andy Rhodes, QPM, OBE and the National Police Chief Lead for Wellbeing) and began working towards a National Service almost ten years ago, to develop what is OK today. He also supports the National Forum for Health and Wellbeing at Manchester University. He holds a PhD in Management and Social Psychology and an MBA from Lancaster University and is a qualified teacher. His research interests are centred on Wellbeing, Resilience and Leadership and, most notably, he introduced the concept and phenomena of Leaveism to explain human behaviours associated with workplace workload and stress. This is now measured annually in the CIPD Health and Wellbeing at Work survey. Dr Hesketh has written and published over 50 peer-reviewed journal articles, numerous books and book chapters. He has been recognised with a Literati Award for outstanding paper by the *International Journal of Emergency Services* and as having penned one of the top five management articles by the Chartered Management Institute.

Prior to working for the College of Policing, he previously served as a police officer. He spent 30 years with Lancashire Constabulary. During his service, he was seconded to the UN Mission in Bosnia and Herzegovina, and the OSCE Mission in Kosovo. He also worked for the EU in Serbia on their accession programme. During his operational years, Ian worked in Response Policing as a Neighbourhood Policing Officer, Armed Response Vehicle Officer, Custody Officer, PACE Inspector and on the Mounted Branch.

Dr Hesketh is an Honorary Fellow of Durham University Business School, an Honorary Researcher at Lancaster University and a Visiting Fellow at the Open University. He is a Chartered Manager, a Fellow of the Chartered Management Institute, a Fellow of the Royal Society of Arts and a Member of the Society for Education and Training.

Dr Hesketh lives in the Northwest of England with his wife and has two children.

ABOUT THE EDITOR

INTRODUCTION

Dr Ian Hesketh

This book begins by looking at the most critical aspect of delivering wellbeing in policing: creating the evidence base. Although all who have contributed to this publication have done exactly that, the first chapter unpacks the underpinning of all that follows, largely providing the basis on which it was undertaken. The team at Durham University Business School, led by Professor Les Graham, have conducted over 100 surveys in UK policing. These have been used as a critical tool by all UK forces to inform their Wellbeing Strategy and monitor progress around the milestones they set. Some of these milestones were focused on discrete business areas, while some of them were at a force-wide level. Our work on the NPWS was focused on the national picture in the UK, and as you can read in Chapter 1, this work was vital to informing the other areas you will read about later in the book. Natalie Brown, an experienced policing researcher at Durham University Police Research Unit, provides the setting, outlining some of the key areas of concern and the validated scales used to unpack each of these areas in detail. Playfully described as 'the good, the bad and the ugly,' the narrative provides a compelling opening to this book.

The second chapter, written by the very experienced Dr Noreen Tehrani, explores the practicalities of operational police work from a psychological risk management perspective. This is the first chapter in the book that looks at the fascinating field of psychology. Moving the reader seamlessly into how they may use research in practice, this chapter provides expert instruction on risk, how to identify it and how to deal with it. Psychological risk is inevitable in a profession such as policing, or other emergency or trauma-related occupations, making this chapter the ideal source of reference. Dr Tehrani outlines the many high-risk roles that exist in policing and how they can be effectively looked after in an ever-challenging environment.

DOI: 10.4324/9781003518860-1

The third chapter is penned by an experienced operational police officer and offers a practical view on the role of peer support. A further style is added as the chapter moves away from academia, giving a practical account of how useful this can be on a day-to-day basis. PC Lee Taylor explains what it is, what it isn't and how to practically set up and deliver peer support in an operational policing environment, including what and what not to do. He draws on his considerable experience in helping UK forces successfully achieve this.

The fourth chapter returns to theoretical constructs. Written by two experienced academics, Professor Jason Roach and Dr Liam Scott Curran, who explore the subjects of resilience, control and wellbeing in policing. The duo begins with the observation that policing is amongst the most stressful of occupations, as Professor Roach often comments, *stating the bleedin' obvious*. This, as they concede, begins most narratives on police and wellbeing, in whatever format. Setting their discussions, they cite evidence from Professor Graham *et al.'s* survey findings outlined in Chapter 1. They draw on their vast experience of research within the investigator field to provide examples of the value of personal resilience and how it can impact positively on those in policing.

The fifth chapter is the first written by what has become popularised as a *pracademic*. Dr Yvonne Taylor is a very experienced police officer, a Chief Inspector with West Yorkshire police, who Dr Hesketh head hunted to carry out the research on sleep and fatigue for the National Police Wellbeing Service. Dr Taylor's PhD focused on this very area and as such provided the perfect recipe to form the evidence base to design some of the services available to our officers and staff in policing today. The 'behind the scenes' lesson here is to garner a network of like-minded experts in the field to collaborate and advise. Within this workstream, Dr Taylor coordinated research in UK universities as well as drawing on expertise in the US. Acknowledgements must go to Dr Lois James at Washington University for her devotion to the UK effort. Ably assisted by her equally talented husband, Dr Steve James, who has also dedicated numerous hours to our research in this field of study.

Chapter 6 is penned by the personification of a British police officer. The recently retired Dr Foley, now a dedicated academic, unpacks some of the main challenges of policing in the UK from a wellbeing perspective. This fascinating chapter provides years of senior leadership experience with a read across to literature to give a solid grounding for why mental health in policing is critical to success. Dr Foley exhibits in his submission a perfect example of a research study to provide solid evidence of the tenets that help officers and staff cope with the many challenges of policing, a blueprint for anyone studying this subject.

Chapter 7 provides a further angle, with a look at the role of dogs in policing, other than to assist with crime and public order. A well-renowned expert, Garry Bottrill, walks readers through the field of service dogs and their many uses within the wellbeing sphere. Garry has a lifetime of experience with service dogs, both in the armed forces and the emergency services. In the chapter, Garry explains how dogs can assist in the delivery of peer support and help with post-traumatic stress, and takes readers through the history of using dogs in this arena right up to the present use through the NPWS and OK9. Dr Hesketh and Garry Bottrill, then a police sergeant, set up (and named) OK9 in 2022. It has been a huge success, with now over 250 dogs (and handlers) nationwide.

Chapter 8 is written by another very experienced (recently retired) officer. Dave Brewster is the national expert on police assaults, now garnering and coordinating reports from all 43 forces in England and Wales. He is also the lead for the so-called Operation Hampshire that addresses the reporting and recording of police assaults nationwide. Dave is extremely dedicated and passionate about this unfortunate aspect of policing. In this chapter, readers will hear, from the horse's mouth, how assaults on police are recorded and investigated, using Operation Hampshire as the framework to describe the process and rationale. This chapter shines a light on pure operational practicalities. In policing, the Op Hampshire strategy has been adopted across the entire UK and has received significant support through key stakeholders (Police Federation/ National Police Chiefs Council/UNISON) as the industry standard. With this chapter, his key message is that it is essential for colleagues to feel valued as victims of assault and aggression. This, in many respects, means a change in culture to recognise that every assault, regardless of injury, has a potential impact. How employers manage that impact can have long-term effects on individuals, the wider workforce and beyond. The response promoted through Op Hampshire calls for authentic, supportive leadership and a recognition of the incredible work police do against a backdrop of the realities they face. Op Hampshire now features as a priority work stream within the Home Office Police Covenant, which continues to drive forward on a consultancy basis providing management training inputs and senior-level strategic development advice.

The following chapter is written by the chief medical officer for policing in the UK, Professor John Harrison. Prof Harrison is also a practicing medical doctor and academic. Chapter 9 explores student officer wellbeing and the introduction of the covenant, a hugely successful element the NPWS can be rightly proud of. Prof Harrison guides the readers through his work in developing these services, explaining how they benefit officers throughout the UK and guide occupational health services in their provisions. Prof Harrison discusses the vision for veteran-friendly GP services and how complex the health service system is to navigate to achieve this goal. Prof Harrison concludes the chapter with a discussion about the national health and wellbeing strategy for policing in the UK.

Staying with the theme of the policing covenant, Chapter 10 unpacks the family's perspective. Written by Claire Long, she leans on her decades of working with police to present the main themes and what they can bring to police and their families. The whole family is given consideration, from toddlers to retirees.

Chapter 11 stays with the theme of the Covenant. Written by Dr Ceri Jones and ex-Chief Superintendent Stuart Noble, the chapter unpacks the process of retiring from the Police Service and the support initiatives to smooth the transition. With record numbers leaving the service, this is a critical area for policing, especially when one considers that 50% of those who left were voluntary resignations. The chapter models research carried out by the authors and discusses some of the research that is useful for those leaving the service.

Chapter 12 is written by the very experienced Dr Jess Miller, who has worked with police almost all her life. She unpacks the science behind the policing brain and illustrates why police think and do and how they behave. Jess explains neuroscience, the policing brain and what can happen if issues go unchecked. This fascinating insight is certain to leave readers wanting to learn more about this aspect of wellbeing.

Following on, and in a similar vein, the National Police Wellbeing Service expert psychologist, Dr Zoe Davenport, explains the practical work undertaken by the police service in the UK to address issues associated with psychological safety. Echoing much of Dr Miller's research, we see how the evidence is used to create practical interventions that benefit those involved in policing. Both Chapters 12 and 13 give great insight into the world of police psychology.

Chapter 14 will take the readers into the realm of social support. Written by ex-UK Chief Inspector and renowned academic Dr Gareth Stubbs, this chapter explains the academic world of how police think and behave, and what the likely influences on these actions and behaviours are likely to be.

Chapter 15 is penned by Liz Eades, a veteran in the policing landscape and one of the most knowledgeable OH professionals in the UK. Liz takes readers through the OH landscape for policing, discussing what works and what could work in this impressive discussion about occupational health services.

Chapter 16 is written by a group of academics that have been engaged with Police Wellbeing from the very start. Upon request, they report on the state of affairs in current home working practice, a contemporary issue for most organisations as they wrestle with the post-pandemic world of work. They draw a line of pre- and post-COVID and explore how policing can adapt to home working as it moves forward. They discuss both police officers and police staff in this research and provide recommendations for future practice.

Chapter 17 explores the world of communications and engagement. In this fast-paced world, there is hardly a day goes by without mention of communications failures. Jenna Flanagan, an expert in the field, who has been with the National Police Wellbeing Service since conception, explores the many benefits of getting this right, both in reputational terms and ultimately for the wellbeing of all those who serve. This comprehensive account of the discipline is certain to give readers a valuable insight into how professional comms and engagement can lead to far better outcomes all round. Jenna uses a mixture of evidence and models her own case study in setting up what is now the Oscar Kilo brand and the daily management of it.

Chapter 18 looks at the future, in particular wearable technology. Written by the NPWS service Director, Andy Rhodes and Dr Carol Cox from Liverpool John Moores University, this chapter provides a fascinating and in-depth insight into data analytics and the use of tech to promote and monitor health and wellbeing in the police service. Covering areas such as sleep, fatigue, trust and confidence, they track the research to date in policing and not least their own substantial body of work.

The penultimate chapter is penned by Dr Tony Parnell, an experienced clinical governance lead. He outlines the services available to the UK police occupational health professionals, providing a brief overview and description of these provisions, including treatments and therapy. The chapter has outlined these psychological support systems and how they address specific psychological impacts and mental health issues. Dr Parnell stresses that when discussing support systems within UK policing, it is important to note that there is a significant difference in the support offered across the 43 Home

Office police forces in the UK. Further, these differences have a direct impact on the type and range of support systems that will be available within different forces in the UK.

The final chapter of this book provides a summary of the amount of work that has been garnered to inform the evidence base for what works in relation to police wellbeing. This 'as is' account, authored by Professor Emma Williams and Professor Sarah-Jane Lennie from Anglia Ruskin University, is a perfect way to conclude the book. In short, there is a lot more to do in terms of research and practical interventions. However, all contributors have undoubtedly shown that with hard work and expertise, policing is getting there and is often the 'go to' resource for other agencies and organisations when it comes to workplace health and wellbeing.

1

THE GOOD, THE BAD AND THE UGLY

Organisational Factors Impacting Wellbeing in Policing

Natalie Brown

Policing is a very demanding and stressful role in nature. Research findings consistently point to wellbeing as a major issue for many individuals across the policing workforce. The research evidence supports that police officers face high average levels of exposure to emotionally demanding situations when carrying out their work duties, such as dealing with violent criminals and responding to incidents of serious harm and trauma. While the work pressures and demands policing face are reported at high average levels, of note is that research highlights that the average levels of wellbeing have declined since the first National Police Wellbeing Survey was conducted in 2019. High levels of burnout and fatigue, anxiety symptoms, difficulty 'switching off' outside of working hours and disturbed sleep have been identified as contributing factors for declined wellbeing.

In this chapter, we draw upon research evidence in policing from studies conducted by the Policing Research Unit at Durham University to identify key factors that are found to have a positive or negative impact on individuals' wellbeing. This chapter will be discussed in four sections:

- **Section 1 – Introducing Wellbeing:** We start by defining wellbeing; following that, we address the importance of wellbeing, how wellbeing is measured and the key wellbeing trends observed in policing data.
- **Section 2 – The Good, the Bad and the Ugly: The Research Evidence:** In this section, we refer to the body of evidence from over 100 research studies conducted by Durham University's Policing Research Unit, in collaboration with local police forces and the National Police Wellbeing Service.
- **Section 3 – What Works:** Of particular interest to practitioners, we highlight wellbeing initiatives that have been deployed by several UK police forces and have shown positive results.
- **Section 4 – Concluding Comments:** In the final section, we summarise key concerns as shown in police wellbeing trend data and offer some concluding thoughts.

DOI: 10.4324/9781003518860-2

Section 1 – Introducing Wellbeing

What Is Wellbeing?

Wellbeing is a broad term comprising numerous factors and can be assessed using multiple lenses – for example, by considering an individual's life satisfaction, mental health, emotional energy, job satisfaction, positive emotions or physical health. These factors highlight higher levels of wellbeing, while lower wellbeing can be reviewed by assessing key factors including – but not limited to – burnout, fatigue, cognitive resource depletion and mental ill-health symptoms.

Having higher wellbeing may look like a person being able to respond to and action work tasks, engage in and have enthusiasm for work challenges or overcome demands with confidence. Conversely, lower wellbeing may result in a person feeling overwhelmed and overstretched as though work demands exceed their capacity to respond, feeling withdrawn from their job and organisation, feeling weary and exhausted or finding it difficult to meet the daily challenges of their job.

The Importance of Wellbeing

Research evidence highlighting the important role of wellbeing at work is not in short supply. In fact, it is well-established in the research literature that low levels of wellbeing are associated with negative consequences for both individuals and organisations. For example, prior studies have linked lower levels of wellbeing to key individual outcomes, such as increased anxiety and depression, lower fatigue and decreased self-esteem. Moreover, research studies have that found lower wellbeing is related to negative organisational outcomes including decreased organisational commitment, and higher turnover and absenteeism.

Research studies in policing have also found a link between lower wellbeing and negative organisational outcomes including reduced work engagement, decreased discretionary effort and higher turnover intentions. Across policing more broadly, it is consistently recognised that wellbeing is a major issue for many individuals in the policing workforce, and that police officer and police staff wellbeing should be regarded as a key priority.

His Majesty's Inspectorate of Constabularies and Fire & Rescue Services (HMICFRS) has identified the importance of police officer and police staff physical and mental wellbeing for the achievement of improved force-level efficiency and effectiveness – while acknowledging that only in relatively recent history have police leaders begun to take the subject of wellbeing seriously. Further work has identified the importance of prioritising the wellbeing of the policing workforce by acknowledging wellbeing as a fundamental ethical issue faced by organisations due to the impact it has on individuals, organisations and service delivery for the public.

Wellbeing Trends over Time from the National Police Wellbeing Surveys (2019–2023)

The National Police Wellbeing Survey was first conducted in 2019, and to date has had three subsequent iterations (2020–21, 2021–22, 2020–23). A key aim of the National

Police Wellbeing Survey research was to assess the state of wellbeing from the perspective of the policing workforce and to review change over time. The four iterations of the survey have facilitated trend data to be analysed, and the insights highlighted have provided a valuable, yet often concerning, view of the extent to which the wellbeing of the policing workforce has changed since 2019.

As can be seen in the graph below (Figure 1.1), police officer wellbeing saw an improvement in the pandemic period,[1] but the findings show a decline since 2020/21. Of particular note is that the 2023 survey sees the lowest average level reported in the four-year period for police officers. While a small decline is also reported for police staff, the trend is less pronounced. Police staff, on average, reported significantly higher levels of wellbeing than police officers.

Overview of Wellbeing by Police Officer Rank and Police Staff Grade

The demographic groupings measured in the 2023 National Police Wellbeing Survey facilitated more granular insights on which groups experience higher – or lower – average levels of wellbeing. The 2023 analysis identified that Constables and Sergeants reported the lowest average levels of wellbeing and job satisfaction and the highest levels of mental ill-health symptoms. While the police officer analysis showed a general improvement of wellbeing as rank increased, interestingly, analysis investigating the differences between the police staff grade groupings showed that middle managers and above reported the lowest average levels of wellbeing and job satisfaction and the highest levels of mental ill-health symptoms.

Overview of Wellbeing by Police Officer and Police Staff Tenure in Policing

Analysis of the police officer sample revealed that average levels of wellbeing declined during the first 5 years of service from a moderate level (for less than 1 year of service) to a low level (for 3–5 years of service). Average scores for wellbeing then steadily increase to a moderately low level for the remaining police officer tenure groupings. Within the

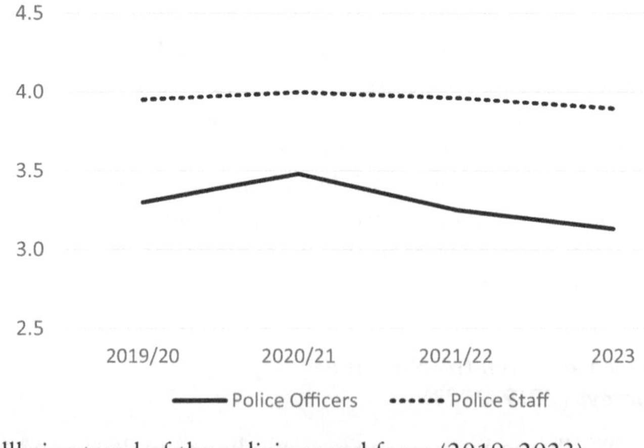

FIGURE 1.1 Wellbeing trend of the policing workforce (2019–2023).
Source: Graham, Brown and Plater (2023).

police staff analysis, average scores of wellbeing were reported at a moderately high level for those with less than one year of service, followed by a decline to a moderate level for those with 11–20 years of service. A slight increase is then observed for the remaining police staff tenure grouping.

Section 2 – The Good, the Bad and the Ugly: The Research Evidence

Now that we've set the wellbeing scene and illustrated its importance, we turn to the body of evidence conducted and collated by Durham University's Policing Research Unit from over 10 years of research in collaboration with police forces and the National Police Wellbeing Service. The body of research evidence comprises over 100 policing studies at local and national levels and provides an overview of organisational factors that are associated with enhanced or reduced wellbeing. Let's start with the positives:

The Good: Factors Positively Impacting Wellbeing in Policing

This section explores various organisational factors that have been found to be positively associated with wellbeing in policing. The identified organisational factors have been grouped into several core themes, including *organisational tone*, *supervisory leadership*, *team support*, *psychological needs*, *social impact* and *recovery experiences.*

Organisational Tone and Wellbeing

Perceived Organisational Support

Perceived organisational support refers to individuals' beliefs regarding the degree to which the organisation values their contributions and cares about their wellbeing. Organisational support is associated with a feeling of assurance that the organisation will provide support when individuals face particularly difficult or challenging circumstances when carrying out their duties. When individuals perceive their organisation as being supportive, their socioemotional needs of respect, being cared for and receiving approval are met. The research findings from Durham University's Policing Research Unit highlight that when individuals feel supported by their force, this is related to higher levels of job satisfaction and wellbeing. A further research study in policing indicates that perceptions of organisational support are linked to higher physical wellbeing and life satisfaction.

Organisational Procedural Fairness

Organisational procedural fairness concerns the extent to which individuals perceive the processes used to determine the distribution of outcomes among individuals at work as fair. Organisational procedures are considered fair when the following six rules are adhered to: *consistently applied, free from bias, based on accurate information, ethical, correctable* and *show consideration towards those impacted by the outcome of the decision.* It is established in the academic literature that fairness communicates whether the other party values an individual and will deliver on their obligations. The research findings in policing suggest that procedural fairness is associated with higher job satisfaction, life satisfaction, work engagement and wellbeing. Furthermore, additional analysis indicates that procedural fairness plays a key role in determining individuals' wellbeing through a process of increasing perceptions of organisational support.

Supervisory Leadership and Wellbeing

Supportive Leadership from Supervisor

Supportive leadership – also known as servant leadership in the academic literature – stresses the importance of personal integrity and serving others such as employees and communities. It focuses on the development of people to their fullest potential through an understanding of each person's different characteristics, strengths and interests. Supportive leaders serve as role models, build trust and provide feedback and resources to their people. It is argued that supportive leadership combats negative outcomes associated with the promotion of self-interest which underlies many incidents of unethical behaviour.

Research in policing indicates that supportive leadership has a positive impact on individuals' job satisfaction, wellbeing, optimism and life satisfaction. Furthermore, studies in policing have found that cognitive resource depletion – *the feeling of having insufficient levels of the cognitive resources required for self-regulation* – is reported as lower when supportive leadership is reported as higher. To add to this body of evidence, policing research studies delve deeper still by examining the pathways through which supportive leadership leads to increased wellbeing. The findings highlight that there are multiple pathways that operate; they include increasing subordinates' role clarity and access to resources required to complete work tasks. Moreover, additional analysis indicates that supportive leadership plays a key role in impacting subordinates' wellbeing through a process of reducing the barriers and frustrations they face in their role, and by fulfilling individuals' psychological needs of autonomy (*not feeling pressurised*), competence (*feeling skilful*) and relatedness (*feeling belongingness*).

Inclusive Leadership from Supervisor

Inclusive leaders appreciate, respect and value the differences between individuals in their team by creating a non-threatening environment in which people can reveal their 'true' selves without suffering adverse consequences and by encouraging team members to resolve misunderstandings or personal conflicts that occur at work. The research findings in policing indicate that inclusive leadership from the supervisor is linked to higher wellbeing and improved job satisfaction of the subordinate. Further analysis highlights that inclusive leadership is related to a higher sense of belonging and increased authenticity at work.

Felt Trust from Supervisor

Feeling trusted can be thought of as a 'vote of confidence' by a leader in their people. Feeling trusted focuses on the willingness of the supervisor to take responsibility and accept vulnerability for their subordinates' actions. Feeling trusted acts to increase the person's confidence in their own abilities, improve their sense of being valued, boost motivation to complete difficult tasks and enhance performance. The research findings in policing show that when individuals feel trusted by their supervisor, their wellbeing is reported as higher.

Team Support and Wellbeing

Team Cohesion

Team cohesion refers to the togetherness team members perceive that their team has, in terms of positive working relationships between members and how close-knit the group feels. Cohesion can be influenced by both task-related and social aspects of working in a team and has been found to relate to feelings of pride and levels of team performance. High team cohesion can also act as an important element of social support which helps to maintain wellbeing when facing difficult situations. Research studies in policing suggest that when higher team cohesion among team members is perceived, individuals working within the team are more likely to experience higher job satisfaction and increased wellbeing.

Team Inclusion

Team inclusion is the way in which people at work enable those in their teams to feel valued, treated as equals, have a sense of belonging whilst being able to be their authentic selves, feel respected, have a voice and fully contribute. Evidence from policing research indicates that team inclusion is associated with higher job satisfaction, life satisfaction and wellbeing and lower intention to quit.

Social Support from Co-Workers

Social support refers to the extent to which individuals believe their co-workers are caring, friendly, competent at their jobs and helpful in getting the job done. In prior research more broadly, the perceived quality of workplace social support has been identified as an important factor that is related to a variety of work outcomes, including lower burnout and increased job satisfaction. Research evidence in policing shows that social support from co-workers is positively related to wellbeing and job satisfaction.

Psychological Needs of Autonomy, Competence and Relatedness and Wellbeing

Research has suggested that people have three universal psychological needs such as autonomy, competence and relatedness, which need to be satisfied to maintain optimal performance and wellbeing:

1. *Sense of Autonomy at Work* – Autonomy relates to an individual feeling a sense of choice in their actions at work and being able to act in accordance with their core values and personal beliefs without feeling pressurised.

2. *Sense of Competence at Work* – Competence relates to an individual's feelings of being skilful, capable, effective and able to contribute.
3. *Sense of Relatedness at Work* – Relatedness refers to the degree to which an individual feels a sense of belonging and part of a team where they feel respected and valued.

The research evidence in policing suggests that feeling a sense of autonomy, competence and relatedness at work is positively related to wellbeing, job satisfaction, life satisfaction and physical wellbeing. To add to this, a further study found that when the psychological needs of autonomy, competence and relatedness are fulfilled, fatigue was reported as lower. Of note is that research outside of policing has identified that when the three needs are frustrated, this results in individuals becoming defensive or passive and negatively impacts wellbeing.

Social Impact and Wellbeing

Public Service Motivation

Public service motivation is considered a core attribute of those working in public service roles that provides them with a desire to have a positive impact on the local community through their work. The four components of public service motivation are: *self-sacrifice*, *attraction to public policy making*, *commitment to public interest* and *compassion*. Research findings in policing indicate that public service motivation is positively associated with wellbeing, job satisfaction and life satisfaction. However, it is important to acknowledge that the research evidence suggests that a high level of public service motivation can lead police officers and police staff to make very high investments of their personal time (such as taking work home, working longer hours, working while on holiday) and have difficulty engaging in recovery experiences outside of work time – both of which can be costly for wellbeing.

Social Impact

Social impact relates to whether individuals feel that their work has a positive impact on the community and makes a positive difference in society. In policing data, perceived social impact is found to be positively related to wellbeing. Additional studies in policing indicate that when individuals feel more strongly that their work has a positive impact on society, this is associated with higher job satisfaction and life satisfaction.

Feeling Appreciated by the Public

Felt appreciation can be considered as an external validation of a person's contributions that involves acknowledgement of their value, conveys positive regard and confidence in their efforts. A recent policing study measured the extent to which individuals felt their work efforts and the challenges they face in their role were valued and appreciated by the public they serve. The research findings suggested that felt appreciation from the public was associated with increased wellbeing through a process of fulfilling individuals' psychological needs of autonomy and relatedness. Moreover, the research evidence supports that felt appreciation from the public is associated with increased job satisfaction, and that this relationship is found to occur through fulfilment of the psychological need of relatedness.

Feeling Valued by the Public

Feeling valued by the public can be considered as the extent to which individuals perceive that the public recognises the relative worth and importance of policing. The research evidence indicates that feeling valued by the public is associated with higher job satisfaction, life satisfaction and wellbeing and lower fatigue. Further analysis identifies that feeling valued by the public is found to be positively related to job satisfaction through increasing the extent to which individuals view their police role as an important part of who they are.

Recovery Experiences and Wellbeing

Disturbed Sleep

Disturbed sleep refers to the extent to which individuals have trouble getting to sleep, have restless sleep, wake during sleep time and find it difficult to get back to sleep and wake up earlier than expected. The importance of sleep for restorative daily functioning is well recognised. A lack of good sleep quality can have serious impacts on individuals' long-term health issues, performance, risk of workplace injury, bias and reactivity to emotional stimuli and an inability to effectively lead others. Research studies in policing suggest that experiencing high workload and high levels of hindrance stressors (*bureaucratic barriers to completing work tasks*) were associated with higher disturbed sleep. In addition, a policing study found that when disturbed sleep was reported as higher, wellbeing was lower. To support this finding, a further study found that disturbed sleep was related to lower wellbeing and increased incivility towards the public.

Psychological Detachment from Work

Psychological detachment from work refers to an individual's state of mind when they are not working, and their ability to distance themselves from job-related issues, problems or opportunities (such as receiving job-related phone calls at home). It demonstrates an individual's ability to switch off and distance themselves from their job, not only physically but also mentally. In policing studies, psychological detachment from work is found to be related to higher wellbeing and lower disturbed sleep. In addition, the research findings indicate that when individuals engage in psychological detachment from work, the negative impact of work intensity on wellbeing is reduced (Table 1.1).

TABLE 1.1 Summary of the 'good' organisational factors

'Good' organisational factors	*Key outcomes*
Perceived Organisational Support	• Higher job satisfaction and wellbeing • Higher physical wellbeing and life satisfaction
Organisational Procedural Fairness	• Higher job satisfaction, life satisfaction, work engagement and wellbeing • Higher perceived organisational support
Supportive Leadership from Supervisor	• Higher job satisfaction, wellbeing, optimism and life satisfaction • Lower cognitive resource depletion • Higher wellbeing by increasing role clarity, access to resources and reducing hindrance stressors • Fulfilment of psychological needs of autonomy, competence and relatedness
Inclusive Leadership from Supervisor	• Higher wellbeing and job satisfaction • Higher sense of belonging and authenticity at work for team members
Felt Trust from Supervisor	• Higher wellbeing
Team Cohesion	• Higher job satisfac tion and wellbeing
Social Support from Co-Workers	• Higher wellbeing • Higher mental wellbeing and job satisfaction
Psychological Needs (Autonomy, Competence and Relatedness)	• Higher wellbeing, job satisfaction, life satisfaction and physical wellbeing • Lower fatigue
Public Service Motivation*	• Higher job satisfaction and life satisfaction
Social Impact	• Higher wellbeing • Higher job satisfaction and life satisfaction
Feeling Appreciated by the Public	• Higher wellbeing through fulfilment of psychological needs of autonomy and relatedness • Higher job satisfaction through fulfilment of the psychological need of relatedness
Feeling Valued by the Public	• Higher job satisfaction, life satisfaction and wellbeing • Lower fatigue
Disturbed Sleep	• Lower wellbeing • Higher incivility towards the public
Psychological Detachment from Work	• Higher wellbeing • Lower disturbed sleep

*Please see the main text above for the research evidence showing the negative outcomes associated with public service motivation.

The *Bad*: Factors Negatively Impacting Wellbeing

Workplace demands can be faced across all levels in organisations. There are no roles or tenure groupings that are exempt or able to sidestep these pressures. While experiencing a manageable level of pressure can motivate and mobilise positive effort at work, what is commonly observed is that workplace demands can accumulate, outweigh internal and external resources, and become difficult to overcome. This section examines key workplace demands that have a negative relationship with wellbeing in policing. The factors include *hindrance stressors*, *challenge stressors*, *emotional demands*, *work intensity* and *felt uncertainty at work*.

Workplace Demands and Wellbeing

Hindrance Stressors

Hindrance stressors refer to work-related demands that are constraining in nature. They act as barriers to individuals doing their jobs well and obstruct valued goals and achievements at work. Examples of hindrance stressors include red tape, poor systems and workplace politics. In multiple studies in policing, hindrance stressors are found to be negatively related to individual wellbeing. Notably, experiencing hindrance stressors at work is found to be associated with lower wellbeing through a process of increasing disturbed sleep. Moreover, in another study, hindrance stressors were found to be related to lower wellbeing through a mechanism of individuals experiencing higher anger and frustration.

Additional studies in policing have identified that the negative relationship between hindrance stressors and wellbeing occurs through increasing the extent to which individuals ruminate about work-related issues and by reducing the extent to which individuals feel supported by their force. Hindrance stressors are also found to be negatively related to job satisfaction, work engagement and mental wellbeing (particularly when challenge stressors are perceived at a higher level).

Challenge Stressors

Challenge stressors reflect people's perceptions of work-related demands. For example, workload, time pressures and levels of responsibility. People who experience challenge stressors, although they may find them a strain, may view them as an opportunity for the achievement of important outcomes or personal development. The research findings in policing support this and suggest that while challenge stressors can deplete wellbeing (of note is that the strength of this effect is significantly lower for challenge stressors than for hindrance stressors), challenge stressors are also linked to higher motivation, work engagement and preparedness to engage in discretionary effort. Furthermore, a study in policing found that challenge stressors, while positive for work engagement, deplete wellbeing. However, if individuals are able to switch off during non-work hours, this impact is greatly reduced. Of particular note is that additional analysis has identified that while challenge stressors can have positive effects on individuals, such as through increased work engagement and discretionary effort, what the data also suggests is that when challenge stressors are faced at a consistently very high level, this can have a detrimental impact on wellbeing.

Emotional Demands

Emotional demands are also considered a form of work-related demand. High levels can be viewed as the extent to which individuals experience high exposure to emotionally demanding work tasks and experiences in their role, such as facing emotionally impactful or distressing situations or interacting with difficult people. While overcoming such situations and/or helping people through challenging circumstances can be a rewarding and meaningful part of work, dealing with such emotional demands requires sustained emotional effort to self-regulate and depletes personal resources in the process. Interestingly, a study of police officers found that their level of wellbeing was most negatively impacted by emotional demands when compared to hindrance stressors and challenge stressors. Moreover, for police staff, the findings showed that their level of wellbeing was negatively impacted by emotional demands and hindrance stressors, but no impact was found for challenge stressors. Further analysis highlighted that emotional demands and hindrance stressors showed the largest negative association with job satisfaction.

Work Intensity

Work intensity describes the extent to which individuals feel that there are too many responsibilities or activities expected of them considering the time available, their abilities and other constraints. Research studies in policing have found that work intensity is associated with lower wellbeing directly, and indirectly through pathways of higher work–family conflict and lower psychological detachment from work.

Felt Uncertainty at Work

Felt uncertainty at work refers to how unsettled and uncertain individuals feel about work in general, and the level of uncertainty they perceive exists in their workplace. Research in policing has found that felt uncertainty at work is negatively related to individuals' wellbeing. Of note is that felt uncertainty at work is linked to higher cognitive resource depletion (Table 1.2).

The *Ugly*: Factors Negatively Impacting Wellbeing

A concerning part of organisational life which often is not addressed or minimised is that of social injustice in the workplace. Social injustice comprises multiple aspects of mistreatment at work. Put simply, it arises when treatment towards others violates respect and dignity. Those responsible for social injustice in the workplace can include co-workers and supervisors. The research investigating social injustice in the workplace highlights its concerning level of occurrence and the harm it causes.

Workplace Social Injustice and Wellbeing

Workplace Incivility from Co-Workers

Workplace incivility can be thought of as a generalised form of low-intensity, subtle, harmful behaviour directed towards others, which can be verbal (being rude or disrespectful) or non-verbal (excluding or ignoring someone). Research in policing identifies that experiencing workplace incivility from co-workers is related to negative outcomes

TABLE 1.2 Summary of the 'bad' organisational factors

'Bad' organisational factors	*Key outcomes*
Hindrance Stressors	• Lower wellbeing through increased disturbed sleep • Lower wellbeing through increased anger and frustration • Lower job satisfaction, work engagement and mental wellbeing
Challenge Stressors*	• Lower wellbeing
Emotional Demands	• Lower wellbeing • Lower job satisfaction
Work Intensity	• Lower wellbeing directly, and indirectly through increased work–family conflict and reduced psychological detachment from work
Felt Uncertainty at Work	• Lower wellbeing • Higher cognitive resource depletion

*Please see the main text above for the research evidence showing the negative outcomes associated with public service motivation.

for individuals and organisations, including lower levels of job satisfaction and wellbeing, and higher intention to quit. One mechanism through which these relationships were found to occur was through violating individuals' psychological needs (*autonomy, reduced sense of competence,* and *relatedness*). Furthermore, experiencing workplace incivility from co-workers is linked to lower life satisfaction and increased levels of fatigue and disturbed sleep. Additional research findings suggest that a further cost of experiencing incivility from co-workers is a reduction in mental wellbeing and a lower sense of belonging.

Workplace Harassment (Interpersonal Mistreatment) from Co-Workers

The National Policing Diversity, Equality and Inclusion Survey conducted in 2019 highlighted that workplace harassment can be thought of as a form of interpersonal mistreatment from a co-worker based on an individual's personal protected characteristic which is perceived as derogatory and demeaning. The national research findings indicate that experiencing harassment at work from co-workers is negatively associated with wellbeing, job satisfaction and life satisfaction. A further policing study in 2019 found experiencing harassment in the workplace from a co-worker was again related to frustration of psychological needs (*autonomy, reduced sense of competence,* and *relatedness*), and in turn lower wellbeing.

Team Incivility Norms

Team incivility norms reflect the extent to which uncivil interpersonal behaviours are normalised within work teams. Examples of uncivil interpersonal behaviours include team members humiliating and shaming each other, making jokes at each other's expense, gossiping and being rude and disrespectful to team members. A team with high incivility norms typically allows these uncivil behaviours to be demonstrated without sanction or repercussions. Of note is that, similar to the research findings for other social injustice measures, team incivility norms are found to be related to lower wellbeing through a process of frustrating individuals' psychological needs (*autonomy, reducing their sense of competence,* and *relatedness*).

Abusive Supervision from Supervisor

Abusive supervision refers to the extent to which an individual perceives their supervisor to engage in hostile or cruel verbal and non-verbal behaviours directed towards them, excluding physical contact. A recent study in policing found that exposure to abusive supervision was related to higher fatigue, and lower job satisfaction, wellbeing and psychological detachment from work (Table 1.3).

Section 3 – What Works

In this section, we introduce two initiatives which have been adopted by a number of UK police forces with the intent to improve workforce wellbeing by using insights provided by research studies conducted by Durham University's Policing Research Unit.

Reducing Hindrance Stressors – The '100 Little Things' Initiative

As previously acknowledged in this chapter, hindrance stressors are found to have a negative association with job satisfaction, wellbeing, work engagement and discretionary behaviour. It has been asserted that reducing hindrance stressors at work would be worthwhile in the effort to improve workplace wellbeing.

The '100 Little Things' initiative places the members of the workforce at the centre of incremental workplace improvements by inviting them to consider and submit ideas that are intended to alleviate the unnecessary barriers and irritations that obstruct

TABLE 1.3 Summary of the 'ugly' organisational factors

'Ugly' organisational factors	*Key outcomes*
Workplace Incivility from Co-Workers	• Lower job satisfaction, life satisfaction and wellbeing • Higher fatigue, disturbed sleep and intention to quit • Reduced feelings of autonomy, competence and relatedness • Lower mental wellbeing • Lower sense of belonging
Workplace Harassment (Interpersonal Mistreatment) from Co-Workers	• Lower wellbeing • Lower job satisfaction and life satisfaction • Lower wellbeing by reducing feelings of autonomy, competence and relatedness
Team Incivility Norms	• Lower wellbeing by reducing feelings of autonomy, competence and relatedness
Abusive Supervision from Supervisor	• Higher fatigue • Lower job satisfaction • Lower wellbeing • Lower psychological detachment from work

individuals from efficiently completing work tasks. This collaborative approach taken to resolve and remove hindrance stressors at work signals to police officers and police staff that the force values their contribution and input, and views them as the experts who are best equipped to identify the workplace improvements needed to assist workforce functioning, productivity and wellbeing. HMICFRS (2017) gave the '100 Little Things' initiative high acclaim by recognising it as best practice and named it an outstanding and inclusive approach to seeking new ideas and generating workplace improvements.

The '100 Little Things' initiative has been widely adopted across policing. Notably, the importance of addressing hindrance stressors faced by the policing workforce was identified in the "Policing Front Line Review (FLR)" in 2019 and again in the "FLR Stocktake Report" in 2023 as a key recommendation for managing internal demand and the impact it has on wellbeing.

National Police Chiefs' Council (NPCC) Project

Equipping Leaders with the Skills and Knowledge to Set an Example and Build Inclusive Teams

Following the publication of research findings from the 2019 National Diversity, Equality and Inclusion Survey in policing, and the identification of the need to reduce unacceptable attitudes and behaviour within policing, Professor Les Graham (Durham University) was requested to act as academic lead to develop a training intervention to meet these challenges by Chief Constables Martin Hewitt Queen's Police Medal (QPM) (then Chair of the NPCC), Mike Cunningham CBE QPM (then Chief Executive of the College of Policing) and Ian Hopkins QPM (then NPCC Workforce Lead for Diversity, Equality and Inclusion).

The purpose of the NPCC project was to create a training intervention designed to enhance frontline supervisors' leadership knowledge and skills, through drawing upon research evidence to improve wellbeing, reduce inappropriate behaviour and build inclusive team cultures. The aims of the intervention were to develop frontline supervisors' understanding of key processes of leadership and wellbeing, and how to deal with the harm caused by inappropriate behaviour in the workplace by providing attendees with the opportunity to critically evaluate the evidence and underpinning theory from research conducted by Durham University's Policing Research Unit.

As of July 2024, over 2,700 frontline supervisors from across five UK police forces have attended the leadership intervention. The research evaluations deployed to assess the effectiveness of the intervention provide encouraging evidence of the benefits for enhancing supervisors' leadership skills, such as increasing their self-confidence and personal commitment towards resolving mistreatment in their work teams, and reducing amotivation (*a lack of motivation*) for resolving mistreatment in their work teams.

Section 4 – Concluding Comments

The research evidence summarised in this chapter illustrates the broad array of organisational factors which can be beneficial or detrimental to workforce wellbeing in policing. While it is insightful to review the factors which are associated with higher wellbeing and which cause harm, the research evidence also holds significant value in assessing the trend of wellbeing and other related measures from the past four National Police Wellbeing Surveys. The wellbeing trend findings in policing act as a stark reminder that, on average, there is a reduction in individuals' wellbeing and job satisfaction, a decline in the extent to which individuals feel valued by the public, and an increase in police officers' quitting intentions. According to the data available, these are significant challenges that require attention.

To address these trends, proactivity and commitment to improve the state of wellbeing across the policing workforce from all levels are required. Encouragingly, there is a growing body of evidence which supports this, where initiatives are designed using science and research findings, workforce wellbeing is shown to improve. In summary, the research evidence highlights that when organisations seek feedback and innovations from their workforce for the improvement of work processes, beneficial wellbeing outcomes can be realised by police officers and police staff. Moreover, the research supports that adopting a supportive leadership approach instead of an authoritarian leadership style provides benefits for workforce wellbeing and the creation of inclusive team cultures in policing.

Note

1 In discussion with senior police leaders, we note that during this period there was a severe reduction in demand due to the lockdown restrictions and suggest that this was the reason for the reported increase in wellbeing.

Bibliography

Åkerstedt, T., Fredlund, P., Gillberg, M., & Jansson, B. (2002). A prospective study of fatal occupational accidents – relationship to sleeping difficulties and occupational factors. *Journal of Sleep Research*, *11*(1), 69–71.

Ashford, S. J., Blatt, R., & Van de Walle, D. (2003). Reflections on the looking glass: A review of research on feedback-seeking behavior in organizations. *Journal of Management*, *29*(6), 773–799.

Bakker, A. B., & Heuven, E. (2006). Emotional dissonance, burnout, and in-role performance among nurses and police officers. *International Journal of Stress Management*, *13*(3), 423–440.

Barber, L. K., & Budnick, C. J. (2015). Turning molehills into mountains: Sleepiness increases workplace interpretive bias. *Journal of Organizational Behavior*, *36*(3), 360–381.

Barnes, C. M., Lucianetti, L., Bhave, D. P., & Christian, M. S. (2015). 'You wouldn't like me when I'm sleepy': Leaders' sleep, daily abusive supervision, and work unit engagement. *Academy of Management Journal*, *58*(5), 1419–1437.

Baruch-Feldman, C., Brondolo, E., Ben-Dayan, D., & Schwartz, J. (2002). Sources of social support and burnout, job satisfaction, and productivity. *Journal of Occupational Health Psychology*, *7*(1), 84–93.

Bolino, M. C., & Turnley, W. H. (2005). The personal costs of citizenship behavior: The relationship between individual initiative and role overload, job stress, and work-family conflict. *Journal of Applied Psychology*, *90*(4), 740–748.

Brown, N., Graham, L., Zheng, Y., Lockey, S., & Hesketh, I. (2020). *The Importance of Perceptions of Fair Treatment and Organisational Support for Well-Being and Discretionary Effort in Policing*. Available at SSRN 3553689.

Cavanaugh, M. A., Boswell, W. R., Roehling, M. V., & Boudreau, J. W. (2000). An empirical examination of self-reported work stress among US managers. *Journal of Applied Psychology*, *85*(1), 65–74.

Colquitt, J. A., LePine, J. A., Piccolo, R. F., Zapata, C. P., & Rich, B. L. (2012). Explaining the justice–performance relationship: Trust as exchange deepener or trust as uncertainty reducer? *Journal of Applied Psychology*, *97*(1), 1–15.

Daniela, T., Alessandro, C., Giuseppe, C., Fabio, M., Cristina, M., Luigi, D. G. & Michele, F. (2010). Lack of sleep affects the evaluation of emotional stimuli. *Brain Research Bulletin*, *82*, 104–108.

Deci, E. L., & Ryan, R. M. (2012). Self-determination theory. *Handbook of Theories of Social Psychology*, *1*(20), 416–436.

Demerouti, E., Bakker, A. B., Vardakou, I., & Kantas, A. (2003). The convergent validity of two burnout instruments: A multitrait-multimethod analysis. *European Journal of Psychological Assessment*, *18*, 296–307.

Diener, E., Suh, E. M., Lucas, R. E., & Smith, H. L. (1999). Subjective well-being: Three decades of progress. *Psychological Bulletin*, *125*(2), 276–302.

Eisenberger, R., Huntington, R., Hutchinson, S., & Sowa, D. (1986). Perceived organizational support. *Journal of Applied Psychology*, *71*(3), 500–507.

Firth, H., & Britton, P. (1989). 'Burnout', absence and turnover amongst British nursing staff. *Journal of Occupational Psychology*, *62*(1), 55–59.

Ford, M. T., Cerasoli, C. P., Higgins, J. A., & Decesare, A. L. (2011). Relationships between psychological, physical, and behavioural health and work performance: A review and meta-analysis, *Work & Stress*, *25*(3), 185–204.

Greenglass, E. R., Burke, R. J., & Konarski, R. (1997). The impact of social support on the development of burnout in teachers: Examination of a model. *Work & Stress*, *11*(3), 267–278.

Graham, L., Brown, N., & Plater, M. (2023). *National Police Wellbeing Survey 2023: Summary of Evidence and Insights*. Durham University. Available at: https://www.oscarkilo.org.uk/news/national-police-wellbeing-survey-2023-results Accessed December 10, 2025.

Graham, L., Gracey, S., Plater, M., Brown, N., Legate, N., Al-Khouja, M., & Weinstein, N. (2020). *Summary of Research Findings: Diversity, Equality and Inclusion in Policing*. Durham University. Available at: https://news.npcc.police.uk/releases/action-to-address-findings-of-first-employee-led-assessment-of-workplace-culture

Graham, L., Plater, M., & Brown, N. (2022). *National Police Wellbeing Survey 2021: Summary of Evidence and Insights*. Durham University. Available at: https://www.oscarkilo.org.uk/news/national-police-wellbeing-survey-2021-results Accessed December 10, 2025.

Graham, L., Plater, M., & Brown, N. (2023). *Summary of Policing: Key Issues and Common Themes*. Durham University and the National Police Wellbeing Service. Available at: https://www.oscarkilo.org.uk/news/national-police-wellbeing-survey-2023-results

Graham, L., Plater, M., Brown, N., Zheng, Y., & Gracey, S. (2019). *Research into Workplace Factors, Well-being, Attitudes and Behaviour in Policing: Summary of Evidence and Insights*. Durham University. Available at: https://www.gov.uk/government/publications/front-line-policing-review

Grandner, M. A., Hale, L., Moore, M., & Patel, N. P. (2010). Mortality associated with short sleep duration: The evidence, the possible mechanisms, and the future. *Sleep Medicine Reviews*, *14*(3), 191–203.

Her Majesty's Inspectorate of Constabularies and Fire and Rescue Services (HMICFRS). (2017). *Durham PEEL 2017 – Efficiency*. Available at: https://hmicfrs.justiceinspectorates.gov.uk/peel-assessments/peel-2017/durham/efficiency/

Her Majesty's Inspectorate of Constabularies and Fire and Rescue Services (HMICFRS). (2018). *PEEL: Police Leadership 2017: A National Overview*. Available at: https://hmicfrs.justiceinspectorates.gov.uk/publications/peel-police-leadership-2017/

Home Office (2023). *Front Line Review Stocktake Report: Progress on Key Deliverables and Next Steps*. Available at: https://www.gov.uk/government/publications/front-line-policing-review/front-line-review-stocktake-report-progress-on-key-deliverables-and-next-steps-accessible

Jackson, S. E., & Maslach, C. (1982). After-effects of job-related stress: Families as victims. *Journal of Organizational Behavior*, *3*(1), 63–77.

Jackson, S. E., Schwab, R. L., & Schuler, R. S. (1986). Toward an understanding of the burnout phenomenon. *Journal of Applied Psychology*, *71*(4), 630.

Johnson, R. E., & Lord, R. G. (2010). Implicit effects of justice on self-identity. *Journal of Applied Psychology*, *95*(4), 681–695.

Kahill, S. (1988). Symptoms of professional burnout: A review of the empirical evidence. *Canadian Psychology*, *29*(3), 284–297.

Kaldenberg, D. O., Becker, B. W., & Zvonkovic, A. (1995). Work and commitment among young professionals: A study of male and female dentists. *Human Relations*, *48*(11), 1355–1377.

Kim, S. (2011). Testing a revised measure of public service motivation: Reflective versus formative specification. *Journal of Public Administration Research and Theory*, *21*(3), 521–546.

Leiter, M. P., & Maslach, C. (1988). The impact of interpersonal environment on burnout and organizational commitment. *Journal of Organizational Behavior*, *9*(4), 297–308.

Leventhal, G. S. (1980). *What Should Be Done Equity Theory? New Approaches to the Study of Fairness in Social Relationships*. In K. Gergen, M. Greenberg, & R. Willis (Eds.), *Social Exchange: Advances in Theory and Research*. New York: Plenum.

Liden, R. C., Wayne, S. J., Zhao, H., & Henderson, D. (2008). Servant leadership: Development of a multidimensional measure and multi-level assessment. *The Leadership Quarterly*, *19*(2), 161–177.

Lockey, S., Graham, L., Zheng, Y., Hesketh, I., Plater, M., & Gracey, S. (2022). The impact of workplace stressors on exhaustion and work engagement in policing. *The Police Journal*, *95*(1), 190–206.

Martela, F., & Ryan, R. M. (2016). The benefits of benevolence: Basic psychological needs, beneficence, and the enhancement of well-being. *Journal of Personality*, *84*(6), 750–764.

Mayer, R. C., Davis, J. H., & Schoorman, D. F. (1995). An integrative model of organizational trust. *The Academy of Management Review*, *20*(3), 709–734.

Nishii, L. H. (2013). The benefits of climate for inclusion for gender-diverse groups. *Academy of Management Journal*, *56*(6), 1754–1774.

Paulin, D., & Griffin, B. (2017). Team incivility climate scale: Development and validation of the team-level incivility climate construct. *Group & Organization Management*, 42(3), 315–345.

Perry, J. L. (1996). Measuring public service motivation: An assessment of construct reliability and validity. *Journal of Public Administration Research and Theory*, *6*(1), 5–22.

Quick, J. C., & Quick, J. D. (1984). *Organizational Stress and Preventative Management*. New York: McGraw-Hill.

Rhoades, L. & Eisenberger, R., (2002). Perceived organizational support: a review of the literature. *Journal of Applied Psychology*, *87*(4), 698–714.

Shirom, A., & Melamed, S. (2005). *Does burnout affect physical health? A review of the evidence*. In A. S. G. Antoniou, & C. L. Cooper (Eds.), *Research Companion to Organizational Health Psychology* (pp. 599–622). Northampton, MA: Edgar Elgar Publishing.

Snape, E., & Redman, T., (2010). HRM practices, organizational citizenship behaviour, and performance: A multi-level analysis. *Journal of Management Studies*, *47*(7), 1219–1247.

Sonnentag, S., Binnewies, C., & Mojza, E. J. (2010). Staying well and engaged when demands are high: The role of psychological detachment. *Journal of Applied Psychology*, *95*(5), 965–976.

Stocker, D., Jacobshagen, N., Semmer, N. K., & Annen, H. (2010). Appreciation at work in the Swiss armed forces. *Swiss Journal of Psychology*, *69*(4), 117–124.

Tepper, B. J., Simon, L., & Park, H. M. (2017). Abusive supervision. *Annual Review of Organizational Psychology and Organizational Behavior*, *4*(1), 123–152.

Vandekerckhove, M., & Cluydts, R. (2010). The emotional brain and sleep: an intimate relationship. *Sleep Medicine Reviews*, *14*(4), 219–226.

Wright, B. E., Hassan, S., & Park, J. (2016). Does a public service ethic encourage ethical behaviour? Public service motivation, ethical leadership and the willingness to report ethical problems. *Public Administration*, *94*(3), 647–663.

Zellars, K. L., Perrewe, P. L., & Hochwarter, W. A. (2000). Burnout in health care: The role of the five factors of personality. *Journal of Applied Social Psychology*, *30*(8), 1570–1598.

Zheng, Y., Wu, C. H., & Graham, L. (2020). Work-to-non-work spillover: The impact of public service motivation and meaningfulness on outcomes in work and personal life domains. *Public Management Review*, *22*(4), 578–601.

2

PRACTICALITIES OF OPERATIONAL POLICE WORK FROM A PSYCHOLOGICAL RISK MANAGEMENT PERSPECTIVE

Noreen Tehrani

Introduction

Operational police work involves a range of psychological challenges that require a robust risk management approach to safeguard officers' mental health and effectiveness. Police officers are often exposed to high-stress situations, traumatic incidents and challenging environments, which can lead to cumulative psychological strain, causing mental health problems and impaired decision-making. From a psychological risk-management perspective, risk reduction measures include regular mental health screening and surveillance, resilience training and access to interventions, including therapy or counselling. Organisational practices, such as dealing with overload, developing a supportive leadership culture and providing post-incident interventions and support following traumatic exposures, are essential to the promotion of the psychological wellbeing of workers. Proactively addressing these individual and organisational factors improves police officers' mental health, operational efficiency and the public's confidence in a competent and effective police service.

The transactional stress model (Cox, 1992) provides a helpful way of examining the interaction between workers and their working environments. It suggests that stress and trauma occur when officers' perceptions of the demands placed upon them exceed their perceived ability to cope. Stress and trauma symptoms arise when officers fear not being able to deal with complex policing demands or threats to their wellbeing when coping is important to them and when failing would cause distress. Stress occurs when there is a realisation of being unable to cope with important demands rather than confidently dealing with a familiar task with a feeling of mastery and challenge, leading to a sense of competence and capability.

Any risk management approach's focus must address the causes of stress and trauma at three levels (Murphy & Sauter, 2004). Primary-level interventions involve creating organisational policies to minimise avoidable stressors, such as long working hours,

DOI: 10.4324/9781003518860-3

inadequate resources, lack of support, unclear role expectations and lack of career development. In policing, this may involve looking at shift patterns and working hours, providing adequate and timely training for high-risk roles and fostering a culture that recognises the need to address diversity and promotional opportunities.

At the secondary level, risk management involves the early detection of hazards to mental wellbeing, facilitated by regular psychological screening and surveillance, the training and development of the supervisor role as a primary source of support and the identification of officers struggling with debilitating symptoms of stress and trauma. Such practices can prevent long-term psychological harm and ensure officers remain operationally active.

Tertiary interventions focus on rehabilitation and recovery, which are crucial for officers who develop conditions such as anxiety, depression, PTSD, compassion fatigue and burnout. Where treatments are necessary to respond to mental health conditions, evidence-based treatments, structured rehabilitation programmes and a process to facilitate a gradual reintegration into the workforce must be adopted.

In policing, where there can be stigma around mental health, structured and organisationally endorsed approaches are vital for encouraging help-seeking behaviours. The College of Policing has tried to address the need for a structured approach by introducing psychological risk assessments at individual and organisational levels (Hesketh & Tehrani, 2019), which recognises that mental ill health is caused by individual coping and capacity in addition to organisational issues, such as poor selection, a lack of resources and training, limited career development opportunities, inadequate leadership, lack of diversity and cultural barriers to seeking help.

The transactional approach encourages police forces to take responsibility for creating supportive environments and addressing structural contributors to stress by using evidence to guide staff selection, training, development and the interventions utilised to maintain capacity and capability. In policing, an evidence-based approach is essential as it provides the opportunity to identify and evaluate the effectiveness of implemented measures and a means to improve practices continuously. For example, psychological surveillance and surveys can inform policies and training tailored to the unique demands of police work.

Integrating risk assessment and management principles into policing aims to create healthier, more supportive environments that enhance officer and staff wellbeing and operational effectiveness. This approach benefits the officers and contributes to safer communities and more trusted policing practices.

The National Police Wellbeing Service (NPWS) is responsible for police forces in England and Wales. The NPWS programme aims to coordinate activities, events and measures to deliver the vision, associated change and benefits of a holistic approach to psychological health and wellbeing, supporting police forces in sustainably growing and managing their workforce.

The first section of this chapter will examine the nature of psychological risks in policing and how they impact police officers and police services. The second section will explore groups with exceptionally high levels of risk in more detail. The third section will focus on interventions and the need for evidence-based practice.

Section 1: Identifying Psychological Risks in Mainstream Policing

Psychological risks in policing relate to the inherently challenging nature of policing, including exposure to traumatic events, highly stressful situations and circumstances with high uncertainty and intense public scrutiny (Tehrani & Hesketh, 2018). Officers frequently encounter violence, threats and traumatic incidents such as serious accidents, natural disasters and violent crimes. In addition, officers and staff are affected by organisational factors, which include poor leadership and management, enforced moves between teams and roles, unrealistic demands, shift working, a lack of career progression and unmet expectations, which increase the psychological strain (Roach et al., 2024). Over time, these organisational issues can lead to mental health conditions, including anxiety, depression, post-traumatic stress disorder (PTSD) or burnout, which impair the officers' ability to perform effectively (Porter & Gavin, 2024). Officers and staff consistently report that organisational failings are more significant than job-related stress and trauma in creating mental health problems due to dissatisfaction, stress and trauma (Charman & Bennett, 2021).

Role-related mental health challenges in policing are complex, requiring an understanding of the relationship between stress and trauma-related mental health conditions. Stress-related conditions, including anxiety, depression, burnout and compassion fatigue, are related to prolonged exposure to high-pressure environments, organisational demands and interpersonal challenges that exceed the officer's perceived capacity to cope. Chronic stress causes include a lack of knowledge, skills and resources; inadequate feedback and encouragement; a lack of effective IT and other systems to handle tasks and demands; constant changes in teams and team leadership; negative media coverage; and insufficient recognition and support.

In contrast, trauma-related conditions, including post-traumatic stress disorder (PTSD), secondary trauma and complex trauma, are related to earlier life experiences of trauma together with current personal and role-related trauma. The causes arise from exposure to death, threats of death, serious injury and sexual violence. Traumatic exposure includes direct experience, witnessing or learning about a trauma that happened to a close relative or friend. For occupational groups such as emergency services, indirect exposure to trauma in the course of professional duties is included (APA, 2025).

Some officers and staff will have experienced earlier life traumas in their childhood, personal life or employment. These earlier life events can be reactivated by their policing role where traumatic exposure can involve acute or repeated traumatic events, such as murder, violent crimes, traffic accidents and terrorist attacks or witnessing human suffering in cases involving domestic violence, sexual violence or child abuse.

While the causes of stress and trauma may differ, these two hazards are interconnected and mutually reinforcing. Officers experiencing personal or occupational stress-related symptoms can find themselves more vulnerable to trauma-related conditions. Chronic stress can reduce the capacity to self-soothe and regulate emotions, with coping skills being reduced and increasing sensitivity to traumatic triggers, causing increased levels of trauma-related symptoms. For instance, an exhausted officer experiencing burnout or compassion fatigue may have a lower resilience threshold when faced with a traumatic event, such as a cot death or suicide, increasing their risk of developing PTSD or complex trauma. Similarly, an officer with secondary trauma caused by their empathic engagement with a rape victim can find themselves experiencing high levels of anxiety, depression, compassion fatigue and burnout.

The reciprocal relationship between stress and trauma complicates the way that mental health can be managed within policing. Addressing one dimension without considering the other can be ineffective or limited in its effectiveness. For example, mitigating chronic stress may reduce overall vulnerability, but without targeted trauma support, officers who have already experienced significant traumatic events may continue to struggle. Conversely, trauma-focused therapies may not yield lasting results if the underlying personal and organisational stressors remain unaddressed (Figure 2.1).

Understanding the underlying interaction between stress and trauma recognises the importance of developing an integrated approach to mental health care in policing. Strategies need to differentiate between stress-related and trauma-related conditions whilst addressing their shared and compounding effects.

Role-Related Risks

Stress, Burnout, Anxiety and Depression

Stress and anxiety are bio-psycho-social responses to challenging or overwhelming demands. Biologically, stress and anxiety activate the autonomic nervous system and the associated fight, flight, freeze and appease responses. Psychologically, the impact of chronic stress and trauma can be difficulty in focusing, forgetfulness, lack of self-confidence and difficulty making decisions, and the social outcomes include isolation and aggression. Demands can be short-term, such as a work deadline, argument, or exam or long-term, such as bereavement, discrimination or chronic illness.

The transactional model of stress and coping (Cox, 1992) suggests that people appraise demands and resources differently. This is often related to their previous experiences dealing with similar demands and whether there was a successful outcome. Cox has shown that this appraisal of the demand rather than the actual demand determines the level of apprehension and stress experienced. Similarly, the appraisal of the resources available to deal with the demands is important. Where there is previous experience of

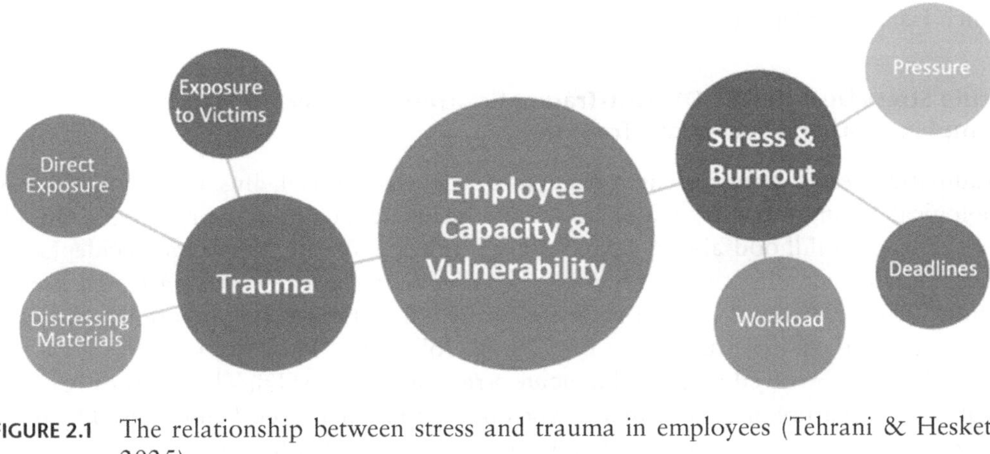

FIGURE 2.1 The relationship between stress and trauma in employees (Tehrani & Hesketh, 2025).

having access to appropriate resources and support in dealing with demands, it can be seen as a challenge rather than a stressor.

In policing, more than half of officers believe their demands are excessive, and almost a third do not get adequate support from their supervisor (Charman & Bennett, 2021). Where the perceived demands increase and there is a lack of support, symptoms can become more persistent, and the condition may become chronic and meet the criteria to be diagnosed as an anxiety disorder.

Burnout, like stress, is recognised as an occupational phenomenon rather than a medical condition. Burnout is caused by chronic workplace stress that has not been managed. Burnout has three symptoms: emotional exhaustion, mental detachment, cynicism and a loss of professional self-esteem.

Clinically recognised anxiety disorders need to meet specific characteristics; this means that the magnitude of the symptoms must be severe and should have been present for at least six months; there is also a need to meet the range of clinically significant symptoms for the condition, the level of distress caused and the impact on social, occupational and other areas of functioning. Some of the common clinically significant anxiety disorders found in policing include phobias, which are relatively common in policing and include fears of a whole range of objects or situations, including heights, exams, blood, dogs and social events. Panic disorder is caused by a sudden surge of fear, leading to palpitations, sweating, shaking, difficulty breathing, dizziness and nausea. The most commonly diagnosed anxiety disorder is known as generalised anxiety disorder, which includes excessive anxiety, which is difficult to control and is associated with restlessness, fatigue, a mind going blank, irritability, muscular tension and problems sleeping.

There are two types of depression: biogenic depression, which occurs without an apparent external trigger and is due to genetic or biological factors and reactive depression, which occurs in response to a specific identifiable event, such as bereavement, relationship breakdowns and other kinds of unresolved stress or trauma. The symptoms of both types of depression include depressed mood, loss of interest or pleasure, insomnia or hyposomnia, fatigue, feelings of worthlessness, lack of concentration and suicidal ideation. Frequently, these conditions are mild and short-term, but they can progress into a major depressive disorder involving constant, severe sadness and social withdrawal, which can last for months. Persistent depressive disorder is a chronic form of depression which lasts for at least two years.

Acute Stress Disorder (ASD), Post-Traumatic Stress Disorder (PTSD), Complex PTSD and Secondary Trauma

Traumatic stress is a response to a traumatic event that overwhelms an individual's psychological coping capacity. Traumatic events include exposure to war, physical attacks and injuries, childhood abuse, sexual abuse, kidnap, torture, disasters, accidents and domestic violence directly, as a witness or discovering a trauma has affected a close family member. Around 70% of people globally will experience a potentially traumatic event during their lifetime. In the first month following exposure, between 20% and 50% of people involved will develop acute stress disorder (ASD). The levels of ASD are related to the nature of the traumatic exposure, with higher levels being caused by interpersonal trauma. The symptoms of ASD are similar to PTSD but are temporary.

Only a minority of people exposed to trauma (5.6%) will develop PTSD (Kessler et al., 2017). To be diagnosed with PTSD, there is a need to show that the traumatic exposure has affected physical, psychological and social functioning for more than one month. There are three trauma symptoms which must be present for a diagnosis of PTSD to be made. These are (a) re-experiencing, including visual re-experiences in dreams and flashbacks, plus physical and emotional re-experiences of physical responses and emotional distress experienced at the time of the trauma; (b) hyperarousal, including irritability, reckless behaviour, hypervigilance, jumpiness, difficulties sleeping and poor concentration; (c) avoidance of any reminders of the trauma including people, places, activities or situations related to the trauma.

Complex post-traumatic stress disorder (CPTSD) is a response to multiple traumatic life events. It is characterised by the three trauma symptoms of re-experience, avoidance and sense of threat (hyperarousal), along with symptoms showing disturbances in self-organisation, including chronic and pervasive disturbances in emotion regulation, identity and relationships. Individuals with CPTSD will have sustained or multiple exposures to trauma, such as childhood abuse and domestic or community violence. The disorder has a prevalence of 1–8% in the population, with higher levels in emergency services.

Secondary trauma, also known as vicarious trauma, occurs when individuals indirectly experience the distress and suffering of others who have undergone traumatic events. Secondary trauma is commonly observed among professionals who emotionally support trauma survivors and occurs through a process of empathetic engagement with the experiences of the trauma survivors. When individuals closely interact with or listen to the stories of those who have endured traumatic events, they may involuntarily internalise the emotional and psychological distress of the survivors, which can cause symptoms similar to PTSD.

Organisational Risks

Overload, Absenteeism, Presenteeism, Retention and Culture

Overload is a common complaint from police officers, who regard the organisation's expectations of them to be unreasonable based on the level of resources and the time available. There are several types of overload, including being under extreme pressure to work at a high pace, having insufficient time or skills to complete a task to the required quality and having a conflict between balancing work and family obligations. Many officers describe working additional hours, often without breaks, to complete work and achieve targets (Charman & Bennett, 2021). Overloading from work, role and personal responsibilities significantly affects employees. The adverse effects include stress, anxiety, depression and burnout, with increased vulnerability to physical and mental ill health.

The risk of employees taking time off work due to a mental health condition is 76% higher among workers exposed to high demands, a lack of control and other stressors than in non-exposed workers (Duchaine et al., 2020). Currently, the level of absence in policing is 9.4% (NPCC, 2022). This is significantly higher than the UK level of 2.7% (ONS, 2022). Understandably, police forces are keen to reduce absence levels.

However, if officers work under extreme pressure, some may feel a "duty" to stay at work to support their supervisor and team, and others concerned about strict attendance management practices may feel unable to take time off work, leading to an increase in presenteeism (going to work when unwell). However, presenteeism can be more costly than sickness absence, as Deery et al. (2014) found working while ill increased physical and psychological strain on the mind and body, requiring employees to expend extra effort to complete regular tasks and leaving them exhausted with no reserves when met with additional job demands. Allowing or encouraging presenteeism results in reduced performance, poorer decision-making and an increasing likelihood of developing more serious conditions requiring more prolonged absences.

An increasing number of newly recruited officers and staff are leaving because the policing role differs from what they expected. In the current occupational climate, policing is losing talented officers and staff to better-paying or less stressful occupations, leaving police recruiters continually needing to recruit and train a revolving door of employees. Turnover figures provide an indication of policing's culture, the effectiveness of its recruitment and retention policies and the way its people are managed and developed. Pay levels, particularly for recruits, opportunities for career advancement, family-friendly policies, work-life balance, inclusivity and satisfaction with management all influence turnover. Nevertheless, the leaver rate in policing is 6.6%, significantly lower than the national level of turnover, with around a third of employees changing their jobs annually. However, the make-up of joiners and leavers in policing is concerning (Charman & Bennett, 2021), with voluntary leavers currently exceeding those leaving through retirement, dismissal and death in service.

Police culture has been under scrutiny following a series of scandals related to the behaviour of serving officers. The "Casey Report" (2023) highlighted the extent of inappropriate behaviours in parts of the Metropolitan Police. The most recent list of barred officers shows a significant increase in dismissed officers, including chief officers who were found dishonest, abused their powers or committed a sexual offence. One of the fastest-growing areas in policing is professional standards, yet despite this growth, cases of bullying, sexual harassment and abuse frequently go underreported. A survey (Charman & Bennett, 2021) found that 24.4% of leavers named discriminatory behaviour by managers and 10.9% by colleagues as their main reason for leaving policing.

Whilst important in maintaining standards, the time taken by the Independent Office for Police Conduct (IOPC) and Professional Standards Department (PSD) to investigate police conduct can take many months and sometimes years to complete. The investigation often results in a "no case to answer" or "words of advice" for the officer. For the officers involved, this is a highly stressful time that frequently leads to significant mental health problems (Police Federation, 2021).

Failing to address organisational problems can significantly impact performance and wellbeing. Decreasing job satisfaction can reduce the quality of decision-making, increase reliance on alcohol and substance abuse and increase physical health problems (Craddock & Telesco, 2022). Chronic and acute organisational stressors have been found to erode officer resilience, compromising their capacity to respond effectively to high-pressure demands (Caceda et al., 2014). The impact of organisational stressors can affect personal relationships, straining family dynamics and leading to marital conflict, separations and divorce (Campbell & Renshaw, 2018).

Moral Injury, Sanctuary Trauma and Embitterment

Three stress and trauma-related psychological conditions have been identified as being due to failings in the management, in particular, the management of mental health in policing. Whilst they are not recognised as clinical conditions, they help in the understanding of the development and maintenance of stress and trauma symptoms in policing.

Moral injury refers to the experience of long-term negative emotions, including guilt, shame, contempt and anger. It occurs when deeply held values are betrayed or violated by ourselves, our leaders, institutions and the government. Moral injury in policing can be related to a belief that victims have been let down due to delays in the investigation or that a prosecution would have been possible with more time. Individual officers may blame themselves or the organisation for these failures.

Sanctuary trauma occurs when someone who has experienced a traumatic event expects their team, manager and organisation to be supportive, only to discover a lack of care, leading to a loss of trust and more trauma. There is an expectation that their supervisor and team will be supportive, but this may not always occur, leaving stressed and traumatised officers and staff feeling abandoned due to the lack of care and support. Officers who have returned after a challenging job may expect some recognition or understanding from their supervisor. If this does not happen, they will feel upset and let down.

Failure to resolve moral injury and sanctuary trauma can lead to officers becoming embittered, which occurs when people perceive themselves as unjustly treated. The person's distress is attributed to the action or inaction of an alleged perpetrator of the injustice, often a manager or organisation. The embitterment becomes associated with a strong sense of entitlement and desire for retribution. The embittered person can become vigilant for other instances of perceived injustice and will use this to convince others of injustice.

Section 2: High-Risk Roles in Policing

The NPWS has identified several roles as being at a higher level of psychological risk (College of Policing, 2020) and has offered police forces an opportunity to access NPWS-funded annual screening for officers and staff in these roles. The NPWS used a role risk assessment tool to identify high-risk roles (Tehrani & Hesketh, 2018). These were all specialist roles with regular exposure to a known stressor, thus falling under the duty of care requirements of the health and safety legislation (HSE, 2013).

Several roles have been selected for further study, and the results have been published in peer-reviewed journals. In this section, we will look at six roles to demonstrate the benefits of psychological surveillance in gathering information to identify hazards and resilience factors related to that role, together with the advice provided to improve mental health and wellbeing. Each police group was involved in an annual psychological surveillance programme. The surveillance questionnaires are fully described in Tehrani and Hesketh (2018) and included four clinical measures: Goldberg Anxiety and Depression

Scale (Goldberg et al., 1988); post-traumatic stress with the Impact of Event Scale – Extended (Tehrani et al., 2002); and burnout and secondary trauma with ProQOL (Stamm, 2010).

There were also some hazard and resilience measures, including the Eysenck Personality Questionnaire (Eysenck & Eysenck, 1975), Sense of Coherence (Antonovsky, 1987), COPE (Carver, 1997), Emotional Awareness (Steiner & Perry, 1999), Workability/ Health Beliefs (Thorsen et al., 2012) and a Lifestyle measure based on NHS lifestyle guidance. The levels of clinical scores are shown in Table 2.1, which also provides the mean level of symptoms in the general public (the levels of burnout and secondary trauma are not available).

Table 2.1 provides information on the proportion of officers and staff in the six high-risk groups above the clinical cut-off level for a clinically significant symptom. Clinical depression is very high in all groups, with workers in the contact centre, forensics and occupational health being most affected. These three roles also have the highest symptom levels in all the other conditions. Burnout is exceptionally high in Negotiators, where most officers undertake negotiation in addition to their substantive role. Occupational health practitioners have lower levels of secondary trauma and the highest level of primary trauma of the six groups, which suggests that the OH role may be reactivating earlier life traumas rather than the trauma being absorbed empathetically from their interactions with distressed clients. The results of the main findings from the six high-risk groups are summarised below.

Contact Centre

The study found that PTSD was significantly related to the number of years in the contact centre. This finding is consistent with other studies into high-risk roles in policing where an increased incidence of clinical symptoms is related to being in a psychologically high-risk role for four or more years (Tehrani, 2018).

Anxiety, depression and PTSD were all significantly related to poorer levels of workability. Workability is the capacity to manage job demands within mental resources. Managers should pay attention to the need for regular wellbeing checks with the opportunity for psychological interventions for those developing mental health symptoms. Improving workability, particularly for the older team members, is essential given the age distribution in this team.

Forensics

Forensic investigators (FI) are police staff and experience a similar, if not higher, level of risk compared to their police officer colleagues (Tehrani, 2023). The study confirmed the value of using the single-item workability and health beliefs measures to identify the hazards and resilience factors within FIs. Lower levels of workability and health beliefs were found in the older FIs; illness and sick days during the previous year were also strong predictors of lower workability and health. Physical fitness and more exercise were also significant in supporting both measures. The results also showed that several lifestyle factors were related to higher health beliefs, including not smoking, caffeine consumption and eating regularly. The results also emphasised the importance of

TABLE 2.1 The percentage of police officers and staff with clinically significant scores working in six different roles (Tehrani & Hesketh, 2025)

Clinical symptom	*Contact CENTRE (n = 815)*	*Forensics (n = 696)*	*Online child abuse (n = 961)*	*Negotiator (n = 2546)*	*Offender management (n = 1526)*	*Occupational Health Advisor (OHA) (n = 127)*	*General public*
Anxiety	29%	29%	21%	19%	20%	25%	3.5%
Depression	35%	34%	25%	23%	25%	31%	8–12%
PTSD	11%	10%	6%	6%	6%	17%	3%
Burnout	18%	21%	17%	22%	15%	19%	NA
Secondary Trauma	22%	25%	13%	15%	15%	11%	NA

engaging in a meaningful role and having social support from colleagues. Higher levels of problem-solving and willingness to get involved in problem-solving and make decisions were important resilience factors.

Online Child Abuse Teams (OCAT)

The study (Tehrani, 2018) found OCAT officers were experiencing symptoms of secondary traumatic stress, and female officers reported more adverse effects than their male colleagues. The results also found neuroticism was associated with an increased reporting of anxiety, depression, burnout, PTSD and secondary trauma. However, the proportion of OCAT officers experiencing primary and secondary trauma symptoms was lower than those reported by teams without surveillance programmes. Less emotionally stable OCAT officers were at greater risk of experiencing secondary trauma from exposure to internet child abuse. It was suggested that emotional sensitivity could be beneficial as it may result in the OCAT intuitively picking up important evidence that a more emotionally stable investigator may miss. Valid and reliable screening as a mechanism of support was recognised as a key means of identifying those at the highest risk and valuable for highlighting wellbeing needs and training opportunities. It was also recognised that reflection and social support increased OCAT resilience and can create post-trauma growth.

Negotiators

When compared with other groups, the Negotiators had lower levels of anxiety and depression than their colleagues (Tehrani & Hesketh, in press). There were also slightly lower levels of secondary trauma and around the average for primary trauma. This study gathered qualitative data, which provided insight into their increased resilience. The negotiator role was regarded as engaging and purpose-driven, contrasting with the perceived monotony or stress of other policing roles. Whilst the negotiator and the primary roles may be stressful, the nature of the stress is seen as different. The stress of the primary role often stems from bureaucracy and workload, whereas the stress of the negotiator role is linked to its emotional and physical demands. The combination of a challenging role, heightened job satisfaction, clarity of mission and a sense of being looked after appears to be the recipe for improved or enhanced personal resilience.

Offender Managers (OM)

The role of offender management is transitioning, with an increasing emphasis on reducing reoffending while ensuring that the community is protected from offenders' criminal activities. Increasing resilience requires developing strong wellbeing skills, a healthy lifestyle and a positive attitude to work. Working with a sense of purpose requires a clear understanding of where one's role fits and there is a manageable workload. The study (Tehrani, 2023) showed that being male, extroverted and emotionally stable were associated with higher levels of psychological resilience, so it would be premature to suggest that OMs with these personal characteristics would be the most successful in their role.

Empathy can lead to higher levels of exposure to the emotions of others, which may account for the difference in resilience.

Occupational Health

The study (Tehrani, 2024) showed that manageability, which measures the extent to which people believe they have the available resources to cope with the demands of their role, is related to lower clinical symptoms. Workability, which measures positive attitudes towards work, is related to lower levels of anxiety and depression. Coping skills, including higher levels of physical fitness, assertiveness, social support, involvement and time planning, are also associated with increased levels of wellbeing. The results also showed several risks, including drinking above the NHS-recommended levels of alcohol or caffeine, insufficient sleep, using denial as a way of handling stress and pretending or hiding symptoms. Where the ability to manage the work was depleted, there were higher levels of all the psychological symptoms, suggesting that improvements in psychological wellbeing would require a review of the work and workloads to ensure they were being managed effectively.

The results of the six studies identify the importance of regular screening and wellbeing checks to provide an early indication of mental health risks. There is also an important need to invest time and resources in building a range of coping skills, particularly those related to problem-solving, team building and recognising the importance of providing social support. Mental health is improved, and physical wellbeing is seen as important. Regular exercise, following a healthy diet and maintaining a balanced lifestyle can increase resilience when dealing with the stress and pressure of a high-risk role. It is essential to ensure that supervisors and teams have a clear sense of purpose and find meaning in their work, as this increases job satisfaction, engagement and resilience.

Support needs to be tailored at several levels. First, each team faced different challenges, and the surveillance identified the key risk factors that needed to be addressed at the team level. Supervisors are essential in working with the team and will need information and support in dealing with team-level issues. However, there is also a need to provide individually tailored assessments, interventions and therapy for officers and staff with clinically significant mental health conditions.

This structured approach involves managers and occupational health professionals developing effective strategies to improve high-risk teams' overall wellbeing, resilience and productivity.

Section 3: NPWS and Other Interventions and Evidence-Based Practices

The National Police Wellbeing Service (NPWS) was launched in 2019 to support and guide police forces across England and Wales in improving and building organisational wellbeing. The service aims to help police forces build wellbeing support for officers and staff and strengthen knowledge and understanding of the available help and support. This approach is designed to reduce the stigma around seeking support or assistance and to encourage people to support themselves and realise their full potential through improving personal resilience and self-help skills. The NPWS has funded some of the services described in this chapter to encourage a broader engagement in a risk management and control approach to responding to stress and trauma. However, each police force remains responsible for supporting its officers and is expected to augment the support provided by the NPWS through their Occupational Health and Wellbeing Services. Stress and trauma-informed care and treatment (STRICT) guidance has been produced to assist police forces in meeting the standards required and is available on the NPWS website.

The risk management model of psychosocial support provides an easy-to-follow aide-mémoire on what is required to reduce stress and trauma in organisations in six simple steps (Figure 2.2).

Finding Out

Role Risk Assessments

There are several ways to assess the risks officers and staff face. The first is a role risk assessment, a tool that assesses ten risk factors in roles. At least three assessors undertake the assessment online. The assessments are reviewed regularly, and a directory of role risk assessments is available.

Individual and Organisational Risk Assessments (IO-RA)

Trained supervisors can use these assessments with their teams or individual team members. The simple assessment tool assesses personal stress and trauma hazards, as well as organisational hazards, based on the HSE Management Standards.

Situational and Personal Risk Assessments (SP-RA)

Following a traumatic exposure, the situational and personal risk assessment tool can be used to identify the likelihood that a particular trauma would require additional interventions and treatment. Two elements are involved: the nature of the traumatic exposure

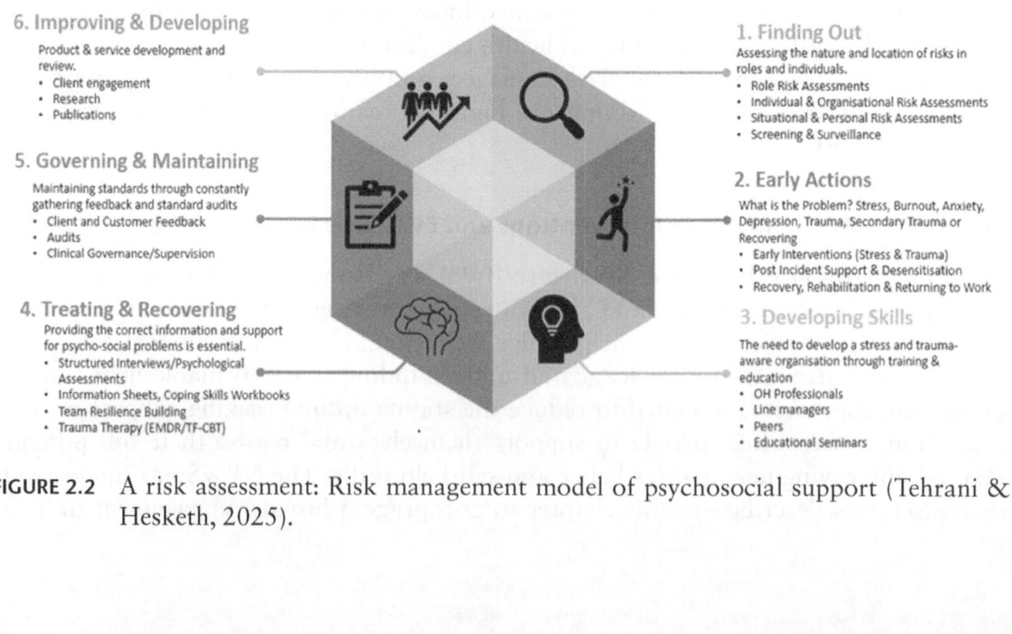

FIGURE 2.2 A risk assessment: Risk management model of psychosocial support (Tehrani & Hesketh, 2025).

itself and the vulnerability of those exposed. Taken together, this assessment enables fast-tracking for anyone at higher risk.

Screening and Surveillance

Online psychological screening questionnaires provide a way to use valid and reliable clinical questionnaires to identify officers and staff who are experiencing above the clinical cut-off level of anxiety, depression, PTSD and secondary trauma, as well as information on organisational and personal risk and resilience factors (see Section 2). The high-risk groups are generally screened annually as part of health surveillance, with approximately 20% requiring some support. In other groups, the need for screening is identified through the IO-RA, SP-RA or by an occupational health practitioner, and an online referral screening can be arranged.

Early Interventions

Early interventions must be initiated and implemented as close as possible to officers and staff experiencing distress to be effective. Surveys have shown that after speaking to family and friends, the most likely person employees will go to with mental health concerns is their supervisor. Therefore, supervisors must see themselves as the primary provider of psychosocial support for their teams. Peers also play a role in providing early interventions, particularly when a major incident occurs.

Peer Support

The evidence on the effectiveness of peer support is mixed (Tehrani & Hesketh, 2023). However, there is a role for well-trained and managed peers to provide support, mentoring and signposting to OH or other sources of professional support.

Supervisor Wellbeing (Stress)

The recommended early intervention for stress is the supervisory wellbeing session, in which the supervisor asks the officer or staff member to complete the IO-RA as a basis for a wellbeing discussion. The approach is solution-focused, where the supervisor works with their team members to identify the nature of their problems, a valued outcome and a plan to achieve the desired outcome. The wellbeing assessment tool identifies where a referral is required to HR or occupational health for specialist support.

Demobilising and Defusing

Supervisors undertake demobilising to acknowledge when a team member has been exposed to something that may cause them to become distressed. This requires the supervisor to have a close relationship with their team, which allows them to distinguish between the events within their capacity and those that may cause distress. This is a discussion with an individual or a whole team that recognises what has happened, offers immediate information and advice and where necessary, organises a time for defusing.

Supervisors typically carry out defusing but may also involve peers, particularly when there has been a major incident involving the supervisor. The defusing consists of listening to what happened, checking physical, social, emotional and psychological wellbeing for signs of distress, offering information and support and following up with referrals to occupational health for anyone whose symptoms are not reducing.

ESTIM/Debriefing

The College of Policing took expert advice to develop the Emergency Service Trauma Intervention Meeting (ESTIM). Occupational health practitioners and trained peers undertake this more in-depth intervention, which explores the nature of the traumatic exposure and identifies potential trigger spots that can activate re-experience. All models, including TRiM, follow a similar pattern: (a) an introduction, (b) an exploration of events before, during, and after the primary trauma, and a detailed examination of the sensory information related to the trauma, (c) identifying symptoms and (d) trauma education, advice and referral where appropriate.

Post-Incident Support and Desensitisation (PISD)

The PISD programme was developed for officers and staff involved in incidents that have led to death or serious injury following police contact. The programme is involved in supporting a return to work for officers and staff who have developed a phobic response to some aspect of the death or near-death event. The support programme involves taking the officer through a tailored desensitisation process with the support of a trainer or experienced peer. This intervention has been used within firearms, where returning officers must be assessed as safe when returning to firearms duties.

Recovery, Rehabilitation and Returning to Work (RRR)

The final evidence-based intervention is the RRR programme. It aims to help officers and staff recover from incidents that may have been identified in IO-RA, SP-RA, screening and surveillance, D&D, ESTIM or PISD. The approach is also a practical tool for supervisors when officers and staff return to work following an absence. The handy workbook provides the steps to support recovery, rehabilitation and return to work.

Developing Skills

As identified in the introduction to this chapter, secondary-level interventions are vital. These interventions include training for all levels of police personnel, including frontline officers and staff, supervisors, senior management and professional staff such as human resources and occupational health.

Occupational Health Professionals

Occupational health professionals need training in managing psychosocial problems, including recognising symptoms of mental health problems and understanding when to use the evidence-based interventions described. Occupational health practitioners and counsellors should be members of a professional body requiring them to have achieved a postgraduate qualification in their work area. They also need to have training in:

- Using the data from online screening to help in case formulation and treatment
- Undertaking structured interviews
- Planning and managing graded desensitisation programmes
- Supporting recovery, rehabilitation and return to work
- Understanding of the transactional model of stress management

Line Managers

Supervisors' role is crucial in managing stress and trauma in the workplace. Without their knowledge of their team's personalities, strengths and weaknesses, signs of mental health and wellbeing issues would go unnoticed until they become chronic and more difficult to treat. The essential toolbox for line managers is an awareness of the signs and symptoms of stress and trauma and emotional intelligence in being able to deal with negative behaviours and issues with sensitivity. A willingness to help team members develop their solutions to personal problems is essential. In addition to more general leadership training, they need the following training to deal with stress and trauma:

- Supervisor Wellbeing Assessments
- Demobilisation and Defusing
- Recovery, Rehabilitation and Returning to Work

Peers

Peers and colleagues are often the first to notice a team member struggling. If the force's culture is stress and trauma-aware, issues can be picked up and resolved very quickly. Some peers may be trained to provide early interventions, including:

- Peer Support
- Demobilising and Defusing
- Post-Incident Support and Desensitisation

Educational Seminars

Psychological surveillance identifies resilience factors and hazards in individual teams and policing in general. To be cost-effective, it is important to identify the areas where training would be beneficial and which groups or individuals would most benefit from the educational input. The following areas identified by the surveillance data have led to the development of (Table 2.2):

TABLE 2.2 Educational seminars (Tehrani & Hesketh, 2025)

• Time Planning	• Sleep
• Problem Solving	• Diet
• Physical Wellbeing	• Exercise
• Psychological Wellbeing	• Mindfulness
• Assertiveness	• Self-Soothing
• Relaxation	• Body Focusing
• Social Support	• Guided Imagery
• Involvement	• Dealing with Bullying

Treating and Recovery

For counsellors or psychologists, the first stage of engagement is to fully understand the person, their background and influences and what they want to get out of the treatment or therapy session. The following interventions are all involved in formulation (developing a plan for doing something).

Structured Interviews and Psychological Assessments

A structured interview ensures that all the relevant areas of life are fully considered when looking for appropriate interventions. Psychological assessments take the next step of providing opinions and guidance on how cases should be handled. In policing, officers and staff with marginal scores are offered structured interviews. OH practitioners undertake them, while psychological assessments are undertaken by psychologists for people with clinical-level scores.

Self-Help Information Sheets and Coping Skills Workbooks

Evidence-based self-help information sheets and workbooks are provided for supervisors and occupational health practitioners to use in a targeted way to address identified needs.

Team Resilience Building

The team resilience-building session is designed for teams that experience a heavy burden of compassion fatigue or secondary trauma. The model adopted involves an in-depth examination of the nature of the problem, when and where it happens, when it does not happen, and how similar problems have been solved in the past. The person presenting the problem then defines their valued outcome, and after this has been explored, the rest of the team provides added support and feedback.

General and Trauma Therapy

Occupational counselling should be solution-focused and short-term. Some police forces have recruited counsellors; others have a bank of associated counsellors, or an external

Employee Assistance Programme provides generalist counselling. Trauma therapy is a specialism. The effective trauma therapy models are trauma-focused cognitive behavioural therapy (CBT) and Eye Movement Desensitisation and Reprocessing. The recommended number of hours required for trauma therapy is between 9 and 12 hours.

Governing and Maintaining

Clinical governance and the maintenance of standards are critical to the establishment of a high-quality, evidence-based service.

Creating the Evidence (EBP)

Evidence-based practice is a systematic process for making decisions, taking action or undertaking activities using the best evidence available and removing as far as possible subjective opinions, unfounded beliefs or biases from organisational decisions and actions. However, despite the importance of evidence in policing, EBP is frequently ignored and untried, resulting in a proliferation of untested interventions being adopted or existing ineffective interventions being retained. It has been suggested (Mathieson et al., 2019) that failure to adopt EBP is the low level of priority given to EBP by management, a lack of awareness or access to the evidence and inadequate resources or training, difficulty developing the management systems to deliver the intervention and a preference for more exotic solutions.

Feedback

Feedback is actively sought from customers and clients as part of the delivery process. It is gained from structured interviews, psychological assessments, counselling, training and seminars. The feedback is generally undertaken online, and the results are published regularly. Comments are evaluated, and where opportunities for improvement are identified, these are implemented.

Audits

Audits are undertaken based on standards agreed upon during training. Although there is some latitude for personal style, the nature of the training or intervention cannot be fundamentally changed apart from where there has been a decision to make a change, which would then form the standard against which future audits would take place.

Clinical Governance and Supervision

The ownership and clinical governance of the training, surveillance and other materials rests with Noreen Tehrani Associates (NTA). Police forces that adhere to the standards set out in the STRICT guidance and elsewhere will be under the protection of NTA clinical governance provided they have abided by the standards. Some occupational health teams have sought clinical supervisors for their professional staff.

Improving and Developing

Client Engagement

Most programme improvements and innovations have come from conversations with clients or customers. Gathering comments and feedback from clients and customers helps to understand what interventions, training and other products mean to the recipients. Rather than trying to defend existing ways of doing things, listening to what is not working or could work better allows continual improvement.

Research and Publications

There is a constant desire to evaluate and share the programme's results. With a database of around 80,000 individual screenings, there are enormous possibilities for undertaking research that helps understand mental health in policing. Choosing to publish in peer-reviewed journals can take time and may result in rejections or major revisions, but it does mean that peers have reviewed the research. One of the most significant papers led by the University of Greenwich (McCrone et al., 2024) demonstrated the programme's economic benefits as three times the delivery cost.

Conclusions

In this chapter, we have shown how policing poses significant psychological risks due to the exposure of officers and staff to trauma, high-pressure environments, and organisational challenges like poor leadership and excessive demands, contributing to conditions such as stress, PTSD and burnout. The National Police Wellbeing Service addresses these issues by promoting organisational wellbeing and resilience, reducing stigma and providing evidence-based interventions, including risk assessments, peer support, trauma-informed care and recovery programmes. Annual psychological screening, especially for high-risk roles, helps identify hazards and foster resilience through tailored interventions, therapy and lifestyle improvements. Training for occupational health professionals, supervisors and peers ensures effective stress and trauma management, while educational seminars enhance coping skills and resilience. Clinical governance, feedback and audits uphold service quality, but challenges like limited resources and resistance to evidence-based practices hinder full implementation.

The transactional model developed by Cox (1992) helps remind organisations of the importance of primary and secondary risk prevention. Rather than focusing on tertiary or treatment solutions, the model emphasises demands and how these demands can be reduced by changes in procedures, improvements in IT and better management.

This requires a fundamental assessment of whether the perceived overload is due to a failure to manage demands by senior management where there is a need to have an open dialogue with the public and politicians on ways to reduce the actual demand by redefining the role of policing or changing the perception of the demand by improved processes or systems which could involve a recalibration of the expectations of the public and the criminal justice system.

Senior management is responsible for responding to emerging issues around employment churn, absence, presenteeism and leaveism. While interventions to treat stress and trauma can help, there is a clear need to consider the importance of having the resources, technology and people to deal with the volume of work and sometimes unrealistic expectations of the public and politicians (Hesketh et al., 2017).

References

American Psychiatric Association (APA). (2025). *Diagnostic and statistical manual of mental disorders* (5th ed.). American Psychiatric Publishing. https://doi.org/10.5555/appi.books.9780890425787.x00pre.

Antonovsky, A. (1987). Health promoting factors at work: The sense of coherence. *Psychosocial Factors at Work and Their Relation to Health*, 153–167.

Caceda, R., Nemeroff, C. B., & Harvey, P. D. (2014). Toward an understanding of decision making in severe mental illness. *The Journal of Neuropsychiatry and Clinical Neurosciences*, *26*(3), 196–213.

Campbell, S. B., & Renshaw, K. D. (2018). Posttraumatic stress disorder and relationship functioning: A comprehensive review and organizational framework. *Clinical Psychology Review*, *65*, 152–162. https://doi.org/10.1016/j.cpr.2018.08.003

Carver, C. S. (1997). You want to measure coping, but your protocol is too long: Consider the brief cope. *International Journal of Behavioral Medicine*, *4*(1), 92–100.

Casey, L. (2023). *The casey report baroness casey review final report*. https://www.met.police.uk/SysSiteAssets/media/downloads/met/about-us/baroness-casey-review/up Retrieved August 8, 2025.

Charman, S., & Bennett, S. (2021). Voluntary resignations from the police service: The impact of organisational and occupational stressors on organisational commitment. *Policing and Society*, *32*(2), 159–178. https://doi.org/10.1080/10439463.2021.1891234

College of Policing. (2020). *Strict guidance: A practical guide. Ryton on Dunsmore: College of Policing*. Retrieved August 8, 2025. https://www.oscarkilo.org.uk/services/psychological-and-trauma-risk-management/psychological-surveillance Accessed December 10, 2025.

Cox, T., & Cox, S. (1992). Occupational health: Past, present and future. *Work & Stress*, *6*(2), 99–102. https://doi.org/10.1080/02678379208260343

Craddock, T. B., & Telesco, G. (2022). Police stress and deleterious outcomes: Efforts towards improving police mental health. *Journal of Police and Criminal Psychology*, *37*(1), 173–182. https://doi.org/10.1007/s11896-021-09488-1.

Deery, S., Walsh, J., & Zatzick, C. D. (2014). A moderated mediation analysis of job demands, presenteeism, and absenteeism. *Journal of Occupational and Organizational Psychology*, *87*(2), 352–369.

Duchaine, C. S., Aubé, K., Gilbert-Ouimet, M. et al. (2020). Psychosocial stressors at work and the risk of sickness absence due to a diagnosed mental disorder: A systematic review and meta-analysis. *JAMA Psychiatry*, *77*(8), 842–851. https://doi.org/10.1001/jamapsychiatry.2020.0322

Eysenck, H. J., & Eysenck, S. B. G. (1975). *Manual of the Eysenck Personality Questionnaire* (Junior and Adult). Kent: Hodder & Stoughton.

Goldberg, D., Bridges, K., Duncan-Jones, P., & Grayson, D. (1988). Detecting anxiety and depression in general medical settings. *British Medical Journal*, *297*, 897–899.

Health & Safety Executive. (2013). *Workplace health, safety and welfare. Workplace (Health, Safety and Welfare) Regulations 1992. Approved Code of Practice and guidance*. Workplace health, safety and welfare – L24.

Hesketh, I., Cooper, C., & Ivy, J. (2017). Wellbeing and engagement in policing: The key to unlocking discretionary effort? *Policing: A Journal of Policy and Practice*, *11*(1), 62–73. https://doi.org/10.1093/police/paw021

Hesketh, I., & Tehrani, N. (2018). *Responding to trauma in policing*. College of Policing Ltd. Retrieved August 8, 2025, from https://assets.college.police.uk/s3fs-public/2021-02/responding-to-trauma-in-policing.pdf

Hesketh, I., & Tehrani, N. (2019). Psychological trauma risk management in the UK police service. *Policing: A Journal of Policy and Practice*, *13*(4), 531–535.

Kessler, R. C., Aguilar-Gaxiola, S., Alonso, J., Benjet, C., Bromet, E. J., Cardoso, G. et al. (2017). Trauma and PTSD in the WHO World Mental Health Surveys. *European Journal of Psychotraumatology*, *8*(sup5), 1353383. https://doi.org/10.1080/20008198.2017.1353383

Mathieson, A., Grande, G., & Luker, K. (2019). Strategies, facilitators and barriers to implementation of evidence-based practice in community nursing: A systematic mixed-studies review and qualitative synthesis. *Primary Health Care Research & Development*, *20*, e6.

McCrone, P., Tehrani, N., Tehrani, R., Horsley, A., & Hesketh, I. (2024). Economic evaluation of a psychological surveillance and support programme in the UK police force. *International Journal of Emergency Services*, *13*(4–5). https://doi.org/10.1108/IJES-03-2024-0020

Murphy, L. R., & Sauter, S. L. (2004). Work organisation interventions: Stage of knowledge and future directions. *Social and Preventive Medicine*, *49*, 79–86.

NPCC. (2022). *Update on the national police absence rate and Coronavirus FPNs issued by forces in England and Wales*. Retrieved August 8, 2025, from https://news.npcc.police.uk/releases/update-on-the-national-police-absence-rate-and-coronavirus-fpns-issued-by-forces-in-england-and-wales

ONS. (2022). *Sickness absence in the UK labour market: 2022 Sickness absence rates of workers in the UK labour market, including number of days lost and reasons for absence*. Retrieved August 8, 2025, from https://www.ons.gov.uk/employmentandlabourmarket/peopleinwork/labourproductivity/articles/sicknessabsenceinthelabourmarket/2022

PolFed. (2021). Federation chair backs criticism of the IOPC. Retrieved August 8, 2025, from https://www.polfed.org/westmercia/news/2021/federation-chair-backs-criticism-of-the-iopc/

Porter, C. N., & Gavin, P. (2024). 'Constant pressures from all angles': Understanding the mental health of UK police officers. *The Police Journal: Theory, Practice and Principles*, *98*(2), 306–323. https://doi.org/10.1177/0032258X241280217

Roach, J., Curran, L., Cartwright, A., & McCarthy, R. (2024). A study of police personnel wellbeing in England and Wales whilst working during the Covid-19 pandemic. *Policing and Society*, *35*(6), 773–794. https://doi.org/10.1080/10439463.2024.2424808

Stamm, B. H. (2010). *The concise ProQOL manual*. Pocatello, ID, ProQOL.org.

Steiner, C., & Perry, P. (1999). *Achieving emotional literacy*. Bloomsbury Publishing.

Tehrani, N. (2018). Psychological wellbeing and workability in child abuse investigators. *Occupational Medicine*, *68*(3), 165–170.

Tehrani, N., Cox, S. J., & Cox, T. (2002). Assessing the impact of stressful incidents in organisations: The development of an extended impact of events scale. *Counselling Psychology Quarterly*, *15*, 191–200.

Tehrani, N., & Hesketh, I. (2018). The role of psychological screening for emergency service responders. *International Journal of Emergency Services*, *8*(1), 4–19.

Tehrani, N., & Hesketh, I. (2023). Employee support: Where have we come from, and where are we going? *Journal of Community Safety and Well-Being*, *8*(Suppl 1), S57–S63. https://doi.org/10.35502/jcswb.289

Tehrani, N. & Hesketh, I. (2025). Hostage and Crisis Negotiators: Responding to the challenges of the role Hostage and crisis negotiators: Responding to the challenges of the role. *Journal of Police and Criminal Psychology*. Springer Nature.

Thorsen, S. V., Burr, H., Diderichsen, F., & Bjorner, J. B. (2012). A one-item workability measure mediates work demands, individual resources and health in the prediction of sickness absence. *International Archives Occupational Environmental Health*, *86*(7), 755–766.

3

PEER SUPPORT

PC Lee Taylor

Brief History

Peer support has been around for hundreds of years. Research shows that Larry Davidson, a Psychiatry Professor from the Yale School of Medicine, tracks the beginning of peer support to a psychiatric hospital in the late 18th century.

Jean Baptiste Pussin was a governor of the Bicêtre Psychiatric Hospital in Paris. Jean Baptiste Pussin recognised the value of employing recovered patients as hospital staff. The chief physician at the hospital, Philippe Pinel, praised these peer staff for being "gentle, honest, and human", "averse from active cruelty", and "disposed to kindness". Hiring former patients marked a shift in mental health care that led the way in the "moral treatment" era (Love and Respect, n.d.).

Workplace Peer Support

In the workplace, peer support is about co-workers, known as "peers", who help one another through confidential discussions. In the general population, an employee's personal problems can affect their job performance and, if left unchecked, these issues may lead to a decrease in their ability to function. The main objective of a peer support programme is to resolve employee and workplace problems before they escalate to crisis levels by providing an extra network of support in the workplace (Wallace, 2016).

What Is It?

Peer support itself is not difficult or rocket science. Peer support is when people use their own experiences to help each other. In peer support everyone's views and experiences are equally valued, rather than anyone being seen as more of an expert than others. How much support you give and receive can vary depending on what feels right for you at different times. It's not always about getting or giving advice. It's also about having a

DOI: 10.4324/9781003518860-4

safe space to get things off our chests and occasionally sharing a laugh about it all. Peer support is run for and by its members. Police peer supporters will have experience and knowledge of police work and culture, with lived experiences of dealing with a variety of life's challenges. Lots of people find peer support improves their wellbeing and helps them cope with mental health problems. For example, it could: help you to open up about what you are feeling and experiencing, introduce you to ideas and approaches that others have found helpful, reassure you that you're not alone in how you are feeling, help you to connect with others and give you a sense of belonging, encourage you to value your strengths, build your self-esteem and confidence and help you to feel more hopeful about the future.

If we look at what support is offered to policing personnel, you will often find that if you have a problem, you are signposted to supervisors/line managers, occupational health, human resources or an employee assistance programme (EAP). Notwithstanding, these sources of support are very helpful and can give you the support and assistance you require. Some of the options, however, are not an immediate source of support and can be a formal process. They can take weeks before you get an appointment to speak to anyone and can appear to be policy-led. Supervisors/line managers are an excellent source of support and are easily accessible. What happens, though, if it is your line manager/supervisor who is causing your concern, or if you work in a department where your supervisor is replaced every few months? If you are struggling with something personal and you don't want everyone knowing about it, then you may not want to repeat yourself, so you find you don't approach your supervisor/line manager. You may find that some people won't approach human resources as some human resource personnel sit on promotional panels; it is policy-led. There is a thought that everything I say will end up in my file. Likewise, some individuals feel they don't want to approach occupational health departments due to their rank/grade: "I'm a senior officer/staff member, I don't want people who may be waiting in reception to see me also waiting for help" or having a misheld belief that "If I go to Occupational health then it will go on my record and my supervisors will find out what I have said". One main concern for individuals is, "They don't understand what it feels like to be police. It can be hard for them to relate to police culture".

As we are becoming more aware of trauma and the effects of trauma, most of us are not speaking to family and friends about things that are bothering us and jobs we have dealt with, as we know we don't want to traumatise anyone else. There is also one common theme about these sources of support: it is down to you, the individual to make the first move, for you to put your hand up and ask for help. Now, for some people, this will never happen; they won't put their hand up and say, "I'm struggling, I need help". So, what happens to them? Well, they could end up suffering or struggling alone, suffering or struggling in silence.

So where can I go for support and assistance? This is where peer support can help. A good peer supporter in your team or department will notice if there are changes in someone's behaviour and their personalities; they notice when a colleague is struggling or looks and acts under pressure. Peer supporters can make the first move and approach their colleagues to offer support. Often just asking "How are you? You seem different today. I've noticed that you don't seem yourself; are you ok"? This can initiate a conversation with someone who may be struggling. Offering to make them a cuppa and a listening ear is sometimes all some people require.

Role of Peer Supporter

So, what do peer supporters actually do? The first thing they do is listen. Now, you may think that's easy or not that difficult, and we all do this on a daily basis. Or do we? Yes, we do listen to people, but do we truly hear them? Do we hear what is being said and, sometimes more importantly, pick up on what isn't being said? Now, think about your last conversation with someone. Did they allow you to speak without interruptions or over-talking? Did they actively listen to you? Did they offer you that safe place to talk freely about anything you wanted, without judgement or offering any critical comments back to you? Did they offer empathy towards you, offer you support and, more importantly, offer the knowledge that whatever you say is going to be kept in strictest confidence? Now, we are aware there are going to be some caveats to confidentiality. These will be disclosing a significant immediate risk of harm to yourself or others, disclosing a criminal offence or a misconduct issue; then, yes, confidentiality may be breached. Apart from that, confidentiality is key.

Offering this safe place for someone to openly talk can be very powerful for the speaker as it's not always that we get the chance to just freely talk. Safe spaces serve as a foundation for nurturing healthy individual and team dynamics and fostering a culture of trust, respect and open communication.

"A space that is supportive, and non-threatening, where each person feels comfortable to express themselves without fear of discrimination or judgement. To put that into simple terms, it's essentially a space to show up and be you!" (Overall and Gorham, 1962).

If you think of what we do in the police, we are fixers, problem solvers and rescuers. This is something that the majority of us do on a daily basis. Now guess what we don't do in peer support. We don't fix, we don't rescue and we don't problem solve for people we are supporting, what we do is empower our colleagues to see their situation in a more constructive way. We do this by being positive, offering empathy and, most importantly, listening. We will explore options available and help our colleagues problem solve the issue themselves. We will offer options and allow them to make the decision themselves on which way forward they would like to go.

As peer supporters, we don't know everything about everything, but what we do know is where to signpost people to and what options are available. There are lots of experts for a variety of issues around. Some of the best sources of support are staff associations, federations and unions. You will find a full list of your staff associations, contact details for federations and unions on your force's intranet.

As peer supporters, we work to a set of principles and try to stick to a process. There are a number of parts to the peer support process. The first and one of the most important is boundaries. Peer supporters are there to offer support and assistance to someone who needs it. We offer support and assistance and can signpost or refer people to other departments or agencies. We are not therapists or psychologists and will never attempt therapy. We are impartial so won't side with one person over another or the organisation. We only take on what we are comfortable to take on; if for whatever reason we don't feel comfortable with a colleague, then we will work with our colleague and find another peer supporter to assist them. It's always best practice not to get peer support from a line manager or supervisor. They are your supervisor and will support you as a supervisor.

We will always adhere to the College of Policing Code of Ethics (these can be found on your force's intranet).

At the start of any peer support interaction, peer supporters will explain their role and discuss confidentiality and limitations to confidentiality with the person they are supporting. Letting you know how long they have set aside for the meeting and speaking about their availability can also clarify the setting of boundaries with the person who is being supported. Remember, peer supporters are not a 24-hr crisis support.

Peer supporters will offer a listening ear to anyone; most of the time, this is all that is needed. There are times when people do get emotional and upset in meetings. This is fine; you are in a safe place where your peer supporter will offer those silences and that safe place for you. They will give you time to get emotional if needed and offer empathy towards you.

The environment where peer support interactions take place is also important. You will find that peer supporters won't conduct a meeting in the middle of the canteen at lunch time or in a busy office. They will try to get a private room, welfare room or contemplation room. These are ideal as they are quiet and out of sight from onlookers. If no rooms are available, then going for a walk or just sitting in a car can be helpful.

As mentioned above, peer supporters will have a good knowledge of what resources are available internally and externally. If they are unsure, then they will know who to call to get the information. Lots of us don't feel comfortable taking support from within the organisation and feel more comfortable with an external source of support. If this is your preferred option, then let your peer supporter know. Peer supporters will also know what happens with referrals; they will explain the process to you and give you rough timescales.

As part of the interaction, you will find that peer supporters assist the person being supported to re-establish personal control. This is an important part of the support offered. If we think about a problem we may be facing for a moment and ask ourselves this question: what is the outcome I want from this problem? More often than not, most of us will be able to answer this question. The problems/issues come to us when we don't know how to get the outcome we want. This then can cause us to feel frustrated, get stressed out or start to feel anxious about the problem. One of the main reasons for this is because we feel we are not in control of this situation. Talking to a peer supporter who will listen to you, explain to you that it is common to feel like this when facing certain problems/issues, then offering you options and allowing you to make the decision yourself on which way forward you go, is a huge help. This is empowerment. Empowerment means people having power and control over their own lives. For a lot of people who feel under stress, their self-esteem can also be affected. Some tend to use explanations of guilt and self-blame; this may be because they readily fit the situation. Peer supporters try to encourage alternative explanations instead of arguing the point with someone. We would call this reframing. An example of this could be someone struggling because they recently had to do cardiopulmonary resuscitation (CPR) on a person who didn't survive.

The individual could be blaming themselves, thinking, did I remember my first aid training? Did I push down hard enough, fast enough? And with these thoughts could come the self-blame and guilt thoughts: it's my fault this person didn't survive. A peer supporter wouldn't argue the point with you, telling you that you did everything correctly and the person wasn't going to survive anyway. They would acknowledge what you had told them and how it is making you feel. They would say words to the effect of: "I'm sorry to hear this, but thank you for sharing it with me. It is common for people who have dealt with what you have to have thoughts like this, and I can see why you would think that you are to blame, but it is possible there is another explanation for this". The peer supporter would then be quiet and allow the person to take a moment and think of explanations.

I spoke early about confidentiality and how important this is in peer support. No one will go and speak with someone and talk to them about issues/problems they may be facing if they believe that the person who is being told will go and tell others what has been said. Peer support is built on trust, openness, confidence and confidentiality. There are, however, some caveats to confidentiality; as mentioned previously, if someone discloses a serious risk of harm to themselves or others, a criminal offence or misconduct issue has been disclosed, and finally, if the person receiving support consents to the sharing of information (this must be done in writing). Before any breach of confidentiality occurs, the peer supporter will always let you know that due to what has just been told to them, they will need to breach. They may offer you the chance to speak to a line manager or supervisor first and even offer to come with you and give you support. What do we know in the police? If you have done something wrong or made a mistake and you own up to it, then the chances are you will get help and support. However, if you lie or deny something and your integrity is called into question, then the offer of support and help may be withdrawn. If a peer supporter is not sure and thinks they may need to breach confidentiality, they will always speak to a peer support coordinator without naming the individual who is being supported and get some guidance.

Now we have spoken about confidentiality and the importance of it, however, there are things that are recorded within peer support. It's important that we know how many people are using peer support and what sort of issues/problems/concerns people are coming to get support with. Be rest assured that no names or collar numbers should be taken when utilising peer support; nothing that can identify an individual should be recorded. There will be some information which is recorded, but this should be told to the person who is receiving support. Examples of what may be recorded are the following: how contact was made, what department they work in, what division, borough or area they work in, what the presenting issue is, how the interaction is taking place (face to face, telephone) and confidentiality has been spoken about, possibly a rough age and how long they have been working for the police. This isn't an exhaustive list, and different organisations will differ on what they record. Most importantly, nothing should be recorded that can identify the individual seeking support.

How many times do we have a meeting with someone and once it is finished, we think "why didn't I ask this, why didn't I mention that"? Well, don't worry because your peer supporter will contact you, usually within a few days to conduct a follow-up. This is when your peer supporter calls you and asks how everything is going, whether you got the support you were looking for and whether there is anything else the supporter can do for you. This is a key part of peer support. Following up so the person being supported doesn't feel like they have just been forgotten about.

Listening

I have mentioned a few times now the importance of listening. This cannot be promoted enough. Listening is the main thing peer supporters do. They will actively listen to the person who is being supported. Peer supporters use a variety of different skills when they listen. They will use verbal and non-verbal responses; this includes head nodding and the use of facial expressions i.e., smiling. The verbal responses are the short words they use when you are talking, the OK, yes, I see and Hmm (short words). They will ask questions; this will help the supporter truly understand and seek clarification on what has just been told to them. You will more often than not notice that the peer supporter paraphrases back what has just been told to them. This is again to clarify what they have just heard and that they understand what has just been told to them. Also, to let you know you have been heard and understood.

Depending on what you are seeking support for, peer supporters may introduce certain topics of conversation; they may include resilience, self-care techniques, sleep, fitness and nutrition. This may be to give you some extra knowledge on how important these topics are and how they can affect our physical and psychological behaviour and thinking if not looked after.

Most of us through our day-to-day lives don't even think about resilience and take time to think what it actually is. I should imagine that for a lot of people the first time they really sat down and thought about it was when they filled an application form, and one of the questions was "give an example of when you have shown/been resilient". This is when we pull out our mobile phone and search "What is resilience and give me an example of it". Now there are many definitions of resilience, and it may mean something different for each and every one of us. Being able to cope in stressful situations, to adapt and overcome, bouncebackability, the list is endless. I would say that one of the key aspects of being resilient is knowing when to put your hand up and ask for help.

Every single one of us need help at some time throughout our lives, every single one of us need help at some stage throughout our careers and yet sadly for some, asking for help is one of the hardest things they can do. Now this could be due to stigma and having a thought process: "It's a sign of weakness, people will laugh at me, people will think I am not coping". When in actual fact, asking for help can be a sign of strength. It's about knowing and accepting that being resilient isn't about never feeling stressed or being under pressure. Accepting that bad things will happen but having the knowledge that you can overcome this, and you will be happy, you can recover, you can be successful even after something bad or difficult has happened.

Self-Care

Self-care is also very important for us. Working within the police is like no other job. We will hear and come across some very upsetting and emotional situations, incidents. Not everyone will attend these, but I'm sure you will hear about them. Due to a number of distressing things we will come across, it is vitally important that we know how to look after ourselves and what to look out for. Again, this is where speaking with a peer supporter can really help and assist you. Peer supporters can talk to you and offer you a variety of different tools and techniques that may be able to assist you. They can discuss with you physical, interpersonal, emotional, cognitive and behavioural fitness. They can talk about the benefits of mindfulness, meditation, yoga and so on. Wouldn't it be nice if there was something that worked for everyone? Well, I'm sorry to say there isn't. We are all individuals; we are all unique. What works for one person may not work for others. I have been told by many mindfulness coaches that one of the hardest things about mindfulness is finding what works for you. This is something that only you will know. Some people like to go for walks in nature, some like to read, build things out of Lego, listen to podcasts, play sports, appreciate the moment they are in now and breathing exercises. Again, the list is endless. Mindfulness is an awareness which allows you to notice what is happening in the present: surroundings, thoughts, feelings and emotions without judgement.

Your physical fitness is also important. We all know that exercise is good for us. Doing something is better than not doing anything – even if it is going for a walk around your building or taking the stairs instead of the lift. We are all aware of how important having good sleep is for us. We do a tough job, and working for the police – especially if you are a shift worker – means that your sleep patterns are vulnerable to all sorts of challenges. There are a number of sleep webinars on the Oscar Kilo website that may be able to assist you if you have trouble with sleep. These webinars will help you to learn and practise strategies to improve the quality of your rest, no matter how much or how little you get (Oscar Kilo, n.d.).

Goal Setting

Setting yourself goals is a great way of achieving those things we want to do. It's important to remember, though, to make them achievable goals and not to set your goals too high. For a lot of people, setting them too high only leads one way: they never get completed. Peer supporters can assist you with setting up realistic and manageable goals. They won't do this for you but will support and assist you in doing this. They will guide you through a process of how to document your goal settings. More often than not, they will introduce you to the STAR technique. Specific: what is the goal you want to set? Measurable: is it measurable, and how will you measure it? Achievable: is it achievable? It is pointless setting a goal if it's never achievable. Relevant: is it relevant to your end goal or task? And finally, Time: how much time are you going to give yourself to complete this goal? It is always nice to add an R at the end also. R is for Reward. What reward are you going to give yourself once the goal has been reached? Peer supporters are fully aware of these techniques and have found that people find using this way of goal setting to be most helpful.

Summary

In summary, peer supporters are there to give you support and assistance whenever there is something you may be struggling with. They give you hope that just because you are feeling like you are now, you won't always feel like this. Your recovery is defined by YOU; it is down to YOU to be honest with yourself. YOU are the only one who can change your life. Remember, there are people who can assist you and people you can speak to who have that lived experience of going through something the same or similar to you. You will hear throughout your career these words: "Early Intervention." Let's do early intervention with ourselves; let's be there and help each other in the early stages and reduce the chances of our troubles escalating. Remember, you are not alone; support is there for you.

References

Love and Respect. (n.d.). A history of peer support. [online] Available at: https://www.loveandrespectcommunityforrecoveryandwellness.org/blog/history-of-peer-support

Oscar Kilo. (n.d.). Better sleep toolkit. [online] Available at: https://www.oscarkilo.org.uk/services/healthy-living/sleep-and-fatigue-interventions/better-sleep-toolkit Accessed December 10, 2025.

Overall, J. E. and Gorham, D. R. (1962). The brief psychiatric rating scale. *Psychological Reports*, 10(3), 799–812.

Wallace, J. R. (2016). Field test of a peer support pilot project serving federal employees deployed to a major disaster. *Social Work and Christianity*, 43, 127–141.

4

RESILIENCE, CONTROL AND THE WELLBEING OF POLICE OFFICERS

A Complex Investigation?

Jason Roach and Liam Scott Curran

Introduction

Most writings on police wellbeing or trauma feel a need to begin with the line (or something close to it anyway) *Policing is a stressful occupation* (Anshel, 2000). It is but then of course so are many other jobs and roles, but it is worth making the point that up until relatively recently, policing remained rather neglected in terms of research looking at how 'doing the job' could have a negative impact on police officers. We are pleased to say that wellbeing is now a thriving area of policing-focused research the world over.

Before we briefly explore what psychological wellbeing might constitute, let us briefly tap into some current perspectives on what wellbeing and stress look like in policing, beginning with identified 'common stressors' (e.g. organisational factors, roles, and tasks) before focusing on the evidence for what protects officers and staff from these potential assaults on their wellbeing. Namely, the research relating to 'resilience'.

Wellbeing in Policing

The latest UK National Police Wellbeing Survey comprising responses from over 42,000 police officers and police staff respondents (Graham et al., 2023) concluded that

1. Fatigue, anxiety, and stress in police officers is high and very high, but moderate in police staff.
2. Depression levels are 'moderate' or 'moderately low' for police officers and police staff alike.
3. Levels of emotional energy are 'moderately low' as are feelings of organisational support.
4. Police officers and police staff feel valued by their co-workers and direct supervisors, but not as much by their individual police force or indeed the public.

DOI: 10.4324/9781003518860-5

5. Life satisfaction, work engagement, and motivation are high in both police officers and police staff.
6. Feelings of 'work overload' are 'high' in both police officers and police staff.
7. Resilience levels are only 'moderately high' in both police officers and police staff.

Much of the research purporting to measure police wellbeing has reported a consistently noticeable decline in wellbeing levels of UK police officers and staff. For example, since 2019 (Graham et al., 2020), which saw the first sweep of the National Police Wellbeing Survey (the most comprehensive self-report survey of UK police officers and staff available), police officer and staff wellbeing levels have been seen to be on a consistent downward trend. Similarly, evidence from the findings of research employing other (non-self-report) methods of data collection, such as studies using data collected under the UK Freedom of Information Act (2000)[1] requesting aggregate figures for police personnel absences from work, show how those absences where psychological or mental ill-health is cited as the primary reason have been increasing (Cartwright & Roach, 2021). Stevelink et al. (2020) estimate that 9.8% of police officers will have depression, and 8.5% experiencing anxiety.

In terms of what constitutes stress, albeit highly subjective to the individual, for the purpose of clarity and consistency in this chapter, we have favoured Lazarus and Folkman's definition of psychological stress:

> a particular relationship between the person and the environment that is appraised by the person as taxing or exceeding his or her resources and endangering his or her well-being.
>
> *(Lazarus & Folkman, 1984, p. 19)*

Research to identify the prevalence of *Post-Traumatic Stress Disorder* (PTSD) in police officers and staff has been found to vary. For example, Stevelink et al. (2020) estimate that 3.9% of UK police officers will be experiencing PTSD, whereas (Brewin et al., 2020) found that as many as one in five (20%) police personnel could have PTSD. Although Brewin et al. (2020) estimate a much higher prevalence of PTSD in UK police personnel than Stevelink et al. (2020) (20% and 3.9% respectively), this is explained by the fact that Brewin et al.'s (2020) study is more expansive in its classification and measurement of trauma as they also included *Complex Post-Traumatic Stress Disorder* (CPTSD) in their estimate.

What Is Resilience and What Makes a Resilient Person?

According to the website for the American Psychological Association:

> Resilience is the process and outcome of successfully adapting to difficult or challenging life experiences, especially through mental, emotional, and behavioural flexibility and adjustment to external and internal demands.
>
> *(nd)*[2]

The website for the British Psychological Society, on the other hand, provides a simpler (arguably vaguer) definition:

> Resilience is about doing well in the face of adversity; to do better than might be reasonably expected.
>
> *(BPS nd)*[3]

For many, resilience is simply the ability to 'bounce back' (Hesketh et al., 2019) after experiencing a negative event, but we believe that there are other important contributing elements; the identification and degree of influence of each is our primary focus in this chapter.

So, what makes a person 'resilient'? In their book *Extreme: Why Some People Thrive* at the *Limits*', Barrett and Martin (2014) suggest that:

> Resilient people have an approach to life that is characterised by realistic optimism, self-confidence, a sense of humour, the ability to stay focused under pressure, not being easily defeated by failure, and finding meaning in negative experiences. They often have a track record of dealing successfully with stressful situations. They also tend to be happier and more successful than those who are less resilient.
>
> *(2014, p. 166)*

So where does resilience come from and, more importantly, can we 'bottle' it (i.e. teach it, learn it, and pass it on)? Where resilience comes from is contested; some suggest that 'psychological resilience' is a form of positive adaptation where a negative event is eventually followed by a positive response (Fletcher & Sarkar, 2013). As a police officer, such a negative event might be the potentially traumatic effect of attending a fatal road traffic collision, or the sudden unexpected infant death (SUID). It may be less traumatic, such as having to deal with a frustrating supervisor, an irritating colleague, or perhaps even receiving a No Further Action (NFA) decision from the Crown Prosecution Service after you have spent hours and days preparing a court-ready file of case evidence. To use an analogy, it is perhaps the ability to repair and reforge the links in medieval chainmail armour to be able to resume battle. It is how quickly you can get back in the saddle after being bucked off. In terms of wellbeing, it is how well and how fast your mind can be repaired.

For many researchers, resilience is characterised by two elements: adversity (such as those above) and positive adaptation. Resilience, if you like, is the bit in the middle that influences whether such positive adaptation occurs. There can be several protective factors, as highlighted by Fletcher and Sarkar (2013, p. 15), such as hardiness, positive emotions, extraversion, self-efficacy, self-esteem, and positive affect (happiness).

Since resilience is linked to coping (Lazarus & Folkman, 1984), our view is that police officers can be supported to improve their levels of resilience and to support their ability to cope with situations more effectively. Indeed, recent research has shown that those officers who have undergone a resiliency training programme had higher wellbeing scores than officers and staff who hadn't (Hesketh et al., 2019).

Why Understanding Resilience Is Important

Understanding resilience and different levels of it helps us understand why a particular police officer may struggle both psychologically and emotionally with recovering from being involved in an investigation into the sudden and unexpected infant death (SUID) or after having attended a fatal road traffic accident (RTA), where another appears to not be affected at all. Indeed, our same officer may have appeared unaffected by previous SUIDs and RTA cases in the past, but not understanding resilience, what it comprises, and how it works therefore helps us to not just understand why different people can react in different ways to the same event (Southwick, 2014), but also why the same people can react in different ways to the same types of events at different points in time.

Some psychologists suggest that an important debate about resilience is whether it should be seen as 'static', that it doesn't change. It is a fixed trait. As a police officer, if you can bounce back from dealing with a sudden and unexpected death of a person in one instance then you can and will do so again. If you can bounce back from that, then you can bounce back from the unsupportive supervisor, or hearing the unfathomable 'not guilty' verdict that has come back from court when you felt you had a solid case at court. This implies that if you 'have resilience', great; if not, you're out of luck. This is not our view. Our view is that people (including police officers) draw on these resources from situation to situation. Very rarely is someone resilient against any and all stressors thrown at them. Resilience is linked to our experiences, our thought processes, and feelings, all of which can be unique and help to explain the psychology of individual differences (Fletcher & Sarkar, 2013). This describes the view of those who see resilience as a 'process'. What people can be resilient to, or not, can change throughout a person's life and throughout a person's experiences (Lazarus & Folkman, 1984). Our research with Senior Investigating Officers has shown that an officer's personal feelings about an event can shape how resilient they are to it.

Resilience is, however, a complex phenomenon. What makes people resilient to different negative events is best explained as the result of a complex interplay of social, biological, psychological, and environmental factors, as argued by Graham (2023, p. 54) 'While often related to individual differences, resiliency is also influenced by the availability of resources to an individual'.

Roach et al. (Roach et al., 2017, 2018), for example, found that homicide investigations could have a varying impact on the wellbeing of investigators depending on whether the victim was a child or an adult. Their research found that officers investigating adult homicide felt more pressure, but that investigating child homicides, detectives reported feeling more negative impacts on their wellbeing, for example, ruminating about a case when off duty and after the investigation had been completed. Roach et al. (Roach et al., 2017) also highlighted how police investigators often found the emotional effects much more acute, enduring, and harder to deal with when investigating child homicides than investigating adult homicide.

From our recent research on the wellbeing of Senior Investigating Officers (SIOs) (Curran, 2024), we noticed how psychological responses to first time experiences, such as seeing a dead body for the first time, although often considered profoundly awful and distressing, can change over time. SIOs suggested that they had *become more resilient* to such events the more times/occurrences they experienced them. Thus, SIOs felt better equipped, psychologically, to deal with and cope with the potential psychological and emotional trauma that such events can cause. For example, one of our SIO interviewees stated:

> the more bodies that you go to, the more ...each one, you're learning and developing, so the first dead body that you go to [...] you don't want to go near, the smell is awful, it stays with you, and then you become more experienced and confident, you become more interested, and therefore you want to be in there to find out are there any marks on the body, have they been strangled, and what's happened, and with the CSI you work together to try establish what's occurred.

Resilience is partially explained by what is known generally in psychology as *repeated exposure*, whereby we tend to develop a positive preference towards things and events that we are repeatedly exposed because they become familiar and to some degree 'predictable'. Put simply, the more you attend to body identifications, the more you tend to get used to it. However, this does not sufficiently explain what resilience is, as Roach et al. (2017) found that police investigators reported seeing child victims of homicide as more emotionally and psychologically impactful (on their wellbeing) than when they saw adult victims generally. They also reported that the level of violence used to kill a victim often had differing negative impacts, with extreme violence being most impactful to investigator wellbeing (Roach et al., 2017). Of course, repeated exposure is often linked to complex PTSD, so this is a difficult relationship to untangle.

Resilience, therefore, must be more than simply being repeatedly exposed to the same stimuli (e.g. violent crime scenes). Interestingly, Harvey et al. (Harvey et al., 2016) found firefighters:

> suffer from high rates of mental disorders, with rates of post-traumatic stress disorder, depression and heavy drinking continuing to rise in a linear manner with each additional trauma exposure. The level of psychiatric morbidity among retired fire-fighters appears to be particularly high. Our findings have important implications for the ongoing debates surrounding the detection of mental disorders in high-risk occupations and for policy considerations around the welfare of current and retired emergency workers. *(2016, p. 649)*

Some suggest that resilience comprises different elements such as 'hardiness' and 'mental toughness' (Barrett & Martin, 2014: Clough & Strycharczyk, 2015). Both relate to an individual's way of being able to reframe a negative event into a positive one and how we can evaluate growth opportunities in situations of adversity. This may all seem a bit 'robot-like' or far too automated for human beings, but in a way, it is how some of us sometimes look on the bright side or look for that silver lining when faced with potentially traumatic and challenging events and situations. Research has shown that those who are 'hardy' are less likely to burn out or be impacted most by adverse situations and events (Fyhn et al., 2016).

To reuse (sorry, recycle) our 'medieval analogy', if resilience is getting back in the saddle, and repairing the armour, then hardiness is more akin to whether one is knocked off the horse or whether the armour is pierced in the first place. Hardiness is therefore concerned with how we protect ourselves, for example, against the potential trauma of attending a road traffic accident, and resilience with how we deal with, 'or bounce back from', any negative impacts on our wellbeing that come afterwards.

One Important Element of Hardiness and Resilience Is the Idea of 'Control'

Feelings of Personal Control and Police Wellbeing

What do we mean by having a sense of control and why is it important when trying to understand police officer resilience? Rotter (1966) identified *locus of contro*l as a personality construct to show the degree of personal control that an individual feels that they have about what goes on in their world and in the wider world around them. If 'extraversion' is a related personality trait, then is 'control'? Roach (Roach, 2023) uses a crime prevention context to explain further.

> **BOX 7.1 LOCUS OF CONTROL AND ENCOURAGING PEOPLE TO THINK ABOUT PREVENTING CRIME**
>
> Locus of control is a personality construct relating to an individual's beliefs about the extent to which an individual feels in control of what happens to them and the extent to which they can affect their own life.
>
> - Strong external locus of control is when someone believes what happens to them is luck or fate (i.e. they are not in control of their life) all due to external forces in their environment (e.g. living in a high crime area).
> - Strong internal locus of control is when someone believes they are in control of what happens to them (e.g. with better security, I can reduce my chances of being a victim).

Locus of control is of great interest to us here as it is likely to impact on an individual's (including police officers) overall wellbeing. More specifically, for example, the degree to which we feel that we have a sense of personal control in our workplace will likely impact on our sense of wellbeing and resilience at our workplace. Researchers have categorised workplace 'stressors' in policing as being either 'operationally' (e.g. attending a road traffic accident or leading a successful investigation) or 'organisationally' (e.g. shift work and lack of management support) caused (Shane, 2010) stressors in policing including, the extent to which we feel that we have a say in the wider organisation within which we work is meant by having a sense of control and feeling valued in the workplace. Leiter et al. describe it as being:

> An employees' sense of control as a pivotal quality influencing their perspective on other aspects of work life while value congruence provides an integrative function, summarizing their overall evaluation of worklife.
>
> *(Leiter et al., 2010, p. 57)*

Resilience, Control, and Wellbeing

We sought to explore the likely interaction between resilience, sense of personal control, and police officer wellbeing in a recent study (Roach & Curran, 2025) using data collected by the National Police Wellbeing Survey (NPWS) (Graham et al., 2023). The NPWS is the most complete survey measuring the wellbeing of police personnel in England and Wales, with the latest sweep in 2023 achieving responses from over 40,000 UK police personnel (roughly a 20% return rate overall). Analyses of individual levels of sense of control, resilience, and feelings of being valued, across different police personnel demographics (e.g., gender, age, year of service) and groupings (e.g., rank, role, department) were conducted using statistical output provided by our kind colleagues at the National Police Wellbeing Survey (Graham et al., 2023).

Figure 4.1 shows the levels of resilience and control reported by respondents according to their rank or role (in the case of police staff).

As can be seen, both sense/feeling of control and resilience levels were found to increase with rank, with those at Superintendent/Chief Superintendent levels reporting highest for both.

A further finding was that those at greatest risk of having a low sense of control over the work environment, were most likely to be police constables working varying shifts, with only 1–2 years of experience. This is possibly explained as after the first year's service, they generally become less supervised by a sergeant; for example, they achieve

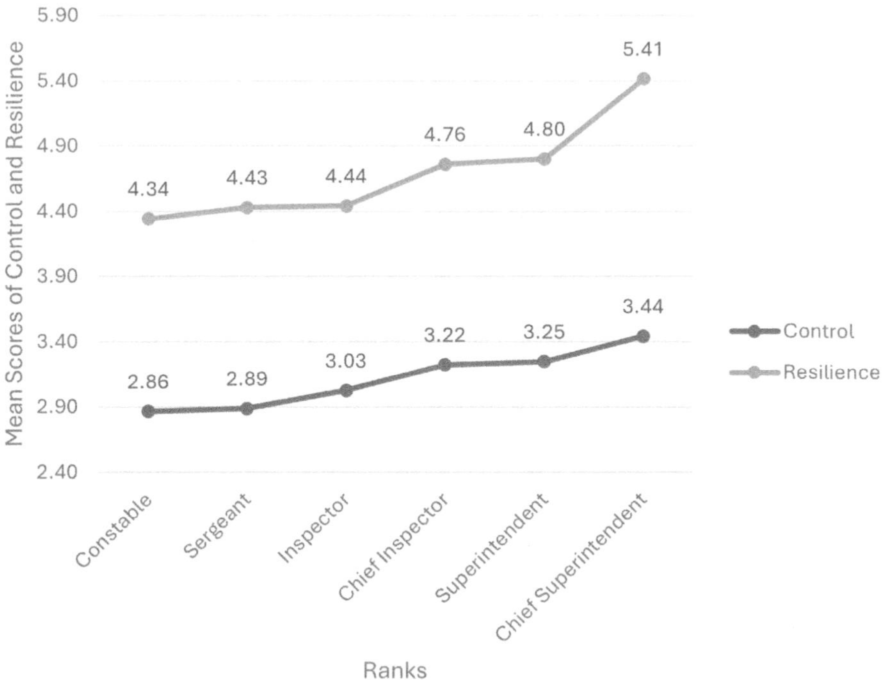

FIGURE 4.1 Mean scores for control and resilience scales according to rank.

Independent Patrol Status (IPS) and therefore feel less in control of their work and organisation (i.e. their police force) as they are left more to make their own decisions.

Next, perceived levels of control in the workplace and resilience were explored according to the respondent's length of experience working in policing. The results are presented in Figure 4.2.

As can be seen, the reported levels of sense/feelings of control rose as experience increased; whereas, contrastingly, reported levels of resilience reduced. This might be explained as although police officers and staff reported that they felt their resilience was reduced over their length of service, for police staff, the picture was slightly different, with those most likely to be at risk of low sense of control at work being those who were practitioners, with no management responsibilities, and having between 11 and 20 years' service, and who work shifts. The longer-term pattern for this cohort of personnel appears to be a more rapidly descending level of resilience as compared to police officers, which declines more steadily by comparison.

So, is there evidence that police wellbeing, resilience, and sense/feelings of personal control have a mutual influence on each other, and if so, to what degrees? Based on the preliminary findings from research, we are currently completing, which explores this exact question in relation to UK Family Liaison Officers (FLO), the answer is 'yes', and they influence each other quite significantly (Roach & Curran, 2025).

We conducted mediation analysis (Hayes, 2018), which, rather than exploring simply a direct 'causal' relationship between an independent and dependent variable (as is commonly assumed), proposes that a third, 'mediating variable' exists which in turn influences the dependent variable. Put simply, the relationship between locus of control and wellbeing is partially explained by levels of resilience. By identifying the effects of a mediator variable, this helps to clarify the nature of the causal relationship between the independent and dependent variables. For example, in our sample of UK Family Liaison Officers, the relationship and degree of influence that feelings of control (i.e. locus of control, LoC) had on reported levels of resilience and wellbeing.

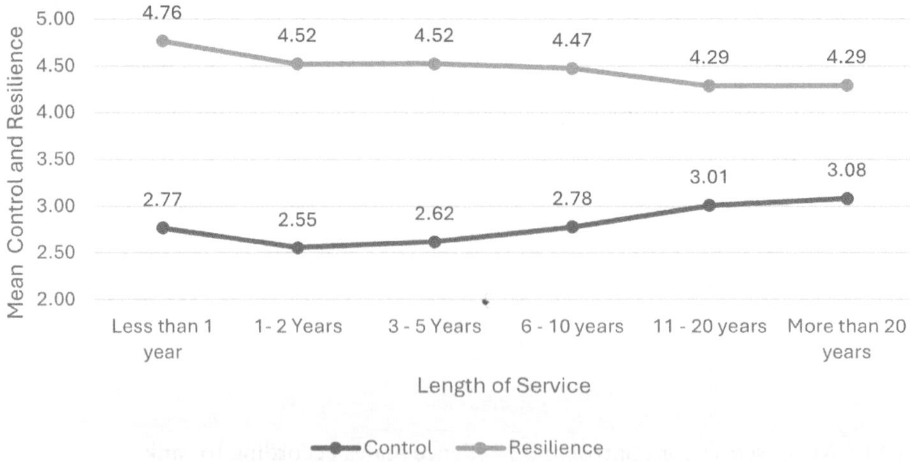

FIGURE 4.2 Control and resilience scale scores according to length of police service/experience.

Our hypothesis was that those reporting low levels of LoC would report having lower levels of resilience and wellbeing than those reporting high levels of LoC. The findings showed that indeed the level of control reported by a Family Liaison Officer (FLO) influenced levels of resilience and wellbeing and vice versa (Roach & Curran 2025). The findings are as follows:

1. Locus of Control positively predicts resilience (i.e. those with internal/high LoC reported having the highest resilience).
2. Those with greater resilience reported greater wellbeing scores.
3. Twenty-three point eight per cent of the effect of Locus of Control on Wellbeing is mediated (explained) by resilience levels.
4. A one unit increase in Locus of Control led to a 0.20 unit increase in resilience.
5. A one unit increase in resilience led to a 1.01 unit increase in wellbeing.
6. A one unit increase in Locus of Control led to a 0.66 unit increase in wellbeing.

Although, admittedly, in the early days, these results do suggest that those with greater perceptions of control have increased levels of resilience and therefore have greater levels of positive wellbeing. These findings suggest that if we can help to improve police officers' and staff feelings of personal control in the workplace (particularly within their organisation), then this is likely to facilitate a corresponding increase in their sense of resilience and overall wellbeing.

Conclusion

To end this chapter in a spirit of optimism, the growing evidence suggests that resilience levels are not set at conception or indeed tied to specific inherited genes. This is primarily because resilience does not appear to be dictated by one source or factor. To quote the American Society of Psychology:

> A number of factors contribute to how well people adapt to adversities, including the ways in which individuals view and engage with the world, the availability and quality of social resources, and specific coping strategies. Psychological research demonstrates that the resources and skills associated with resilience can be cultivated and practiced.
>
> *(APA website n.d.)*

So, if people's levels of resilience can change (more importantly improved), then how can we do this with our police officers and staff? Can we train people to be more resilient?

One study by (Hesketh et al., 2019) used survey questionnaires to explore the impact of a series of resilience training sessions conducted with officers and staff (n = 350). The course sought to brief personnel on (a) what resilience is, (b) how it is shaped by personality, (c) how it can be improved and maintained, (d) what the signs of stress are, and finally, (e) how social support from others impacts on levels of resilience. The following year, the impact of these sessions was measured, and it was found that those who had taken part in *the reported statistically significantly higher levels of* 'resources and communication', 'control', 'work relationships', 'balanced workload', and 'job conditions' than those who had not. These findings suggest that those who undergo resilience training can be helped to adapt more positively to an array of different occupational stressors, and thus better protect their wellbeing. It is unclear, however, whether this change can be definitively attributed to the course, as levels of participant wellbeing were not available prior to the workshops. We are clinging to the fact that participants reported responding positively to the training, indicating that training of this ilk at least shows promise and calls for further research to explore this further.

Miller et al. (2020) found that 20% of police officers might be experiencing a 'trauma-related disorder' (although this figure has been disputed by some e.g. see Stevelink et al. 2020). In a feasibility study they aimed

> to teach new recruits' practical skills to help them adapt to the extraordinary and difficult incidents that lie ahead.
>
> *(Miller et al., 2020, p. 311)*

Jess Miller and colleagues sought to improve the resilience and hardiness levels of police officers by supporting them to be able to 'better process' experiences of trauma. The training comprised three training sessions – two sessions for those taking part in the actual experiment, and one session for a 'control group' (for comparison). In session one, the officers were asked to recall a difficult incident and to put themselves back into their memory of it. Officers were then asked to think of themselves as having a bird's-eye view of themselves at the incident and were taught how to do free-style mapping techniques and free-text recall. In session two, the officers were then asked to shift that bird's-eye view as if they were watching from a bystander's perspective, alongside other timeline techniques. The experiment found that those officers who took part in the training reported feeling generally 'more at ease' about their experience than they had before. Officers felt that they were able to 'depersonalise' the event to a greater degree and more able to shift away from feeling guilty about what they previously felt they should and/or could have done. This training helped the officers to deal with the memory by safely putting 'it into a box', by reprocessing it, as opposed to leaving the traumatic memories in a box – 'unsorted and unprocessed' – a potential ticking trauma time-bomb.

Notes

1 See https://www.legislation.gov.uk/ukpga/2000/36/contents for more information (accessed 5/2/2025).
2 See https://www.apa.org/topics/resilience (accessed 6/2/2025).
3 See https://explore.bps.org.uk/content/report guideline/bpsrep.2018.rep122/chapter/bpsrep.2018.rep122.7 (accessed 6/2/2025).

References

Anshel, M. H. (2000). A conceptual model and implications for coping with stressful events in police work. *Criminal Justice and Behavior*, *27*(3), 375–400. https://doi.org/10.1177/0093854800027003006

Barrett, E., & Martin, P. (2014). *Extreme: Why some people thrive at the limits*. Oxford University Press.

Brewin, C. R., Miller, J. K., Soffia, M., Peart, A., & Burchell, B. (2020). Posttraumatic stress disorder and complex posttraumatic stress disorder in UK police officers. *Psychological Medicine*, *52*(7), 1287–1295. https://doi.org/10.1017/S0033291720003025

Cartwright, A., & Roach, J. (2021). The wellbeing of UK police: A study of recorded absences from work of UK police employees due to psychological illness and stress using freedom of information act data. *Policing: A Journal of Policy and Practice*, *15*(2), 1326–1338. https://doi.org/10.1093/police/paaa033

Clough, P., & Strycharczyk, D. (2015). *Developing mental toughness: Coaching strategies to improve performance, resilience and wellbeing.* Kogan Page.

Curran, L. S. (2024). *"Every contact leaves a trace": Investigating the mental health impact of being a senior investigating officer* [Doctoral thesis, The University of Huddersfield]. https://pure.hud.ac.uk/en/studentTheses/every-contact-leaves-a-trace

Fletcher, D., & Sarkar, M. (2013). Psychological resilience: A review and critique of definitions, concepts, and theory. *European Psychologist*, *18*(1), 12–23. https://doi.org/10.1027/1016-9040/a000124

Fyhn, T., Fjell, K. K., & Johnsen, B. H. (2016). Resilience factors among police investigators: Hardiness-commitment a unique contributor. *Journal of Police and Criminal Psychology*, *31*(4), 261–269. https://doi.org/10.1007/s11896-015-9181-6

Graham, L., Brown, N., Plater, M., Gracey, S., Legate, N., & Weinstein, N. (2020). *National policing wellbeing survey 2019.* https://www.oscarkilo.org.uk/resources/national-wellbeing-survey/2019-wellbeing-survey Accessed December 10, 2025.

Graham, L., Plater, M., & Brown, N. (2023). *National police wellbeing survey 2023.*

Harvey, S. B., Milligan-Saville, J. S., Paterson, H. M., Harkness, E. L., Marsh, A. M., Dobson, M., Kemp, R., & Bryant, R. A. (2016). The mental health of fire-fighters: An examination of the impact of repeated trauma exposure. *Australian and New Zealand Journal of Psychiatry*, *50*(7), 649–658. https://doi.org/10.1177/0004867415615217

Hayes, A. F. (2018). *Introduction to mediation, moderation, and conditional process analysis: a regression-based approach* (2nd ed.). The Guilford Press.

Hesketh, I., Cooper, C., & Ivy, J. (2019). Leading the asset: Resilience training efficacy in UK policing. *Police Journal*, *92*(1), 56–71. https://doi.org/10.1177/0032258X18763101/FORMAT/EPUB

Lazarus, R. S., & Folkman, S. (1984). *Stress, appraisal, and coping.* Springer.

Leiter, M. P., Gascón, S., & Martínez-Jarreta, B. (2010). Making sense of work life: A structural model of burnout. *Journal of Applied Social Psychology*, *40*, 57–75. https://doi.org/10.1111/j.1559 1816.2009.00563.x

Miller, J. K., Peart, A., & Soffia, M. (2020). Can police be trained in trauma processing to minimise PTSD symptoms? Feasibility and proof of concept with a newly recruited UK police population. *Police Journal (Chichester)*, *93*(4), 310–331. https://doi.org/10.1177/0032258X19864852

Roach, J. (2023). *Practical psychology for policing.* Policy Press. https://doi.org/10.46692/9781447325932

Roach, J., Cartwright, A., & Sharratt, K. (2017). Dealing with the unthinkable: A study of the cognitive and emotional stress of adult and child homicide investigations on police investigators. *Journal of Police and Criminal Psychology*, *32*(3), 251–262. https://doi.org/10.1007/s11896-016-9218-5

Roach, J., & Curran, L. (2025). *Locus of control and police wellbeing.* Unpublished report.

Roach, J., Sharratt, K., Cartwright, A., & Skou Roer, T. (2018). Cognitive and emotional stressors of child homicide investigations on U.K. and danish police investigators. *Homicide Studies*, *22*(3), 296–320. https://doi.org/10.1177/1088767918759695

Rotter, J. B. (1966). Generalized expectancies for internal versus external control of reinforcement. *Psychological Monographs*, *80*(1), 1–28. https://doi.org/10.1037/H0092976

Shane, J. M. (2010). Organizational stressors and police performance. *Journal of Criminal Justice*, *38*(4), 807–818. https://doi.org/10.1016/j.jcrimjus.2010.05.008

Southwick, F. S., Martini, B. L., Charney, D. S., & Southwick, S. M. (2016). Leadership and resilience. In *Leadership today: Practices for personal and professional performance* (pp. 315–333). Cham: Springer.

Stevelink, S. A. M., Opie, E., Pernet, D., Gao, H., Elliott, P., Wessely, S., Fear, N. T., Hotopf, M., & Greenberg, N. (2020). Probable PTSD, depression and anxiety in 40,299 UK police officers and staff: Prevalence, risk factors and associations with blood pressure. *PLOS ONE*, *15*(11), e0240902. https://doi.org/10.1371/JOURNAL.PONE.0240902

5

SLEEP, FATIGUE AND SHIFT WORK

Preparing for Duty and Staying Safe

Yvonne Taylor

Introduction

For those joining the policing family, it may be the first introduction to working shifts. The transition into policing and subsequent onset of shift work is a challenging and critical time on a career path (James et al., 2019). Maintaining shift work and wellbeing is complex. As such, it is essential to develop an understanding of the risks involved, along with increasing the level of preparedness for undertaking and coping with shift work.

Around 20% of the workforce worldwide currently work shifts (Harris et al., 2024). Shift work is necessary in many occupations, particularly in policing where we need to be available round the clock to attend emergencies and calls for service.

Shift work can be broadly defined as a pattern of work outside the standard working day and standard working week, ordinarily associated with the Western world office practices of recent years, involving a working week of Monday to Friday, eight hours a day, usually during daylight hours (McCormond, 2004).

Shift working can follow a variety of patterns; for example, shifts can either be fixed, where employees work the same shift regularly depending on the needs and demands of the business or service, or be varied and rotating (Richbell & Chan, 2011). However, shift workers normally work in teams or groups of workers who make up separate shift teams. In UK policing, a rotating pattern is usually followed, at least for those classed as being in frontline roles. Rotating shift workers are prone to more problems than fixed-shift workers. This is believed to be due to sleep deprivation and misalignment of circadian phases (Gold et al., 1992).

Whatever the particular shift pattern that is followed, shift work is generally associated with working and sleeping out of phase with the natural circadian rhythm (Boersma et al., 2023). This causes detrimental effects on sleep health and police officers often report that shift work is one of the most difficult aspects of the job. Add to this are the high demand and high stress of policing; it is no surprise that it is challenging to cope with (Violanti et al., 2009). There is no ideal shift pattern that suits all, but there

DOI: 10.4324/9781003518860-6

are suggestions that make some patterns more favourable than others in terms of psychological and physiological wellbeing. For example, forward rotating systems, with a shift change every few days, limiting the number of consecutive night shifts, along with limiting the number of hours worked on night shifts and stipulating minimum rest hours between shifts are all thought to help the human body better adapt to a schedule (Harma et al., 2006; Cairns et al., 2008).

Rearranging sleep and working times can be highly impactful, not only on those working shifts, but also on their families (Violanti et al., 2009), who also have to adapt to a loved one coming and going at irregular times and a certain level of disruption and sleep disturbance that may cause in the household.

Shift work has been shown to be detrimental to overall health and wellbeing (Harris et al., 2024), including increased sleep problems, sleep disorders, cardiovascular issues and digestive ill-health (Scholarios et al., 2017). In addition, it is linked to increased errors and poorer quality of work. It is for these reasons that it is vital to increase knowledge and preparation. In doing so, we can help to manage shift work safely, mitigate risks wherever possible and help to keep workers healthier, from the moment they begin working shifts.

Sleep and Wakefulness

We spend around one third of our lives at work; we should also spend around one third of our lives sleeping. Sleep needs vary widely; however, most healthy adults need between 7 and 9 hours of sleep in a 24-hour period, ordinarily at night. We don't really adapt to getting less sleep than we need – we may get used to a schedule, but our judgement, reaction time and other functions will suffer (Hirshkowitz et al., 2015). Sleep is a necessity, not a luxury; it is necessary for optimal functioning and therefore needs to be prioritised.

Sufficient, good quality sleep is essential for good health and wellbeing, normal brain function and cognitive performance (Buysse, 2014). Normal sleep consists of a series of repeating cycles, where intensity varies from being awake to light sleep, deep sleep and dream sleep. There are normally four to six of these cycles during a normal night's sleep, with each cycle lasting approximately 90 minutes (Shneerson, 2009). All of these stages are essential for good health.

There are at least two factors regulating sleep timing – the circadian rhythm and the homeostatic drive for sleep. These run over a 24-hour period, strongly influenced by the natural cycles of light and dark. The circadian rhythm is the most prominent pattern of human behaviour, where people are normally active during the day and asleep at night. At night, many of the processes that are active during the day start to slow down as our bodies prepare for sleep. Circadian rhythms direct a wide variety of functions from daily fluctuations in wakefulness to body temperature, metabolism and the release of hormones. They control the timing of sleep and cause you to be sleepy at night and your tendency to wake in the morning. Circadian rhythms synchronise with environmental cues, such as light and temperature about the time of day, but they do continue without these cues. The circadian process stimulates the night-time release of the 'sleep hormone' melatonin, which has the effect of lowering alertness and increasing the desire for sleep (Horrocks & Pounder, 2006). Sleepiness peaks are generally between 03:00–05:00 and

14:00–16:00 hours, and it is at these times that we experience our worst physical and mental performance and therefore, we are most at risk of accident and injury resulting from sleepiness (Alhola & Polo-Kantola, 2007). It is also between these times that there is an increase in fatigue-related road traffic collisions (May & Baldwin, 2009).

The homeostatic process is the drive for sleep that increases the longer we are awake. As time awake increases, sleep pressure increases. It usually reaches a maximum after around 16 hours of wakefulness, decreasing whilst asleep and reaching a minimum at the natural waking time in the morning. If the sleep period is shorter than required, a 'sleep debt' builds up (Wilson & Nutt, 2013).

The circadian rhythm and homeostatic process work together to promote stability in sleep and wakefulness cycles (Dijk & Edgar, 1999). Figure 5.1 illustrates the interaction between the processes. Both your circadian alerting signals and sleep drive, shown here as 'sleep load', increase gradually throughout the day. Your circadian alerting signal peaks just before bedtime and then starts to decrease. This is when the sleep drive overpowers it and causes you to feel sleepy. The sleepiness that results from these processes occurs regardless of training, occupation, education or commitment to stay awake: Only sleep can reduce sleep debt, and eventually your body will dictate that you repay that debt (Connor, 2009).

Disturbed Sleep and Health Implications

Disturbed sleep is probably the major outcome of shift work. Working irregular hours, such as those involved in shift work, disrupts these natural rhythms and levels of alertness when the body is ready for sleep. This makes getting sufficient sleep challenging. Working shifts, particularly night shifts, not only affects the quality of sleep but also the quantity. Studies show that night shift workers get, on average, 2 hours less sleep in

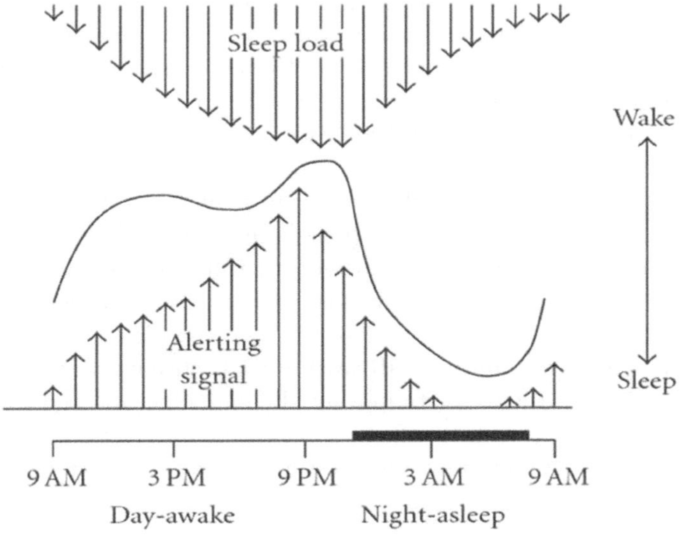

FIGURE 5.1 The interaction between the circadian and homeostatic processes (Dijk & Edgar, 1999).

a 24-hr period when compared with regular day workers (Taylor et al., 2019): So, we need to be smart about protecting the time we have available for sleep and making the most of it.

Unsurprisingly then, complaints from shift workers tend to be related to an inability to get enough good quality sleep following night shifts (Bajraktarov et al., 2011). Poor sleep results in chronic fatigue, job-related injuries and accidents, mental ill-health, adverse effects on the immune system and increased risk of heart disease and other illnesses. In addition, night shift work is associated with an increased rate of sleep disorders, dissatisfaction with the workplace and increased work absences (Muecke, 2005).

Many individuals, including police officers, work at night and are trying to function when the human body is designed to sleep. They are trying to perform when alertness, vigilance and cognitive abilities are at their lowest and trying to sleep at times that others think are peculiar. As most people are awake at these times, society appears to place less importance on protecting the sleep of shift workers during the day. For example, few people would consider making a phone call in the middle of the night; however, the same consideration is perhaps not applied when phoning a night shift worker during the day (Monk & Folkard, 1992).

The National Police Wellbeing Service 2019 Wellbeing Survey (Graham et al., 2020) attracted 35,000 responses from police officers and staff across England and Wales. It highlighted that 45% of police officers reported frequently having less than 6 hours' sleep a night. This is clearly well below the recommended amount of sleep for healthy adults and, as such, places this cohort at risk of chronic sleep deprivation and associated ill health.

Those who continue working irregular hours over a number of years can develop chronic circadian and sleep disruption, sometimes resulting in shift work sleep disorder (SWSD). SWSD is a circadian rhythm sleep disorder, characterised by excessive sleepiness, insomnia or both as a result of shift work. It is often associated with accidental injury, absenteeism and other difficulties (Booker et al., 2018). SWSD, along with other untreated sleep disorders, such as insomnia or obstructive sleep apnoea, increases the risk of accident, injury and road traffic collisions. Sleep disorders are common and largely undiagnosed amongst police officers; as such, it is beneficial to raise awareness of these conditions and to utilise simple sleep disorder screening tools amongst this cohort (Rajaratnam et al., 2013).

On top of the potential risks of these disorders, there are individual differences in tolerance for shift work, including age, personality traits, chronotype (a tendency to be a morning or evening person) and some genetic influence. Some people tolerate shift work well, whereas others develop problems, such as SWSD discussed above (Saksvik et al., 2011).

There is no simple fix to improve shift work for all those workers employed in it. It is for these reasons that shift work is complicated by many factors, and shift workers need to try to understand methods to counteract the negative effects of working shifts that work for them, in order to maximise alertness and performance (Folkard et al., 2005).

Preparing for Duty – Mitigating the Risk

Sleepiness and fatigue are both occupational and personal risk factors; hence, they should be seen as a shared responsibility between an organisation and its workers. Employers have a duty to protect health, safety and welfare. This includes, for example, ensuring a safe working environment (as far as possible); providing schedules and shift rotas that provide enough opportunity for rest and recuperation; offering training and procedures for managing sleepiness and fatigue; providing areas for rest; and establishing means of raising and reporting concerns (Noone & Waclawski, 2018). However, there is also an expectation of personal responsibility on the workforce to ensure they are well rested and prepared for shift work.

New shift workers may have limited techniques for coping with the changes that shift work brings to their sleep, normal bodily rhythms and other lifestyle factors that accompany shift work (Harris et al., 2024). In addition, improving sleep and preparing for shift work will likely involve a degree of behaviour change – something that is not easy for any of us.

We are tired for a number of reasons, over and above our particular working pattern. These include lifestyle, physical or psychological reasons. Humans are the only species that procrastinate over sleep (Kroese et al., 2016). Modern life entices us to extend our days, where we sacrifice sleep for reasons such as entertainment, fun or in pursuit of success, where we are often oblivious to the toll it can take on our health and wellbeing. On the other hand, illness, side effects of medication, stress, depression or anxiety can all interfere with sleep from a physical or psychological point of view.

We can take control of some of these aspects in order to make a difference and develop a greater tolerance to shift work. Personal management strategies including healthy sleep practices to promote sleep and help the circadian clock to adapt to imposed work pattern is a good starting point.

Healthy sleep practices broadly refer to adopting behaviours that facilitate sleep and avoiding behaviours that interfere with good sleep (Shriane et al., 2020, 2023). They are an inexpensive way in which to improve sleep quality and quantity and minimise sleep disorders (Irish et al., 2015).

Healthy sleep practices can be broadly explained in four main areas.

Sleep and Routine

As a shift worker, it is difficult to get enough sleep, so it is important to prioritise and allow sufficient time to get those recommended 7–9 hours. Despite the irregular hours, it is possible to develop a successful sleep schedule. Your schedule will be individual to you and should be based on your lifestyle and working hours. If you struggle to sleep during the day, as most people do, supplement your main sleep period with an additional sleep period later in the day. Strategic napping can also be beneficial for shift workers. Shorter naps (around 20 minutes) can help boost alertness, while longer naps (around 90 minutes) can help to reduce sleep debt (Shriane et al., 2023).

The Environment

Create a comfortable and inviting sleep environment. Keep the room as dark as possible, either by utilising blackout blinds or an eye mask. Keep it cool, and block out noise by closing doors and windows and using earplugs, if required.

In addition to creating your own personal sleep environment, it is also helpful to notify others when you will be working night shifts or sleeping during the day. This should help to minimise disturbances by encouraging family, housemates or neighbours to keep the noise down.

Nutrition

Not only is sleep influenced by light and darkness, appetite and digestion are too. Digestion works much better during daylight hours, so it is important to consider what and when to eat. Eating more nutritious foods helps to balance energy, and foods that provide a gradual release of energy keep you fuller for longer and reduce the desire to snack. Eating too close to bedtime diverts the body's attention to digestion, rather than sleep. Try to avoid heavy, fatty meals that take longer to digest if eating close to bedtime and opt for lighter meals during night shifts. Existing guidelines for adults suggest approximately 2080 calories per day (Crowther et al., 2022).

Keeping hydrated keeps your brain busy, and often when your brain thinks you're hungry, you're actually thirsty, so try a drink first (Benelam & Wyness, 2010).

Caffeine is a central nervous system stimulant, so it can be helpful if used strategically to promote wakefulness and increase alertness when you are tired. It takes around 30 minutes from consumption for caffeine to become active in the body, but it can stay in your system for many hours, so you need to be mindful that when trying to sleep following your shift that, caffeine may still be active, which will increase the time it takes to fall asleep and may reduce your sleep quality (Gardiner et al., 2023).

Exercise

If you can't avoid sitting in a vehicle or at a desk for long periods of time, it is important to get physically active during these times. Regular exercise is good for general health, raising body temperature and increasing alertness, but it also helps you sleep better. Exercise recommendations for adults are a minimum of 150 minutes of moderate intensity or 75 minutes of vigorous intensity physical activity per week. Insufficient exercise contributes to increased mortality rates (Crowther et al., 2022).

Good sleep, physical health and mental health are deeply intertwined and contribute heavily to overall health and wellbeing. Along with independent risk factors, each also has an interactive effect on the others. For example, insufficient sleep is associated with greater calorie consumption (Crowther et al., 2022). It's therefore vital that we pay attention to sleep, along with engaging in exercise and being mindful of nutritional intake, to help us promote good mental and physical health.

Road Safety and Commuting Considerations

Fatigue and sleep deprivation can be problematic when experienced in many day-to-day situations. However, when drivers are affected by fatigue, it can cause extreme danger, bringing a high risk of road traffic collisions, often resulting in serious or fatal consequences. Fatigue can affect any driver, but those who drive as part of their job and/or who are shift workers are more at risk, and there has been a reported increase in road traffic collisions whilst driving home from night shifts (Stutts et al., 2003). Fatigue doesn't just mean falling asleep at the wheel; driving ability can be affected long before this. When drivers begin to notice or struggle with fatigue, they are already impaired (James & Vila, 2015).

Driving while tired is not unusual, with research showing it to be a contributory factor in around 20% of serious road traffic collisions on motorways and monotonous roads (Jackson et al., 2011). Crashes involving sleepy drivers tend to be more serious in nature. They typically involve vehicles running off the road or into the back of another vehicle; they tend to happen at high speed, because drivers who are asleep don't use their brakes! Therefore, the risk of death or serious injury is high (Horne & Reyner, 1995). If you nod off at 70 mph – you could travel 200 metres without knowing it whilst microsleeping.

The dangers of driving under the influence of alcohol or drugs are well documented and have been publicised over the years. Driving whilst fatigued has been shown to be just as dangerous, where the impairment associated with being awake for 24 hours has been shown to be equivalent to a blood alcohol concentration of 100 milligrams of alcohol per 100 millilitres of breath. This is above the current drink drive limit in England and Wales of 80 milligrams of alcohol per 100 millilitres of breath (Dawson & Reid, 1997).

Many factors contribute to driver sleepiness – lack of sleep or disturbed sleep is just one risk involved with shift work. Add to that the other daily pressures that many people have, such as caring responsibilities, undiagnosed sleep disorders, hefty commutes or travelling at times of circadian low, and the risk increases further. Key problems associated with work-related road safety therefore include extended waking or driving hours, reduced sleep and working during the night at times of circadian low – all things that put shift workers at risk.

Conclusions and Further Resources

Healthy sleep is all about duration, timing and continuity (Chaput et al., 2020):

Duration – Getting sufficient sleep is difficult for shift workers.

Timing – When sleep timing isn't in sync with circadian rhythms, as is the case for many shift workers, then it is more difficult to get to sleep, to stay asleep and to get enough sleep.

Continuity – Quality sleep is continuous, with minimal disruption.

By prioritising the time we have available for sleep, whilst being mindful of our circadian rhythm, we can improve and increase our sleep. However, shift work makes getting sufficient sleep challenging, and a reduction in sleep causes safety concerns. Shift work-induced fatigue is a significant risk factor, increasing the likelihood of accidents, injuries and road traffic collisions. Getting good quality sleep makes you feel better and improves learning and memory, strengthens the immune system and makes it easier to maintain a healthier diet. Taking advantage of napping, particularly prior to night shifts, can be an effective countermeasure to deteriorating alertness and performance.

Lack of knowledge about the negative effects of shift work has adverse wellbeing implications and can result in increased work absences, along with the risks associated with road traffic collisions, both on duty and whilst commuting. It is for these reasons that early intervention with new shift workers needs to be the norm. This enables those new workers to begin their career from a well-educated perspective and embed good habits from the outset.

Education is of primary importance so that shift workers, and particularly those who drive, are aware and can take appropriate steps to reduce the impact of these factors, including driving at vulnerable times, where possible.

Self-care is not selfish: It is necessary to keep your own batteries charged in order to stay fit and healthy. Seek out help if you are struggling in this area.

The National Police Wellbeing Service is designed specifically to meet the needs of those in policing. There are numerous resources that are free and easy to access via the website https://www.oscarkilo.org.uk. These are designed for organisations, individuals, families and those leaving the policing organisation and cover all aspects of wellbeing support. There is a specific 'Healthy Living' campaign that provides assistance on all aspects of sleep, nutrition and physical health touched upon here, including hints and tips, healthy eating challenges, recorded webinars and sleep disorder screening.

If you think you may have a sleep disorder, or screen positive in the online screening, seek professional medical help.

References

Alhola, P., & Polo-Kantola, P. (2007). Sleep deprivation: Impact on cognitive performance. *Neuropsychiatric Disease and Treatment*, *3*(5), 553–567.

Bajraktarov, S., Novotni, A., Manusheva, N., Nikovska, D. G., Miceva-Velickovska, E., Zdraveska, N., ... & Richter, K. S. (2011). Main effects of sleep disorders related to shift work—opportunities for preventive programs. *EPMA Journal*, *2*, 365–370.

Benelam, B., & Wyness, L. (2010). Hydration and health: A review. *Nutrition Bulletin*, *35*(1), 3–25.

Boersma, G. J., Mijnster, T., Vantyghem, P., Kerkhof, G. A., & Lancel, M. (2023). Shift work is associated with extensively disordered sleep, especially when working nights. *Frontiers in Psychiatry*, *14*, 1233640.

Booker, L. A., Magee, M., Rajaratnam, S. M., Sletten, T. L., & Howard, M. E. (2018). Individual vulnerability to insomnia, excessive sleepiness and shift work disorder amongst healthcare shift workers. A systematic review. *Sleep Medicine Reviews*, *41*, 220–233.

Buysse, D. J. (2014). Sleep health: Can we define it? Does it matter? *Sleep*, *37*(1), 9–17.

Cairns, H., Hendry, B., Leather, A., & Moxham, J. (2008). Outcomes of the European working time directive. *Bmj*, *337*, a942.

Chaput, J. P., Dutil, C., Featherstone, R., Ross, R., Giangregorio, L., Saunders, T. J., ... & Carrier, J. (2020). Sleep timing, sleep consistency, and health in adults: A systematic review. *Applied Physiology, Nutrition, and Metabolism*, *45*(10), S232–S247.

Connor, J. L. (2009). The role of driver sleepiness in car crashes: A review of the epidemiological evidence. In J. C. Verster, S. R. Pandi-Perumal, J. G. Ramaekers, & J. J. de Gier (Eds.), *Drugs, driving and traffic safety* (pp. 187–205). Birkhäuser Basel.

Crowther, M. E., Ferguson, S. A., & Reynolds, A. C. (2022). Longitudinal studies of sleep, physical activity and nutritional intake in shift workers: A scoping review. *Sleep Medicine Reviews*, *63*, 101612.

Dawson, D., & Reid, K. (1997). Fatigue, alcohol and performance impairment. *Nature*, *388*(6639), 235–235.

Dijk, D. J., & Edgar, D. M. (1999). Circadian and homeostatic control of wakefulness and sleep. *Lung Biology in Health and Disease*, *133*, 111.

Folkard, S., Lombardi, D. A., & Tucker, P. T. (2005). Shiftwork: Safety, sleepiness and sleep. *Industrial Health*, *43*(1), 20–23.

Gardiner, C., Weakley, J., Burke, L. M., Roach, G. D., Sargent, C., Maniar, N., ... & Halson, S. L. (2023). The effect of caffeine on subsequent sleep: A systematic review and meta-analysis. *Sleep Medicine Reviews*, *69*, 101764.

Gold, D. R., Rogacz, S., Bock, N., Tosteson, T. D., Baum, T. M., Speizer, F. E., & Czeisler, C. A. (1992). Rotating shift work, sleep, and accidents related to sleepiness in hospital nurses. *American Journal of Public Health*, *82*(7), 1011–1014.

Graham, L., Brown, N., Plater, M., Gracey, S., Legate, N., & Weinstein, N. (2020). *National police wellbeing survey 2019*. Policing Research Unit, Durham University. Available at: https://www.college.police.uk/News/College-news/Pages/Oscar-Kilo-wellbeingsurvey-results-June-2020.aspx.

Härmä, M., Tarja, H., Irja, K., Mikael, S., Jussi, V., Anne, B., & Pertti, M. (2006). A controlled intervention study on the effects of a very rapidly forward rotating shift system on sleep–wakefulness and well-being among young and elderly shift workers. *International Journal of Psychophysiology*, *59*(1), 70–79.

Harris, R., Kavaliotis, E., Drummond, S. P., & Wolkow, A. P. (2024). Sleep, mental health and physical health in new shift workers transitioning to shift work: Systematic review and meta-analysis. *Sleep Medicine Reviews*, *75*, 101927.

Hirshkowitz, M., Whiton, K., Albert, S. M., Alessi, C., Bruni, O., DonCarlos, L., ... & Hillard, P. J. A. (2015). National Sleep Foundation's sleep time duration recommendations: Methodology and results summary. *Sleep Health*, *1*(1), 40–43.

Horne, J. A., & Reyner, L. A. (1995). Sleep related vehicle accidents. *BMJ*, *310*(6979), 565–567.

Horrocks, N., Pounder, R., & an RCP Working Group. (2006). Working the night shift: Preparation, survival and recovery-a guide for junior doctors. *Clinical Medicine*, *6*(1), 61–67.

Irish, L. A., Kline, C. E., Gunn, H. E., Buysse, D. J., & Hall, M. H. (2015). The role of sleep hygiene in promoting public health: A review of empirical evidence. *Sleep Medicine Reviews*, *22*, 23–36.

Jackson, P., Hilditch, C., Holmes, A., Reed, N., Merat, N., & Smith, L. (2011). Fatigue and road safety: A critical analysis of recent evidence. *Department for Transport, Road Safety Web Publication*, *21*, 44.

James, L., Butterfield, P., & Tuell, E. (2019). Nursing students' sleep patterns and perceptions of safe practice during their entrée to shift work. *Workplace Health & Safety*, *67*(11), 547–553.

James, S. M., & Vila, B. (2015). Police drowsy driving: Predicting fatigue-related performance decay. *Policing: An International Journal of Police Strategies & Management*, *38*(3), 517–538.

Kroese, F. M., Nauts, S., Kamphorst, B. A., Anderson, J. H., & de Ridder, D. T. (2016). Bedtime procrastination: A behavioral perspective on sleep insufficiency. In F. M. Sirois, & T. A. Pychyl (Eds.). *Procrastination, health, and well-being* (pp. 93–119). Academic Press.

May, J. F., & Baldwin, C. L. (2009). Driver fatigue: The importance of identifying causal factors of fatigue when considering detection and countermeasure technologies. *Transportation Research Part F: Traffic Psychology and Behaviour*, *12*(3), 218–224.

McOrmond, T. (2004). Changes in working trends over the past decade. *Labour Market Trends*, *112*(1), 25–36.

Monk, T. H., & Folkard, S. (1992). *Making shiftwork tolerable*. CRC Press.

Muecke, S. (2005). Effects of rotating night shifts: Literature review. *Journal of Advanced Nursing*, *50*(4), 433–439.

Noone, P., & Waclawski, E. (2018). Fatigue risk management systems needed in healthcare. *Occupational Medicine*, *68*(8), 496–498.

Rajaratnam, S. M., Howard, M. E., & Grunstein, R. R. (2013). Sleep loss and circadian disruption in shift work: Health burden and management. *Medical Journal of Australia*, *199*(8), S11–15.

Richbell, S., & Chan, K. W. (2011). Permanent night shifts in the 24/7 economy. *University of York. The York Management School*, 1743–4041.

Saksvik, I. B., Bjorvatn, B., Hetland, H., Sandal, G. M., & Pallesen, S. (2011). Individual differences in tolerance to shift work–a systematic review. *Sleep Medicine Reviews*, *15*(4), 221–235.

Scholarios, D., Hesselgreaves, H., & Pratt, R. (2017). Unpredictable working time, well-being and health in the police service. *The International Journal of Human Resource Management*, *28*(16), 2275–2298.

Shneerson, J. M. (2009). *Sleep medicine: A guide to sleep and its disorders*. John Wiley & Sons.

Shriane, A. E., Ferguson, S. A., Jay, S. M., & Vincent, G. E. (2020). Sleep hygiene in shift workers: A systematic literature review. *Sleep Medicine Reviews*, *53*, 101336.

Shriane, A. E., Rigney, G., Ferguson, S. A., Bin, Y. S., & Vincent, G. E. (2023). Healthy sleep practices for shift workers: Consensus sleep hygiene guidelines using a Delphi methodology. *Sleep*, *46*(12), zsad182.

Stutts, J. C., Wilkins, J. W., Osberg, J. S., & Vaughn, B. V. (2003). Driver risk factors for sleep-related crashes. *Accident Analysis & Prevention*, *35*(3), 321–331.

Taylor, Y., Merat, N., & Jamson, S. (2019). The effects of fatigue on cognitive performance in police officers and staff during a forward rotating shift pattern. *Safety and Health at Work*, *10*(1), 67–74.

The National Police Wellbeing Service – Oscar Kilo. https://www.oscarkilo.org.uk/

Violanti, J. M., Burchfiel, C. M., Hartley, T. A., Mnatsakanova, A., Fekedulegn, D., Andrew, M. E., ... & Vila, B. J. (2009). Atypical work hours and metabolic syndrome among police officers. *Archives of Environmental & Occupational Health*, *64*(3), 194–201.

Wilson, S., & Nutt, D. (2013). *Sleep disorders*. OUP Oxford.

6

'IT'S WHY YOU GET UP IN THE MORNING'

Jim Foley

Mental Health in United Kingdom (UK) Policing

The study of mental health in policing has become a popular area of research and regularly evidences the existence of poor mental health and wellbeing in police officers in the United Kingdom (UK). The mental health charity Mind (2015) in their 'blue light' survey of the UK emergency services evidenced that 91% of police personnel experienced stress, low mood, or poor mental health, with policing having the highest levels of personal experience of mental health disorders amongst all 'blue light' services. A follow-up survey in 2019 (Mind, 2019), highlighted that poor mental health in policing was still an issue, with 70.4% of police respondents stating they had personal experience of poor mental health. Police officer wellbeing is an important area of study, as poor mental health is likely to lead to increased sickness, increased absence from work, and reduced productivity, all of which will influence how an officer is able to respond to the public as well as how they are likely to care for and treat victims of crime (Boag-Munroe, 2017; Hesketh & Cooper, 2014; Houdmont & Elliot-Davies, 2016).

Whilst all roles within policing clearly have their own complexities and demands, those involving child abuse and sexual offences have been recognised as some of the most stressful and high-risk roles in policing (Brown et al., 1999; College of Policing, 2020; Roach et al., 2017). Previous research (Foley et al., 2022, 2023) has maintained that the nature of police trauma and how officers in these high-risk roles cope is not fully understood. Foley et al. (2023) conducted research with officers who investigate child abuse, child sexual exploitation, and rape (n = 343n) and found that 23% (n = 81n) of officers had potentially clinical levels of post-traumatic stress disorder (PTSD); 26% (n = 92n) had moderate to severe levels of anxiety; 35% (n = 122n) had moderate to severe levels of depression, and 12.7% (n = 45n) had moderate to severe levels of anxiety, depression, and potentially clinical levels of PTSD. As this was purely a quantitative study, there was no explanation or context available which looked behind the data to understand what was happening to these officers, what was causing these potentially

DOI: 10.4324/9781003518860-7

clinical levels of PTSD, anxiety, and depression, and importantly, were these officers coping with their roles, and if so, how? Further research was therefore needed in this extremely complex and important area to try to understand how officers in these high-risk roles cope with the work they do on a daily basis.

Method

In order to gain this understanding of how police officers cope with the work that they do, a pragmatic and abductive approach was undertaken utilising grounded theory methodology (Corbin & Strauss, 2008, 2015; Strauss & Corbin, 1990, 1998) as a framework to develop a model of coping.

Purposeful sampling was undertaken where selected officers who worked in rape and child abuse investigation (detective constables, police constables, detective sergeants) within one area of a large police force were contacted via email to ask for their participation in the study. Individual consent was obtained, and semi-structured interviews were conducted and transcribed, and data were initially analysed using open, axial, and selective coding (Strauss & Corbin, 1990). An iterative approach was taken during the process with constant comparative analysis, memoing, and reflection being conducted throughout the research and data analysis stages. This continued until theoretical sufficiency (Dey, 1999) of data was deemed to have been reached and a provisional model of coping was developed. In total, twenty-three interviews were undertaken with nineteen participants (Participants 1–19). Partially anonymised demographic data of the participants (to try to limit identification of individuals) can be seen in Table 6.1.

Data Analysis

Fourteen interviews were initially conducted, and after the data was interpreted and coded, three main concepts relating to 'purpose', 'control', and 'support' were identified. Within each of these concepts, there was the potential for them to be conceptualised as either 'risk' or 'protective' factors, depending on how they were perceived by the participants. After the initial rounds of open and axial coding were complete, selective coding was conducted, as although the three key concepts of purpose, control, and support seemed to be significant to an officer's ability to cope, there were initially difficult to separate, so selecting which was the 'core category' (Given, 2008) was challenging. Theoretical sampling was then undertaken, and a further nine interviews were conducted until it was clear that a core category of 'purpose' was identified, as well as the main risk and protective factors being recognised. A five-step analytical process was undertaken as part of this study.

Step 1 – Initial data collection.
Step 2 – Initial data analysis (open and axial coding).
Step 3 – Selective coding (the emergence of a core category).
Step 4 – Theoretical sampling.
Step 5 – Model development.

The key steps taken as part of this study are further explained in Figure 6.1.

TABLE 6.1 Demographic data of interview participants

	n = 19
Gender	
Male	7 (37%)
Female	12 (63%)
Age	
30–35	4 (21%)
36–40	3 (16%)
41–45	6 (31.5%)
45+	6 (31.5%)
Marital status	
Married	9 (47%)
Unmarried	10 (53%)
Time in policing	
0–10 years	5 (26%)
10–15 years	10 (53%)
15+ years	4 (21%)
Time on unit	
0–5 years	14 (74%)
06–10 years	2 (10%)
10+ years	3 (16%)

Model Development

These interviews led to the development of a tentative model of coping which demonstrated that these officers are continually exposed to organisational and occupational stressors such as high workloads, long hours and listening to traumatic accounts from victims of rape and child abuse. In order to be able to cope with these stressors, an officer will need to rely on their actual or perceived levels of control, support, and purpose. These levels of control, support, and purpose may change frequently and regularly, moving from potentially risky to protective factors (and vice versa), depending on what an officer is being asked to do. This ongoing cyclical pattern of moving between both protective and risk factors throughout the day was referred to as a *whirlpool of misery* by one participant (Participant 3). It was therefore initially hypothesised that when there is a negative relationship either individually or collectively with control, support, and purpose, these risk factors may lead to an officer struggling to cope. Conversely, where there is a positive relationship either individually or collectively with control, support, and purpose, these protective factors may mean that an officer may be better able to cope with the work that they do.

How these three factors fit together is shown in a simple model of coping which can be seen in Figure 6.2.

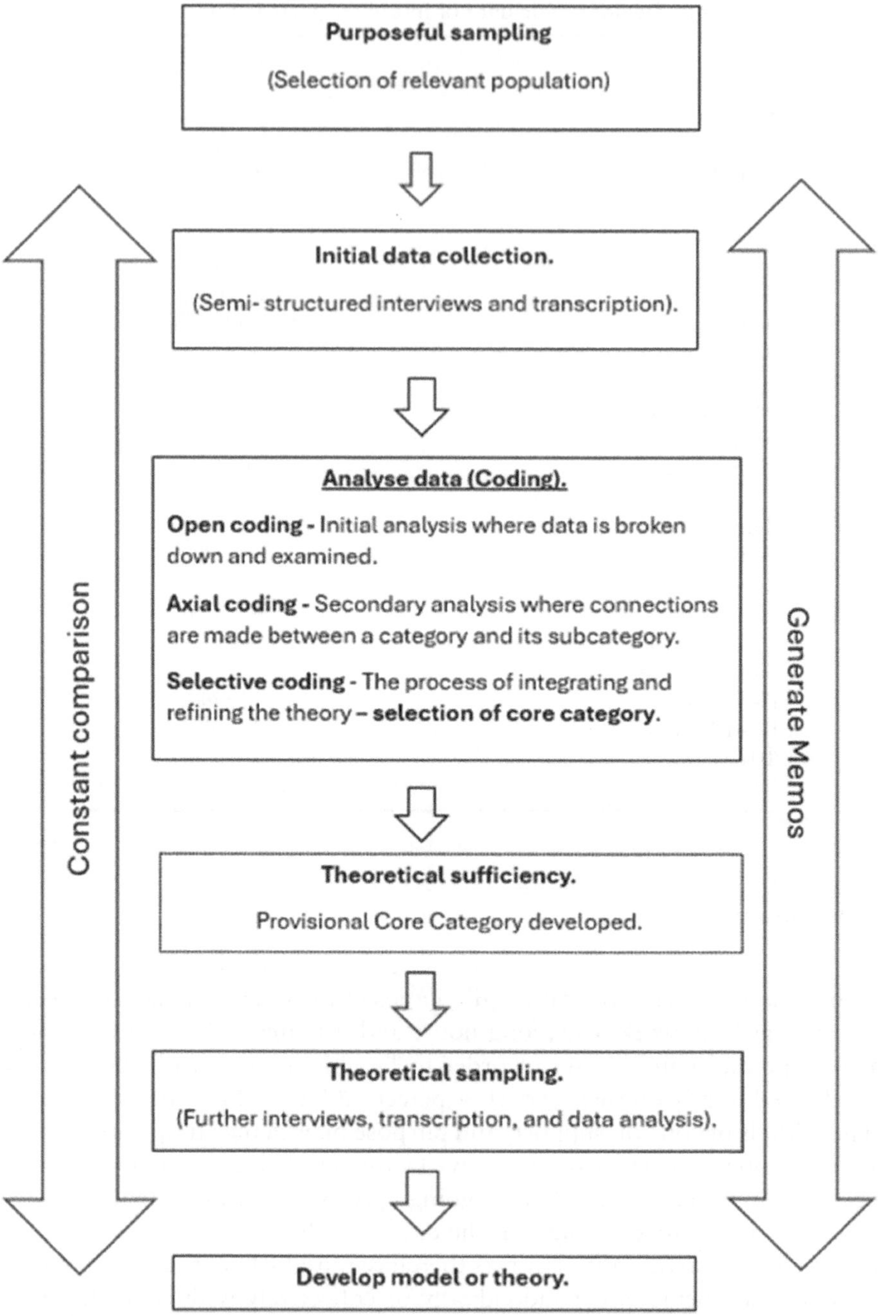

FIGURE 6.1 Grounded theory method employed within this research (based on Strauss & Corbin, 1990).

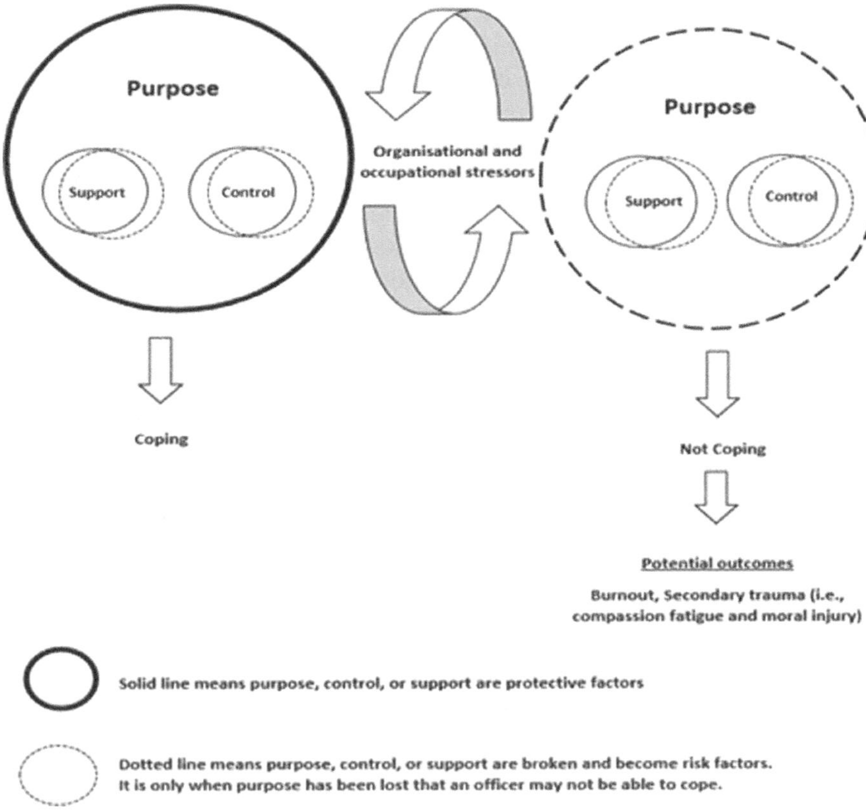

FIGURE 6.2 Simple model of coping.

Discussion

The aim of this research was to develop a model to understand how officers who investigate rape and child abuse cope with the potentially traumatic nature of their work. It was initially hypothesised that listening to repeated disclosures of child abuse and rape would be traumatic and would significantly impact those officers who undertake this particular type of work. However, this study identified that secondary trauma was not as prevalent as first thought, and even though nearly all officers acknowledged that their work was 'horrific', most felt that the nature of the work undertaken (e.g., hearing and seeing victims of rape and child abuse) did not impact on them, although there were findings of burnout, compassion (victim) fatigue and moral injury within the participants.

This research further identified that purpose, support and control may be important to consider regarding how an officer may (or may not) cope in the future, with an officers purpose being the most important factor in relation to *'if'* an officer copes.

Purpose

As interviews were conducted and data analysed, it became apparent that there were a large number of risk factors that were interpreted as relating to an officer's 'purpose'.

This was felt to be an important finding and went some way to explain why some officers appeared to be struggling during the interviews, when others appeared to be coping. This apparent lack of having a sense of purpose led to a number of officers questioning both why they were doing this role and, in some cases, policing altogether.

Purpose is a term that the Cambridge dictionary describes as 'why you do something or why something exists' (Cambridge dictionary, n.d.). Within this study, having a sense of purpose meant officers strongly articulating during the interviews that they originally joined policing as they cared or wanted to make a difference. Although having a sense of purpose appears to be a common theme amongst most police officers, it is tentatively suggested that having a strong sense of purpose may be particularly relevant to those who have chosen to work with vulnerable victims, such as those subjected to child abuse or rape, as they have chosen an extremely challenging area of policing to work in, compared to some other roles. Protective categories related to having emotion and empathy towards victims; being professional in their role; having satisfaction and pride in the job they do, as well as identifying with some victims. A number of officers also felt a greater sense of purpose and importance in the work they were doing, namely helping, and supporting vulnerable victims.

> It is very challenging. It's rewarding. Not every job is ... some jobs are quite simple. Even the rape ones are quite simple. But there's nothing better than ringing them up and saying I'm gonna charge ... this has affected you your entire life. I got a charge.
>
> *(Participant 11)*

Whilst having a sense of purpose may be a protective factor if it is being met, it was apparent that several officers felt that their sense of purpose was being eroded due to factors outside of their control such as third parties like the Crown Prosecution Service (CPS) being barriers.

> I do what I do because I help people, that's what I do. I've got lots of victims, which I'm going to have to leave behind (when the officer changes roles), some of them I'm quite sad about leaving behind. But that that is what I do. I help people, I try and make people's lives a little bit better... Purpose, that's the whole point of coming to work. That's the whole point of doing the job.
>
> *(Participant 19)*

Within the concept of purpose, there were a number of codes that related to the participants' beliefs and values. Risk categories included feelings of responsibility for the victims; caring too much (as well as not caring); guilt towards their victims (as they cannot do the job they want to); the impact that the role was taking on the officers; a general lack of coping and morale within the teams; dealing with sudden unexplained infant deaths (SUDIs); the stigma around disclosing that you are struggling psychologically to cope, as well as experiencing stress and lack of sleep caused by the role. Some officers also had to work through their own personal trauma as well as dealing with the aftermath of suicides by 'their' victims. Within this concept, there was some very strong and emotive language used to describe their experiences, such as 'broken' teams, which was believed to be leading to a lack of charges within rape investigations.

> I've been a police officer for a number of years, you would occasionally … visit the dark place where you felt your confidence, your, you know, your self-esteem was just rock bottom. But these were temporary, you'd be like a tourist to the dark place. Now I feel like I'm there constantly. And it's like I live there.
>
> *(Participant 4)*

Support

A second concept of support, whether it be peer, social, supervisor, or organisational, also appeared to be a significant factor within this study, with the importance of peer, family, and friend support being cited by all participants. The importance of support as both a protective and risk factor was not unsurprising due to a large amount of research which highlights its importance to general policing. The risk factors that were identified in relation to a lack of support included inexperience and the lack of officers within the teams; the impact of poor supervision; the negative impact of the media; the general lack of resources within the units; and a desire to go back to the way things were before the unit transformation, which appeared to be making officers look negatively at the current working arrangements.

> I think it took me to about October, November to start getting back on an even keel. What I was lost in it. I was I was drowning, and I was vocalising that I was drowning, but it was always the same – 'there's nobody else'.
>
> *(Participant 2)*

Officers felt that policing in general was regularly and unfairly criticised in the media which was impacting how they were perceived and supported by the general public. Those who worked within rape investigation also felt particularly strongly about the negative media coverage regarding rape prosecutions and the fact that the senior leaders did not appear to challenge or give any response.

> Within the media, you know, rape is obviously a massive factor and constantly highlighted at the moment for various news stories. But prior to that, as well, there is obviously a massive media circulation around that and the low conviction rates… I think the fact that we don't have that voice, so we can't explain why there are low conviction rates, and you just have to rely on other people putting that out there for us and speaking on our behalf. It's sometimes difficult because you do think why am I doing this job if everything you get is negative response, when we all work really hard.
>
> *(Participant 14)*

Other protective factors also included the need for trust and humour between colleagues and within the office; the importance of strong supervision; a realisation that it is 'not just me' struggling; a suggestion that officers should not work in the role too long and should be moved after a certain time period (referred to as tenure) and a return to their 'specialist status', which was felt would aid recruitment and retention, lessening workloads and improving experience.

> And it was affecting my family. Because when I worked in, I worked a late turn on Saturday, I was on my own, and that that woman rung me up saying, like, saying she's gonna kill herself and then had a go at me for calling the police. I left work that night at 11 o'clock at night, and I rocked up at my parents' house at midnight, in tears saying, 'have I've done the right thing'. I don't know, like, I just, I know, I've done the right thing, we've got a duty of care, and I know, I've done the right thing anyway. But that's what I mean. It's almost like an abusive relationship. Like, I think they call it that gaslighting or something where they think make you think something when actually, you've done the right thing.
>
> *(Participant 6)*

There was also a positive idea to create an informal 'drop-in service', where officers could 'vent, moan, and generally unload' what is on their minds. This, it was suggested, would help the officers both feel listened to and cope better after having got things 'off their chests', but this doesn't currently exist.

> But I do I think there needs to be some sort of drop in – unloading if that makes sense. So, when we were on the other side, I think we were specialised we had someone (Sexual Offences Investigative Technique (SOIT) Coordinator) that looked after us and one of his main roles, which wasn't even probably his real role was that we would, once a month he would and if it wasn't bribery, he would bring in chocolate biscuits or whatever. And he would say right, it's whatever team's time to attend today. And you'd go in, and you would literally just rant about all the things that really pissed you off about what was going on. And you just sit there for an hour and eat twirl bites and just rant and go, well, this is annoying, and that's annoying. You come out and be like, alright, let's go back to work… It wasn't part of his role, and he has decided to do that, and we were really grateful for that. Because you could just sit there without, you could just have, you could just have a moment, you could also unload… that's why I think there needs to be more of like a 'forced support' slash intervention for want of a better phrase, because if you were made to or there was drop-in sessions, for example, and a bit like OST (Officer Safety Training), so every year, we have to do ELS (Emergency Life Support) and OST. We have to make sure that we're physically well enough to do this job, but no one ever makes sure we're mentally well enough to do this job.
>
> *(Participant 1)*

The importance of supervisory support was highlighted as an important factor as to whether an officer copes or not, and interestingly there was also the suggestion that senior officers (particularly those above Inspector) do not know what the officers do and how the work may impact on them. It was suggested that if there was more engagement from senior officers and an acknowledgement of the often difficult and challenging work that officers do, it would go a long way to helping officers feel supported, particularly in the more difficult times (e.g., after working extended hours to deal with a prisoner). Several officers felt that although they knew that their family and friends were there to support them and listen if needed, unless they were in 'the job' they would not fully understand what the officer was going through so they would not open up to them. This in part was due to a fear of traumatising them with the detail of what the officer had dealt with, which meant that speaking to them was usually avoided. Surprisingly, a positive mentality relating to the use of organisational trauma support being made available when needed was an unexpected finding due to the stigma that is usually associated with seeking help. It appeared that once an officer had overcome the stigma and mistrust of occupational health, the counselling provision provided was effective and helped provide improvements to the officer's health and wellbeing.

For this population of officers at least, actual or perceived support from the organisation, peers, supervisors, or family will significantly impact an officer's ability to do the job they do. This support from supervisors and peers is an important aspect of police culture, and there is a need for these formal or informal support mechanisms to be developed and embedded within policing and within these high-risk roles in particular.

Control

The concept of control was the third significant concept which came out of this research and primarily related to an officer's ability to control what they were doing day to day, as well as what is done to them by supervisors and the organisation. The risk factors for control included unnecessary administration (paperwork), some of which was deemed pointless and took up a considerable part of their day; feeling 'helpless' in the role; changes to the roles performed by the Sexual Offences Investigative Technique (SOIT) officers; the impact of COVID on them personally and the ability to work in the usual way; the impact of third-party organisations such as social services and the Crown Prosecution Service (CPS); a poor quality working environment (broken computers, chairs, etc); being posted into or out of the unit with no influence when it happens or even what unit they will be posted to; the significant risk associated with the role; taking time off and being worried about things happening whilst they are away as well as what they will return to; the lack of training and preparation for the role; and the excessive workloads that officers were carrying.

> One of the things that I find surprisingly traumatic, was gonna sound silly is going through the freezer, because first of all, I, I quite like things being organised and neat, and it's the absolute opposite of that…it just feels like this distillation of misery. Seeing an exhibit bag being like, infant nappy, samples of blood and semen. And you just like, whatever circumstances have created that exhibit. It's just awful.
>
> *(Participant 3)*

Protective factors included being able to take a break and being able to 'switch off' away from work; being organised and being able to get on with their job; being (and being seen to be) tough; being desensitised to what they were experiencing; realising they are only one person, so can only do so much (rather than taking everything on); having 'dual roles' such as a work version and a home/family version of themselves; having hobbies including the need to exercise and having a good 'work/life' balance.

> I like to be organised; I think you need to be as you lose track. You know, if you've been pulled in all different directions, you don't know, you know what's going on. You need to try and keep yourself organised otherwise things get lost. You know, people ask you about jobs and you think 'who is that person?' You know, you don't know about you are, so I think to be organised. You know you need to, especially nowadays because you've got kids and you're trying to spin plates a lot of the time. That's what we're doing spinning plates. If you're not organised, it's going to make them all topple off and break.
>
> *(Participant 9)*

Throughout the interviews, it became apparent that several officers used being organised and just focusing on what was in front of them to cope with the daily challenges they were experiencing, such as increased workload as well as the potentially traumatic nature of what they were doing. This became particularly evident when asked about how they would feel if their day and plans (which had been organised) did not happen due to the needs of the role (such as dealing with a prisoner who had just been arrested), and most felt that they would struggle to cope and that it may be a 'bad' day.

Moral Injury

A surprising finding within this research was the potential discovery of what may be described as 'moral injury' (MI) within some officers. Although MI as a concept may be used to explain some of the psychological trauma that individuals are experiencing within this research, there are a number of challenges in linking it to this study and to policing. First, there have been a number of attempts to define what is (and sometimes what is not) moral injury, and it is suggested that the concept of MI has become more nebulous over time with no clear definition (Atuel et al., 2020; Litz & Kerig, 2019). However, the most widely used definition appears to be that by Litz et al. (2009) who suggested that MI can be defined as *perpetrating, failing to prevent, bearing witness to, or learning about acts that transgress deeply held moral beliefs and expectations* (Litz et al., 2009, p. 700). Farnsworth et al. (2017) added to existing literature on MI by defining a number of concepts linked to MI, including a 'morally injurious event' (a violation of something that is morally important to that individual); 'moral pain' (a sense of unhappiness and dissatisfaction in response to the morally injurious event which can present as feelings of guilt, shame, or anger); and 'moral injury' (social, psychological, or spiritual suffering relating to trying to cope with 'moral pain'). As MI was originally conceptualised in relation to combat veterans (Griffin et al., 2019; Litz et al., 2009; Shay, 1995), there has been a limited amount of research relating to UK policing, with only two studies being found which used the same six officers (Doyle et al., 2022 & Tapson et al., 2022) relating to MI in officers viewing indecent images of children and its impact on those officers. Doyle et al. (2022) found that stigma regarding seeking help and exposure to a large amount of traumatic material where the main factors impacting on an officer's trauma and moral injury within the study. Tapson et al. (2022) found that officers were not given the time to be able to process what they were experiencing, leading to the use of dysfunctional coping strategies (e.g., alcohol and cognitive avoidance) as well as issues with identity, which ultimately meant that they were struggling with the moral trauma and injury which they were experiencing.

The findings within this study had some similar findings to the studies of Doyle et al. (2022) and Tapson et al. (2022), in that officers were overworked (so did not have time to decompress), were using maladaptive coping strategies such as using alcohol to cope, and expressed feelings of anger, guilt, and shame. When you consider how and why these feelings of anger, guilt, and shame are articulated by the officers, it appears that this relates to an officer's belief and apparent failure in their inability to do the job that they want to do. It is therefore cautiously proposed that these findings in some officers are not only symptoms of MI, but also linked to an officer's 'purpose'.

> I think it was that it got to that stage where she hung herself…and she never told anyone. I think I felt … not guilty because that would be wrong… maybe a little bit, could have done more? I was very young in service I think, and I was response team. So, it was sort of like, you know, 124d, blah, blah, blah, but my colleague nicked him, I stayed there. I asked all the questions. She didn't respond to them, and then I find out two days later, that she'd hung herself as a result of being a sexual abuse victim and if she told me I could have done something about it, but I didn't know so how was I?
>
> *(Participant 10)*

Whilst burnout, victim fatigue and moral injury may be significant risk factors for this group of officers, it appears that purpose, support, and control were all very important concepts which determined whether these officers would be able to cope with their roles. The need for purpose however is identified as the 'core category' and is felt to be such an important factor that it is suggested that those in high-risk roles such as child abuse and rape investigation may be able to cope better when they feel they are achieving their purpose, which means quite simply that they feel they have done a 'good job'. Significantly, it became very apparent during the interviews that if an officer's purpose was lost, this would lead to them struggling with not only the day-to-day challenges that they were experiencing but also potentially *why* they were working in policing, which ultimately led to one officer resigning from the police during this study.

Practical Implications for Policy and Practice

This study has potential organisational and clinical implications in relation to supporting and treating officers who are not coping within their roles and may be suffering from PTSD and other common mental disorders such as anxiety and depression.

Understanding Trauma

Clinically, an understanding of the pressures that officers are under and the potential importance of having feelings of support, control, and purpose may mean that clinicians can start to understand the 'policing mind'. It is suggested that this is an important step to start to help officers get those positive aspects of support, control, and purpose back, which may in the long term mitigate the effects of trauma and burnout as well as improving an officer's wellbeing and mental health. It is also suggested that with the potential for moral injury to be present within officers, there needs to be a greater understanding of the concept and the fact that due to an officer's 'moral code' being damaged, officers may not be forthcoming regarding the disclosure of the 'morally injurious event' which has led to the 'injury', which could lead to a misdiagnosis and ultimately no help or support for the officer.

Organisational Changes

This research indicates that organisationally a number of changes need to be made in order to mitigate the effects of burnout, compassion fatigue, and moral injury (MI). This includes but is not limited to:

- Reduce workloads (within ethical boundaries) including minimising the 'additional responsibilities' that officers are taking on as part of their role.
- Improve basic working conditions (fix computers, chairs, etc).
- Improve recruitment into these high-risk units but do NOT forcibly 'rotate' officers into them for short periods i.e., 6-month attachments, and only use volunteers.
- Conduct a 'skills audit' within the teams. Are staff suitably trained and are there a number of experienced officers to support less experienced staff?
- Introduce mental health awareness to be part of an annual mandatory training programme. Officers undertake yearly officer safety training and emergency life support, and as highlighted by Participant 1, *we have to make sure that we're physically well enough to do this job, but no one ever makes sure we're mentally well enough to do this job.*

Give Staff the Ability to 'Decompress' When Needed

A key finding from this research was the need and ability for officers to take a break when needed. Taking a break was something that was not routinely done unless the officer was a smoker, due to the large workload each officer has. The ability to talk to someone 'informally' was also discussed and highlighted as something that helped and supported SOIT officers (it was only brought in for their role). Therefore, the following should be developed.

- Create 'wellbeing teams' to support officers and 'wellbeing rooms' within each station.
- Consider developing a support role (similar to the SOIT coordinator role discussed earlier) and conduct 'informal' drop-in appointments for officers to attend and discuss current issues and concerns should they wish to.

Improve Supervisor Support

A key factor in this and other research is the importance of supervisor support. Supervisors need to be properly trained to manage these high-risk teams, understand the roles that their teams perform and, importantly, acknowledge the challenges of the role.

The biggest challenge, however, may be in trying to reinvigorate an officer's 'purpose' within policing. It is suggested that this will not be an easy task, but the first step must be to try and understand the problem, which means greater education and awareness amongst officers and staff. It is argued that only by understanding and raising awareness of the individual concepts of burnout, compassion fatigue and moral injury can we start to support officers and staff operating within this complex area of policing.

Conclusions

The aim of this research was to understand how officers cope with the potentially traumatic nature of their work. As the research developed, it became clear that most officers (although not all) were actually coping well with any trauma they were experiencing, and it was the organisational stressors such as burnout, which were the biggest challenges that officers were facing. As the study progressed, it became apparent that there were three risk or protective factors in relation to coping. These were 'having control', 'having support', and 'having a purpose'. These findings led to the development of a model of coping where 'having a purpose' was the decisive feature as to whether an officer can cope or not. Having a sense of purpose is difficult to properly define as it is a subjective concept and may be different even for those individuals who collectively have the same overarching purpose (e.g., help victims).

There was also a finding of moral injury which was unexpected as there is little empirical research regarding its impact on policing. Examples of potential moral injury included feelings of 'helplessness' in their inability to help victims, seeing children who were physically or sexually abused as well as deceased, sometimes at the hands of their parents. These examples seemed to erode an officer's sense of purpose and cause them to struggle within their role, which may link to the findings of moral injury (feelings of guilt, shame, and anger), as well as one officer questioning (to God) 'why' this was happening. Moral injury appears to be an important but under-researched aspect of policing and further studies are clearly needed in this area.

This model is believed to be the first that specifically looks at coping within this high-risk group of officers within the United Kingdom. While generalisability to other officers cannot be concluded, it is felt that the three factors of support, control, and purpose will be relevant to most officers and should be explored further. If organisations can develop effective support networks, allow officers to take back their sense of control, and reinvigorate their sense of purpose, then maybe this will be enough to allow officers to cope with their daily challenges more effectively and enable them to compassionately support vulnerable victims of child abuse and rape and give them a reason to *get up in the morning.*

References

Atuel, H. R., Chesnut, R., Richardson, C., Perkins, D. F., & Castro, C. A. (2020). Exploring moral injury: Theory, measurement, and applications. *Military Behavioral Health*, *8*(3), 248–255. https://doi.org/10.1080/21635781.2020.1753604

Boag-Munroe, F. (2017). *Police Federation of England and Wales National Detectives Survey, Headline report*. Police Federation of England and Wales. https://www.polfed.org/our-work/operational-policing/detectives/

Brown, J., Fielding, J., & Grover, J. (1999). Distinguishing traumatic, vicarious, and routine operational stressor exposure and attendant adverse consequences in a sample of police officers. *Work & Stress, 13*(4), 312–325. https://doi.org/10.1080/02678379950019770

Cambridge Dictionary. (n.d.). Purpose. In *Cambridge dictionary.* Retrieved 29 November 2022, from https://dictionary.cambridge.org/dictionary/english/purpose Accessed December 10, 2025.

College of Policing. (2020). *Responding to trauma in policing: A practical guide.* College of Policing. https://www.oscarkilo.org.uk/news/trauma-resilience-uk-policing Accessed December 10, 2025.

Corbin, J., & Strauss, A. L. (2008). *Basics of qualitative research: Techniques and procedures for developing grounded theory* (3rd ed.). Sage.

Corbin, J., & Strauss, A. L. (2015). *Basics of qualitative research: Techniques and procedures for developing grounded theory* (4th ed.). Sage.

Dey, I. (1999). *Grounding grounded theory: Guidelines for qualitative inquiry.* Academic Press.

Doyle, M., Tapson, K., Karagiannopoulos, V., & Lee, P. (2022). Impacts of organisational role and environmental factors on moral injury and trauma amongst police investigators in internet child abuse teams. *The Police Journal: Theory, Practice and Principles*, *96*(1), 153–171. https://doi.org/10.1177/0032258X211043331

Farnsworth, J. K., Drescher, K. D., Evans, W., & Walser, R. D. (2017). A functional approach to understanding and treating military-related moral injury. *Journal of Contextual Behavioral Science*, *6*(4), 391–397. http://dx.doi.org/10.1016/j.jcbs.2017.07.003

Foley, J., Hassett, A., & Williams, E. (2022). 'Getting on with the job': A systematised literature review of secondary trauma and Post-traumatic Stress Disorder (PTSD) in policing within the United Kingdom (UK). *The Police Journal*, *95*(1), 224–252. https://doi.org/10.1177/0032258X21990412

Foley, J., Jones, F., Hassett, A., & Williams, E. (2023). *'Holding onto trauma?*' The prevalence and predictors of PTSD, anxiety and depression in police officers working with child abuse, rape, and sexual exploitation victims. *The Police Journal: Theory, Practice and Principles*, *97*(2), 370–393. https://doi.org/10.1177/0032258X231183638

Given, L. M. (2008). Core category. In *The sage encyclopaedia of qualitative research methods* (pp. 131–132). SAGE Publications, Inc. https://dx.doi.org/10.4135/9781412963909.n72

Griffin, B. J., Purcell, N., Burkman, K., Litz, B. T., Bryan, C. J., Schmitz, M., ... & Maguen, S. (2019). Moral injury: An integrative review. *Journal of Traumatic Stress*, *32*(3), 350–362. https://doi.org/10.1002/jts.22362

Hesketh, I., & Cooper, C. L. (2014). Leaveism at work [Editorial]. *Occupational Medicine*, *64*(3), 146–147. https://doi.org/10.1093/occmed/kqu025

Houdmont, J., & Elliot-Davies, M. (2016). *Police Federation of England and Wales 2016 Officer demand, capacity, and welfare survey.* Initial report–descriptive results. Police Federation of England and Wales. https://www.polfed.org/media/14061/welfare-survey-2016-pfew-descriptive-results-report-v30.pdf

Litz, B. T., & Kerig, P. K. (2019). Introduction to the special issue on moral injury: Conceptual challenges, methodological issues, and clinical applications. *Journal of Traumatic Stress*, *32*(3), 341–349. https://doi.org/10.1002/jts.22405

Litz, B. T., Stein, N., Delaney, E., Lebowitz, L., Nash, W. P., Silva, C., & Maguen, S. (2009). Moral injury and moral repair in war veterans: A preliminary model and intervention strategy. *Clinical Psychology Review*, *29*(8), 695–706. https://doi.org/10.1016/j.cpr.2009.07.003

MIND. (2015). *Blue Light scoping survey.* https://www.mind.org.uk/media-a/4583/blue-light-scoping-survey-police.pdf

MIND. (2019). *Mental health in the emergency services.* https://www.mind.org.uk/media-a/4849/2019-survey-police-service-summary.pdf

Roach, J., Cartwright, A., & Sharratt, K. (2017). Dealing with the unthinkable: A study of the cognitive and emotional stress of adult and child homicide investigations on police investigators. *Journal of Police and Criminal Psychology, 32*, 251–262. https://doi.org/10.1007/s11896-016-9218-5

Shay, J. (1995). *Achilles in Vietnam: Combat trauma and the undoing of character*. Simon and Schuster.

Strauss, A. L., & Corbin, J. (1990). *Basics of qualitative research, grounded theory procedures and techniques*. Sage Publications.

Strauss, A. L., & Corbin, J. (1998). *Basics of qualitative research: Techniques and procedures for developing grounded theory* (2nd ed.). Sage.

Tapson, K., Doyle, M., Karagiannopoulos, V., & Lee, P. (2022). Understanding moral injury and belief change in the experiences of police online child sex crime investigators: An interpretative phenomenological analysis. *Journal of Police and Criminal Psychology, 37*(3), 637–649. https://doi.org/10.1007/s11896-021-09463-w

7

OK9 WELLBEING AND TRAUMA SUPPORT DOGS

Garry Bottrill

Introduction

This chapter is written by Garry Bottrill, a former Police Sergeant. It provides a practical operational overview of this groundbreaking work to date. It is not written in an academic style. There is very little academic literature in this area within policing, but both Garry and the Editor are working to build this evidence base. It is worthy of note that a few have introduced this service that nearly all in policing value and appreciate. Garry served in the Royal Navy before becoming a Police Officer, serving for almost 30 years. He co-developed a Police mental health app called *Backup Buddy*, which is now used in many forces in the UK and internationally. Garry won a Churchill Fellowship and travelled extensively to research PTSD assistance dogs. He then set up Service Dogs UK, a successful assistance dog charity for Veterans of the Armed Forces and Emergency Services with PTSD, gaining accreditation from Assistance Dogs International. He is a trustee and volunteer Operations Director for the charity he founded, as well as a trustee for Assistance Dogs UK. He serves on the Access and Advocacy Panel of Assistance Dogs International (ADI) and hosts the Shelter/Rescue dog group within ADI. In 2022, he joined the National Police Wellbeing Service where he initiated and leads nationally with the award-winning Oscar Kilo OK9 Wellbeing and Trauma Support Dogs. As such, this chapter provides a vital narrative of this aspect of Wellbeing in Policing.

The Case for the Introduction of a Canine Connection and Evidence of Benefits

Policing is about helping and protecting the vulnerable, largely by dealing with those who harm others and bringing them to justice. The practical application of this work inevitably means that Police Officers and Staff will encounter and be subjected to traumatic events, stressful situations, hostility, abuse and even assaults. This chapter will show how the introduction of OK9 Wellbeing Dogs into the workplace acts as a natural morale boosting intervention that is based on the foundations of the 'human–animal

DOI: 10.4324/9781003518860-8

bond' and why dogs, historically, are so successful in helping humans cope with the difficulties they face.

Evidence of the Benefits

An ever-growing raft of research clearly indicates the benefits that can be had simply by interacting with dogs. We will look at the science behind the way that dogs can help us and the way that help is delivered, whether through the release of oxytocin, dopamine surges or the therapeutic tactile interactions that buffer social mammals against neurobiological and behavioural effects of stress. Assistance Dogs are used to support humans with post-traumatic stress disorder (PTSD), and we will examine how they do this effectively and what lessons have been learned from this kind of Animal Assisted Intervention.

Who Let the Dogs Out...And Why?

Initial use of 'Welfare' or 'Therapy' dogs in forces was undertaken individually or ad hoc. While they enjoyed much popularity among a small handful of organisations, each was a 'stand-alone' project, and there was no national guidance or support. We will look at how the concept of a national OK9 service was born and how, in the early beginnings, the appetite for this resource grew and enabled forces from around the country to provide a very well-appreciated form of peer support, helped significantly by the presence of OK9 Wellbeing Dogs.

Trauma Support

In August 2024, the OK9 National Lead and a small number of OK9 Handlers from Ambulance, Fire and Police services provided support following the horrible incident in Southport that culminated in the murders of three children and the injury of others. Without respite, the first responders in Merseyside were then hit by violent riots. This is an insight into how OK9 Wellbeing and Trauma Support Dogs responded to the national incident of unprecedented scale for the group.

Challenges, Blockages, and Breakthroughs

The problems and pitfalls that can beset attempts to establish an OK9 entity in an organisation can be numerous. These can occur at the start of the journey or even when the scheme is established. Navigating through these can be a challenge; we will look at how 'blockages' can be overcome, the importance of a vibrant OK9 Network, and how passionate, dedicated people can help each other to achieve success.

The Power of Paws

Monitoring and evaluation of the OK9 service has been key to understanding how the service has landed in each organisation and assessing the impact it has had. Here, we look at the ways the service is utilised and examine the 'real-life' feedback from those who have encountered the OK9 Wellbeing Dogs. We look at the ways the service is delivered to provide a structured, physical and tangible wellbeing offering that is safe, effective and impactive.

OK9 'Fur' Ever?

A look at what the future of OK9 is in the often turbulent, changing environment of policing and why it is important to have reliable, trusted wellbeing options for people to access. Why is it that dogs are able to reach people and help us open up a dialogue or just make things better!

The Case for Canine Connections in the Workplace

Policing is about helping and protecting the vulnerable, largely by dealing with those who harm others and bringing them to justice. The practical application of this work inevitably means that Police Officers and Staff will encounter and be subjected to traumatic events, stressful situations, hostility, abuse and even assaults. The introduction of OK9 Wellbeing Dogs into the workplace serves as a natural morale boosting intervention that is based on the foundations of the 'human–animal bond'. Because dogs, historically, are so successful in helping humans cope with the difficulties they face.

All OK9 Handlers know that when they bring a Wellbeing Dog into the workplace, they will be greeted with an enthusiastic array of smiling people who are simply delighted that a dog is present among them. This is a phenomenon that shows no sign of abating and is quite extraordinary considering dogs in the UK are not exactly a rarity! Many of the people 'charmed' by the furry four-legged visitor have dogs at home, but still the OK9 Wellbeing Dog brings about a change in the atmosphere, an opportunity to engage with a dog at work, to enjoy 'happiness personified' in dog form, complete with wagging tails and wet nose kisses! It is a welcome relief from the serious, sometimes dangerous, and often traumatic work that they do to keep people safe. To be able to step away for a minute and get a precious moment of unadulterated joy or the opportunity to experience something positive during a bleak, stressful shift is both helpful and healthy, and when coupled with the chance to speak to a supportive peer, these interactions can make a significant difference to their wellbeing at work.

But why dogs? For over 30,000 years, humans have enjoyed a partnership with dogs. This has evolved from a basic need to cooperate to hunt for food, share shelter and warmth, to the complex creatures that inhabit our homes today. Studies show that dogs have become proficient at understanding what we want and communicating with us. It seems incredible that they can learn over one hundred words, that they observe and react to our slightest body movements, or that they often seem to know what we are going to do before we do it and be so 'in tune' with us.

In the USA, UK and other countries, Assistance Dogs are now used to support humans with post-traumatic stress disorder. They are highly trained animals with the ability to perform at least three key tasks to reduce or mitigate the symptoms of PTSD. This could be waking the person from a nightmare, interrupting a flashback or guiding the handler to the nearest exit in the event of a panic attack. In addition to this, the dogs will undertake other practical tasks, but a strong bond of trust and mutual emotional support is necessary for this partnership to be highly successful. Typically, those with PTSD found that being with a dog reduced depression, anxiety and feelings of low self-esteem. In addition, veterans from the military and emergency services with PTSD on the Service Dogs UK assistance dog charity reported increased confidence, being able to go out more and being more social after completing the programme. The daily and almost constant presence of a dog in their lives served, at various levels, to counterbalance the negative and debilitating aspects of the illness. Those in the Armed Forces and Emergency Services are used to working in teams; they depend on and support each other. They are used to encountering dogs in the workplace and indeed working alongside them too. It is these mainly 'dog confident' workplaces that benefit from the daily presence of dogs. This may be why the police were so well placed to begin the introduction of a national Wellbeing and Trauma Support Dog initiative and create OK9.

Evidence of the Benefits

An ever-growing raft of research clearly indicates the benefits that can be had simply by interacting with dogs, whether through the release of oxytocin, dopamine surges or the therapeutic tactile interactions that buffer social mammals against neurobiological and behavioural effects of stress.

We have probably always had this deep connection with dogs. As far back as the 1860s, the now legendary nurse Florence Nightingale recognised how well animals provided social support for institutionalised, mentally ill patients. The American Red Cross deployed dogs to military and convalescent hospitals after World War II, and relief organisations used dogs to help Hurricane Katrina victims recover from trauma.

When the University of British Columbia brought in therapy dogs in 2018, providing 246 students with a chance to pet and cuddle during drop-in sessions, the results, published in *Stress and Health*, were impressive: students who were surveyed both before and after engaging with the dogs reported a significant decrease in their stress levels, along with increased happiness and higher energy levels following the session.

'The results were remarkable', said Stanley Coren, study co-author and professor emeritus of psychology at UBC. 'We found that, even 10 hours later, students still reported slightly less negative emotion, feeling more supported, and feeling less stressed, compared to students who did not take part in the therapy dog session'.

Interacting with dogs releases oxytocin in both the dog and the human; this is a stress-relieving hormone that reduces anxiety and helps us feel secure. It is thought to have a positive effect on empathy and trust. When sharing this exchange of oxytocin, the bond between the human and dog is strengthened. Dogs appear to be empathetic towards humans; when a human is upset, a dog will often try to comfort or distract the human from that behaviour. Millions of dog owners around the world will readily testify to their dog's ability to 'read' their mood and understand their body language.

This willingness to interact so closely has endeared them to us; there are instances of dogs being used to help humans with disabilities since Roman times, but they were first widely used as guide dogs in Europe after the First World War. These dogs would assist soldiers blinded by poisonous gases, and this led to the advent of specialised training programmes that trained dogs to help humans as their assistance dogs. The use of assistance dogs has evolved considerably since those early days, and now dogs are used successfully to assist with a wide range of other disabling conditions and help people who struggle with hearing, autism and post-traumatic stress disorder as well as alerting people to imminent medical conditions such as epilepsy.

It is hardly surprising that dogs have gained a huge foothold in the human world; they assist people with disabilities, they fight crime, they help with security and they find lost or injured people and rescue them! Within the emergency services, dogs have been trained to help in a number of ways; they are part of the team and are accepted as such. It is therefore unsurprising that they are welcomed in this environment and are thought of in a positive way. The 'human–animal' bond is born out of working closely together and respecting each other. The bond is made stronger by showing kindness, consistency, fairness, affection and trust. Dogs are renowned for their enthusiasm, courage and loyalty, and these qualities are typical of those that are valued in the police and other blue light services. Big-eyed, sweet-faced, affectionate dogs are always going to be popular, but there is also a fundamental connection of values that makes dogs a very welcome addition to the workplace!

Who Let the Dogs Out? ...And Why?

The initial use of 'Welfare' or 'Therapy' dogs in forces was first undertaken from around 2020 in Southern England with individual organisations having a good level of success which helped show the value of this intervention. Other forces brought in therapy dogs from established providers, but this was on an ad hoc basis, and the handlers were not trained in Peer Support or knowledgeable about the 'job' and the types of work carried out by officers and staff. This meant that these non-police volunteers ran the risk of being subjected to vicarious trauma while listening to details of the incidents attended. There was little or no training or support provided for them and certainly no clinical governance to monitor their own wellbeing. While officers and staff undoubtedly enjoyed the presence of a dog, they would naturally refrain from talking to someone not part of their trusted workplace network about anything relating to their mental health or wellbeing. Those that utilised Police Officers or Police Staff as Handlers enjoyed much more success, and the impact was much greater. There were some great early examples in Sussex Police, the Metropolitan Police, Cheshire Constabulary and Thames Valley Police. The combined number of dogs in this small handful of organisations was less than ten, and each were 'stand-alone' projects doing an excellent job but with no national guidance or support. The potential to build on these beginnings and do something on a larger scale with a framework that could be accessed by all was realised. Through discussions with the Welfare Dog 'pioneers' in each organisation, a small but enthusiastic network of people with a passion for helping colleagues began reaching out to others, and the OK9 Wellbeing and Trauma Support Dog network was started.

Today, all new members of the group are provided with Peer Support training, so they are better equipped to help colleagues. They are also supplied with Risk Assessments and Standing Operational Procedures to help them get up and running, and each must nominate a Single Point of Contact and agree to and sign the Service Level Agreement to help ensure the high standard of the service is maintained. All prospective dogs are required to pass the OK9 Suitability Assessment. Once the Handler has completed the training, they are sent their OK9 dog jackets and Handler clothing so that they can begin, in earnest, to provide a highly visible and accessible service to their colleagues.

The OK9 Network has grown exponentially with now over 30 Police Forces becoming part of the group and others in the process of joining. The dogs in their jackets caught the imagination of those at work, and soon more visits were requested. The dogs are used to promote mental health awareness and during incident debriefs to provide support to officers and staff subjected to trauma. The number of dogs has grown to accommodate the demand, and bespoke OK9 online training, designed in consultation with the Dogs Trust, was introduced to ensure all Handlers are aware of all aspects of animal welfare, safety, body language and how to prepare and plan visits. As colleagues in other emergency services saw the benefits of the OK9 Wellbeing Dogs, they contacted Oscar Kilo, enquiring how they could get their own wellbeing dog scheme. The OK9 National Lead welcomed several Fire and Rescue Services and an Ambulance Service to the OK9 Group and following training and assessments, they were issued with red and green OK9 dog jackets respectively. The demand from other services continued to grow, and a grant secured from the Blue Light Card Foundation enabled more emergency services to enjoy the benefits of membership to OK9.

There are currently over 270 OK9 Wellbeing and Trauma Support Dogs from the Police, Fire and Rescue Service and Ambulance Service, and they work collaboratively to support each other in the UK.

Trauma Support

On 29th July 2024, a mass stabbing targeting children occurred at a dance studio in Southport, Merseyside. This shocking, abhorrent incident was attended by the local emergency services, and police apprehended the suspect at the scene. While the UK was reeling from the incomprehensible, devastating attack on young children, the next night far-right, anti-immigration protests started, and serious disorder broke out. Merseyside Police officers and staff, still trying to make sense of the tragic murders of three children and the attempted murders of ten others, suddenly found they were under physical attack from a mob that was bent on confrontation and violence. On that first night, over 50 officers were injured, 8 seriously, with fractures, lacerations, a broken nose and a concussion. It was reported by the Chief Constable, Serena Kennedy, that some officers on duty were thinking 'they weren't going to make it home to their own children, to their own families'.

The role of the National Police Wellbeing Service in these situations is to provide guidance and advice to help those police forces affected. In this case, communication with the welfare leads of Merseyside Police was established, and the Oscar Kilo Wellbeing Vans were deployed to the area to provide support to the Occupational Health and Wellbeing Team. The offer of OK9 Wellbeing and Trauma Support Dogs was also made when the time was appropriate. Meanwhile, there were further outbreaks of violent disorder in many areas of England which had to be managed by police officers during a particularly busy summer.

On the 9th August, after the situation nationally had calmed, Merseyside Police requested the OK9 Wellbeing Dogs. The OK9 Network was, by this time, somewhat stretched in supporting the officers in many other forces who had policed their own riots or had provided mutual aid to neighbouring forces. The neighbouring forces to Merseyside were unable to supply any police OK9 support as a result. However, during the week commencing 13th August, a small band of OK9 Wellbeing and Trauma Support Dog Handlers and dogs from Police, Fire and Rescue and Ambulance Services arrived in Merseyside to provide OK9 support to those affected by the recent harrowing events. They were volunteer OK9 Handlers who were supported by their service but were giving their time and energy freely to help their emergency services colleagues.

The National OK9 Lead reported:

> We met with the officers who first responded to the murders and they spoke about the incident and we listened. We spoke to other officers, some who had been assaulted in the disorder and we heard about how they witnessed friends and colleagues being badly injured and how awful it was but how proud they were of 'holding the line' looking after each other and regaining order. We heard how officers came into the police stations on their days off to help out, knowing full well they would be putting themselves in harm's way. Other officers came back to work the day after being knocked unconscious or with fractured arms because they wanted to do more. Some officers felt guilty about not being in the right place at the right time to provide more help. We listened, they stroked the dogs and shared their experiences and in some cases we pointed them towards support but mostly we helped them by just listening so they could try to process what they had been through.

Chief Inspector Rob Budden sent this message on X.

> Thanks to all the Trauma Support Dogs that have visited our first responders over the last few days. Something about these characters that elicit responses that humans can't! A definite part of the recovery and wellbeing package for our teams in Sefton.

There were many more positive comments from the Merseyside Police officers and staff. The Wellbeing Team also requested visits to the Coroners' Offices, which were undertaken. The OK9 teams were requested to do return visits to Police, Fire and Ambulance stations because officers and staff who had missed a visit wanted to meet the dogs! The National OK9 Lead thanked those from West Sussex and Norfolk Fire and Rescue Services, the Welsh Ambulance Service, Northamptonshire and Cheshire Police Forces who had stepped up to help.

> I am deeply proud of the extraordinary way that you all responded to heartbreaking events in Southport. In the face of unimaginable tragedy and the unrest that followed, you displayed a true sense of service, going above and beyond to support those in need. Your selfless dedication, driven by a deep sense of compassion has been nothing short of inspiring. A huge thank you for the unwavering commitment of you and your four-legged friends and work colleagues. Thank you, Jo.
>
> *(Jo Shiner, Chief Constable, Sussex Police and OK9 Ambassador)*

This was the first time that OK9 had responded to a national incident in this way to provide support after trauma. The OK9 Lead and OK9 Handlers responding had not previously attended anything on this scale with wellbeing dogs, and it was uncertain how effective or worthwhile the intervention would be, given the tragic and harrowing circumstances. The dogs, wearing Police blue, Ambulance green, and Fire and Rescue Service red jackets, were, in fact, symbols of solidarity and support from all three services to those first responders dealing with tragedy, grief and violence. The dogs brilliantly represent the unique bond between our emergency services and our willingness to come together to help each other.

Challenges, Blockages and Breakthroughs

The problems and pitfalls that can beset attempts to establish an OK9 entity in an organisation can be numerous. These can occur at the start of the journey or even when the scheme is established. Navigating through these can be a challenge. There is within most organisations an inherently cautious approach to trying something new when it comes to wellbeing. Often, these departments are not well funded, and many rely on volunteers and 'Champions' in order to bring additional support to officers and staff. Investing in the wellbeing of the workforce makes sense, and a proactive approach can help with recruitment and retention; it helps the workforce to feel valued and shows the organisation cares about their welfare. This perceived organisational support has been shown to help with resilience, something our officers and staff need, given the increasingly difficult and demanding job that they do.

OK9 has grown as a direct result of the efforts of passionate people who care about colleagues and who believe that dogs have the power and capability to help in the workplace. The enthusiasm that the dogs are greeted with when they conduct a visit is enormous and infectious. As the word spreads about these dogs, forces and services want to know more, and through the NPWS, the process of onboarding new organisations begins. It is seldom an easy journey! Oscar Kilo provides the Peer Support training, and OK9 provides the information, additional training, templates and structure to help get set up. However, the person wanting to introduce OK9 to an organisation can often find that the route is difficult to navigate as there is an absolute need to ensure the scheme is properly managed and maintained. There is a stringent criterion to be met to ensure welfare, safety and standards. If the Senior Leadership Team are 'on board' with the idea, the process runs much smoother, but even so, for some forces it is a 'big leap' to subscribe to a project that relies on their people to invest time and energy to support colleagues.

Helpfully, the early reports and feedback from forces and services have been resoundingly positive about the benefit of having OK9 Wellbeing Dogs and Handlers. As the number of OK9 Wellbeing Dogs has grown, so has the appreciation of them and the demand for visits.

The Power of Paws

Monitoring and evaluation of the OK9 service has been key to understanding how the service has landed in each organisation while assessing the impact it has had. The goal of

OK9 has always been to provide a structured, physical and tangible wellbeing offering that is safe, effective and impactful. Crucial to this is the ability of those within OK9, the SPOCs and Handlers to communicate effectively and share best practice. The monthly OK9 Network meetings that are held are important because they provide the platform for this, and they keep the network connected.

Following a visit, OK9 Handlers are encouraged to complete a short online form that provides anonymised information. Typically, the Handlers will be able to give information about the number of personal interactions with people and the type of visit i.e. morale or general, support following an incident, event, roadshow or outreach, training or team building etc. If a colleague talks to them about an issue, they will record it as part of their Peer Support role, and this will include the type of problem and any advice or signposting that was given. This helps to get a picture of the impact the OK9 Wellbeing Dogs and Handlers are having. In an average month, OK9 Wellbeing and Trauma Support Dogs and their Handlers collectively carry out up to 3,000 personal interactions with work colleagues. Typically, these result in around 30 referrals where the Handlers signpost those met to appropriate help. Here is some of the feedback received following the OK9 interactions:

> The session was a recruitment event, and the numerous positive interactions were able to highlight the welfare support available when joining the organisation.

I attended the patrol room, and two female officers had just returned from taking out a Public Protection Order (PPO) on three children. The officers witnessed that the children were living in horrendous conditions, i.e. human waste all over the house. One of the children had accidentally urinated on the officer. The officers saw the children eating foam because they were so hungry. Bear and I walked into the office, and both officers said 'you are exactly what I need right now. I need a cuddle, I'm so glad you are here – you've arrived at the right time'.

> Just want to say a massive thank you to you and Henley for yesterday. Everyone really appreciated yours and Henley's presence and the opportunity to talk if needed, it has been very stressful here the last few weeks and it definitely broke our week up. Take care and will definitely see you soon. Thanks Again for all the work you do.
>
> 'I was anxious about my bleep test but the dogs made me feel much better – thank you!' 'Having time with a dog just makes everything much better'!

I took Lola to a TRiM assessment. My colleague appreciated Lola being there, and she was happy to talk whilst stroking/cuddling Lola.

'The team had been through traumatic time with a suspect taking their life. Bringing the wellbeing dog in was a massive boost for them and made a big difference to their day seeing her all day'.

Students stated how beneficial it was to have a wellbeing dog in the room whilst discussing an emotive subject. Tutors have also stated that they would like one in each session.

A member of staff died while on rest days; a dog was brought in to provide support to the force chaplain, who was providing the news to the team and explaining the support available.

One female officer shouted 'THIS IS THE BEST DAY EVER' after meeting Duke today!

'Absolutely love the dog; she has really helped me to speak to you today'.

'Thank you for all you have done for helping me with my 30 years of fear of dogs. I am really proud of myself and grateful to you and your dog ...'

Margot attended the Roads Policing FLO PPD day. A heavy topic and very emotive, including a presentation on a Roads Policing colleague who had been killed on duty in a collision. It was very emotive, and everybody commented on how lovely it was to have Margot there to lift their spirits :)

One of my colleagues was talking about a tough time she was going through; Bub picked up on this and cuddled in closer to her when she was getting upset.

Roadshow at Police headquarters to support Mental Health Awareness Week. The event was advertised, and staff all wanted to interact and spend time with the wellbeing dog.

The visit was for the prisoner handling team, and one of them had been in an interview all morning. They walked into the office, saw the dog, and shouted, 'this is so what I need right now'! Then they put their stuff down and dropped to the floor with the dog.

This event was a staff network event with many people saying they had just come down to see the dog, but then once they were there, they were able to receive lots of useful information about the different internal support networks available to them.

This was very beneficial; it was a difficult day for lots of officers at the station and they were happy to see Barney the OK dog. The funeral cortege passed by the police station, and we all stood outside. We attended the video funeral and visited all departments in the station.

During Investigators Wellbeing Week, a colleague entered the room and the first words they said were 'I really needed this today'; they proceeded to sit and stroke the Wellbeing dog and, in doing so, began to open up about not only work-related stresses and issues they were having but also personal stresses that were putting even more pressure on them and the lack of support they felt they were getting from work. Because of this, we were able to signpost this colleague to welfare for further follow-up support.

Successful visit. A few call takers had just taken particularly bad phone calls, and it was perfect timing to speak about it whilst cuddling the dog.

I attended a local station with Woody this week and went into a response team briefing to talk about OK9. After the briefing, I was approached by an officer who wanted to talk with me. The officer is really struggling with their mental health following dealings with a distressing job. They had not spoken with anyone about the struggles, stating that they saw the dog as a good excuse to talk to someone. As a result of our conversation, the officer has now been directed towards appropriate support.

We were attending a station where a shift had to deal with their third child fatality since January. One member of the team with about 7 years' service has now had to deal with the sudden/suspicious deaths of 10 children, and he said that after our visit earlier in the year, he has sought support and encouraged colleagues to do the same.

The variety of comments that OK9 Handlers receive help to illustrate the many ways the dogs can influence wellbeing at work. The use of wellbeing dogs to provide a supportive learning environment when dealing with potentially difficult or even traumatic subject matter such as investigating child death or disaster victim body recovery training has been shown to be helpful to students. In 2024, Dr Jess Miller published a research paper about the effect of using OK9 Wellbeing Dogs in trauma resilience training, which concluded.

> The brief experimental sessions introducing OK9 dogs into the trauma resilience training environment, although at small scale, demonstrated a critical component of any new intervention in this field; that doing so *did no harm*. With the conditions carefully executed by the experienced OK9 team, the deliveries were seen to be constructive, and we overwhelmingly well received, with feedback suggesting a good appetite for more such interventions to come.

OK9 'Fur'ever?

Quite often, people working in policing are totally engrossed in the work they do; their vocational aspirations can lead them to put the welfare of others before their own wellbeing. Many Officers and Staff will be experts at signposting victims of crime or members of the public to the support that they can access but are often unaware of services within their organisation for themselves, that is if they even recognise, they need help! The OK9 Wellbeing Dogs are a living, breathing and often 'wagging' representation of the importance of mental health and wellbeing in policing, and they, together with the Peer Support trained Handlers, help to highlight and connect the strands of support within an organisation. Rather than being a resource to be located on the force intranet, this wellbeing initiative comes to you! The dogs wear the highly recognisable Oscar Kilo branded jackets; they are big and bold and are synonymous with 'wellbeing'. They are also a signal, unambiguously stating the importance of looking after the workforce and a beacon to let people know that there is someone near who cares and will do all they can to help. This is up close and personal, practical support for often 'difficult to reach people', and it works!

The demand for OK9 visits continues to increase, so it is important that the service is inclusive and considers the needs of people with allergies or those who have phobias and are frightened of dogs. It is vital that people who don't like dogs or have cultural concerns about the presence of dogs are not alienated. There are robust policies and operating procedures in place to minimise the risk of upsetting people, and the specific training provided also addresses this to ensure that all OK9 Wellbeing Dog Handlers are sensitive to the needs of all their colleagues and will take positive action to prevent any disruption or upset.

Many other 'bluelight' services are interested in joining OK9 because they see the benefits and they want to be part of the network. To facilitate and maintain the growth of OK9 within the emergency services, it is necessary to have separate national leads for each service. These leads will be responsible for the development, management and maintenance of OK9 in their service. The Fire and Rescue Service and Ambulance

Service, together with the Police, are in the process of forming a national coalition. It is envisaged that other services will join them in time and OK9 membership will be achievable for many more first responders.

The concept of using Wellbeing Dogs and Peer Supporters together to support colleagues originated in policing and has shown so many benefits; it is widely appreciated by officers and staff. The popularity of the initiative shows no sign of abating, but for how long will OK9 enjoy being one of the most popular initiatives in wellbeing? Time will tell, but so also will budgets. While OK9 is a low-cost scheme that has an enormous impact, it still requires compassionate, caring leaders to keep things on track. It needs the SPOCs and Handlers to be given the time and opportunity to do the role and to help colleagues.

In policing, the 'winds of change' are ever present. This turbulence can be overwhelming and unsettling. The 'job' is becoming increasingly complex as new technologies enter the equation, numerous ways of harming people and committing crime online now exist, and no doubt, many more will be found. The finances for ensuring that adequate resources are available to deal with the increasing demand on policing are never certain, and the move away from the traditional vocational 'job for life' to a more transitional occupation for our new police officers may bring further instability. The actions of Police Officers are constantly under the microscope of social media attention, with thousands of 'armchair' experts and 'keyboard warriors' launching visceral attacks at people who are merely trying to do their jobs. Although accepting of accountability, this bombardment of negativity can bring intolerable pressure on those charged with protecting our society. This is amplified if they feel that they have insufficient 'backing' from their senior leaders and can lead to low morale, lack of trust and less productivity. The families of officers and staff may also suffer because of a lack of focus on the wellbeing of their loved ones. These problems and many others contribute to an often tumultuous environment within policing which for some is difficult to navigate.

There is a need for solid, dependable, visible support for those who police. This may come in the form of strong leadership, effective, empathetic, supportive management but is more readily found within the 'Police Family' among peers 'sharing the load'. The NPWS has contributed to 'creating the environment' by introducing the Blue Light Framework. The Oscar Kilo website provides an amazing array of evidence-based wellbeing resources. Oscar Kilo Wellbeing Vans are highly visible, tangible assets that bring welfare to the workplace, whether in response to an incident or to provide health checks and a place to have a 'cuppa' and to step away from the 'coalface' for a few minutes. There are now two OK9 vehicles which are available for all OK9 Handlers to use, to make it easier for them to reach every part of their force. The commitment of Oscar Kilo to those in policing is unwavering; it is forged from experience, sharpened by knowledge and driven by passion. OK9 Wellbeing and Trauma Support Dogs are part of Oscar Kilo and most of the Handlers do their role in addition to their main job. They do it because they can see the difference it makes and how it helps their colleagues. What makes it easier is the 'furry bridge to communication', the dog that gets the conversation started and allows people to 'open up'. For years in cultures all over the world, dogs have been associated with the qualities of love, loyalty and service; the ancients named the brightest star in the sky Sirius the 'Dog Star' in the constellation of Canis Major. Such stellar adoration has been earned by their ability to brighten up our days and lighten our moods. In times of uncertainty and darkness, dogs remain steadfast; they sense how we are feeling and try, in their own ways, to help. They make us laugh and they show us affection; they bring nature into our lives and help us to live in the present, to celebrate life and enjoy the moment!

Spiritual teacher and author of 'Guardians of Being' Eckhart Tolle wrote:

> Dogs emanate a goodness that people respond to. One of the joys of walking a dog is that often people come up to you and immediately their hearts open. They are not interested in you, of course. They want to pat your dog.

And people really do want to pat the OK9 Wellbeing and Trauma Support Dogs, they want to get on the floor with them and enjoy that canine closeness. They know that the dogs are 'on their side' and are there to support them. So too is the Peer Supporter at the other end of the lead, and this is what helps make the use of OK9 as a wellbeing initiative so successful. We hope that our OK9s will continue to shine brightly in the workplace as a beacon of unrelenting, indomitable support.

8

OPERATION HAMPSHIRE

Improving the Response to Assaults on Police

Dave Brewster

Introduction

The author of this chapter is Dave Brewster, a former Chief Inspector with the Metropolitan Police Service, with 30 years' operational and leadership experience across a broad spectrum of challenging policing environments. Dave has always maintained a strong focus on staff wellbeing and meaningful leadership and in the latter part of his career was responsible for developing the national strategy to improve the response to officer and staff assaults for the College of Policing. This was called Operation Hampshire, relating to the county in which it was first trialled. Dave has been the lead for Operation Hampshire, which relates to assaults on police officers and staff. This is a critical area for policing for a long list of reasons. Although this chapter is not written in an academic style, Dave is the unquestionable expert in this area and as such readers can hear the perspective from the horse's mouth, so to speak.

Rationale and Context

Policing has its obvious inherent risks; the nature of the role and the obligations of duty often place officers and staff between the vulnerable and the aggressor. Being assaulted on duty is a regular and increasing operational hazard; it nonetheless does not make it acceptable. Police officers and staff deserve and have the right to full victim support and care where subjected to an assault. Post-assault processes need to be consistent with minimum standards clearly set and delivered.

According to Police Federation statistics, in the year 2023–24, there were around 46,000 assaults on police recorded in the UK, an increase of 13.8% on the previous year. These figures are regularly updated on their site https://www.polfed.org. It is essential

DOI: 10.4324/9781003518860-9

that we have a meaningful response to these incidents to ensure officers and staff are supported as victims of crime.

A victim-focused response is essential. In 2015, I conducted a survey of MPS officer and staff assault victims, an attempt to look through the victim's lens at what mattered to them. The results were not surprising, and they helped break my approach down into two elements: the first being supervision and wellbeing, the second being investigation and criminal justice. Both elements are important, and how each is delivered can make or break the victim's experience. It was through this lens that I developed Operation Hampshire.

Op Hampshire is the initiative that seeks to develop and improve our responses to incidents of assault against police officers and staff. It provides a structure to ensure that the supervision and investigation of all assaults are managed consistently with a strong wellbeing and victim care focus on the individual.

I genuinely believe that the men and women in policing do an incredible job. They do the things that many others could not or would not do. They face some of society's most volatile and unpredictable situations, and they do that in the knowledge that they may get hurt.

As service providers, we are there for victims of crime, but occasionally those victims include our own people. Op Hampshire is simply about recognising the realities and risks of policing so that the same standards of victim care apply to the men and women that provide it for others. Op Hampshire is intended to support the entire police family. While frontline police officers are most likely to be assaulted, we must ensure that police staff are also acknowledged and fully encompassed by the processes.

History and Development

Operation Hampshire was developed and launched in the Metropolitan Police Service (MPS) in 2016 and was based upon a seven-point plan first which had been introduced in Hampshire Constabulary. As the MPS is the largest force in the UK, it was necessary to develop a broader strategy for the MPS as a structure to support the original principles.

The aims and objectives for Op Hampshire are not necessarily groundbreaking. They are, in fact, quite simple and for many they would be considered the basics for any crime type or victim group. The aims are:

1. To provide a consistent approach to wellbeing support and victim care
2. To consider the potential impact of every assault
3. To pursue justice through thorough investigation
4. To increase/improve criminal justice outcomes
5. To improve our understanding of the scale, trends and peaks
6. To drive a change in culture. Being assaulted is *not part of the job*

Progress

Following the success of Op Hampshire in the MPS, the initiative drew the attention of the Police Federation of England & Wales (PolFed) and the National Police Chiefs

Council (NPCC). As a result, there was general agreement that similar approaches should be adopted by all forces. This coincided with the introduction of the Blue Light Wellbeing Framework and the NPCC Officer and Staff Safety Review recommendations, both of which endorsed the need for improvements in the response to police assaults. Consequently, in late 2020, centrally coordinated work commenced through the College of Policing to support the national introduction of consistent assault strategies.

In December 2020, a self-assessment review was conducted to assist forces in establishing a benchmark against a comprehensive range of systems and processes. The analysis demonstrated that there was indeed a level of inconsistency across the UK, with priorities identified to include improving local delivery and communication.

Operation Hampshire leads were subsequently identified for all forces, and a national knowledge-sharing network and a range of College of Policing strategic guidance material were provided to support local development. Through national coordination, Op Hampshire is now a feature in every UK force.

From my experience, the forces who demonstrate a real grip of Op Hampshire are those with a combination of an energised operational lead focused on continuous wellbeing improvement, supported at Chief Officer level providing supportive scrutiny and direction. Leadership, consistency and commitment are essential in maintaining the confidence of the workforce and driving improvement.

Expectations

A significant amount of effort has been applied to driving Op Hampshire into forces, with the provision of guidance material, network knowledge-sharing events and a continued offer of focused development support. The maturity and effectiveness of Op Hampshire processes now lie with forces to progress locally. As a priority work stream within the Police Covenant the HMICFRS (the police inspectorate) have included Op Hampshire in the latest round of Police Effectiveness, Efficiency and Legitimacy (PEEL) inspections. Police forces are expected to formally evidence their commitment and approach. Additional scrutiny is also applied through the PFEW and UNISON (the main police staff union) in ensuring the support which Op Hampshire advocates for is provided locally.

On a local level, there should be a clear commitment to continuous improvement with ongoing senior leadership team (SLT) support to the Op Hampshire principles. Capturing and sharing organisational learning with other forces will drive consistency and enable peer support across all forces. Collaborative approaches between forces can encourage innovation and provide value for money solutions.

Op Hampshire should be embedded as part of any local wellbeing, human resources or people strategy. Improvements and performance should feature in local management meeting structures to ensure focus, governance and compliance. A senior leader should be identified as a point of contact and escalation to own and drive the strategy locally.

Challenges

The culture around police assaults is challenging, and it involves an ingrained mind-set. We provide a service to the public; that service often calls for us to face confrontation and violence on their behalf, and therefore it can be argued that being assaulted is an occupational hazard. For many, however, that has become "part of the job". This is something we really need to change from within. We absolutely must start from a position that being assaulted is not acceptable. If it were, there would not be legislation to cover it. It is the difference between "expecting" and "accepting" the assault.

What's the Point?

This is something that I have heard on many occasions up and down the country (UK). There is sadly a level of despondency among our colleagues, particularly where the lower end of the assaults scale is concerned, those assaults considered as "minor", a term I try to avoid and will explain why later. Current sentencing for these lower end assaults very often receives what is considered minimal or even no additional sanction at court. Victims often wonder what all the effort was for. Was the effort of hours of paperwork and months of memos and follow-ups worth it, only to see the offender walk out of court with a £50 fine? My response to this is that we have to be part of the solution. As I responded to a colleague recently, "we cannot throw the baby out with the bathwater". The criminal justice process starts with us; we have to report offences to ensure that we understand the fuller picture, we have to pursue justice for our colleagues and we have the right to be treated as a victim. If we dismiss this point ourselves, then we are throwing the towel in and exacerbating the problem.

Data Collection and Consistency

As mentioned earlier, for the financial year 2023/24 around 46,000 offences were recorded. This equates to around 126 offences per day and could be considered an emerging problem for policing and society. The figure is currently gathered through the Home Office Annual Data Requirement (ADR) and reported by the Police Federation. It does not provide any detail to determine the context of the issue, nor does the figure include assaults against other frontline police staff.

Any meaningful response must include the ability to identify trends and themes to support organisational learning and inform risk/safety decisions based upon detailed and consistent national data. The current volume of assaults presents an untapped and significant opportunity to positively impact police officer and staff wellbeing. There is also an opportunity to link this work to officer abstraction, retention and training improvements.

As one of the objectives for the initiative is to achieve a national police assaults data set to inform risk/safety management decisions and provide potential wellbeing insights. This would include data such as methodology, injury type, interaction types leading to violence and victim demographics to improve our understanding of the risk posed to colleagues.

A 2019 study conducted by Pang and Pavlou demonstrated how the effective gathering and use of data can lead to a reduction in offences. The key findings of which state:

> Our analyses on police IT use and violence against the police with a six-year panel dataset provide interesting and meaningful findings. We found that a high level of IT

use for intelligence, prediction, or investigation by the police leads to a substantial decrease in violence against officers in the line of duty.

(Pang & Pavlou, 2019)

Many forces do make best use of assaults data, providing local insights to inform improvements, and the NPWS has invested in the infrastructure that could provide meaningful national insights and analysis, should a consistent level of data be available. Work is ongoing to draw a full range of data from all forces through the ADR process.

Victim Focus – Impact versus Injury

In my experience, I have seen incredible levels of support to colleagues who have been seriously injured. There have been some horrific life-changing attacks on colleagues over the years, and we absolutely must respond with the highest standards of care. However, what cannot be lost is the fact that around 65–70% of assaults do not result in any injury. Because of the nature of the role, most of those assaults will be concentrated on frontline policing. As a result, many frontline colleagues are repeatedly assaulted, in some cases 6 times or more in a 12-month period. The potential impact and effects of repeat victimisation cannot be overlooked. We all react differently and have different levels of tolerance. We are only human.

The fact that an assault did not result in an injury is irrelevant as to whether support is offered and provided. As an example, let's consider spitting as an assault method. A vile offence and one which I have experienced personally. When an offender spits in the face of a colleague, that in itself is appalling, but let's expand on this. Let's consider whether the offender claims to have some kind of communicable disease, the spit contained blood perhaps, the victim may then have to undergo tests and commence a course of anti-viral medication. The anxiety of waiting to hear whether you have contracted an illness, whether you have passed it on to a loved one, the nauseating effects of medication, these effects all add up; they all have an "impact". Technically, an offence where spitting is the only factor would probably be recorded as an assault without injury at the lower end of the scale, but the effects are often greater.

The impact of every assault should be considered. We must have a starting point to work from and a process that ensures we don't miss that one incident that can be "the straw that breaks the camel's back". Even if an assault is dismissed by a colleague, we should also consider the impact on our role in society. Is it right to ignore an assault on the office of constable and those that support it? What message does that send to the public or would-be offenders?

Impact of Repeat Assaults on Police Officers' Occupation

In a 2023 study of Operation Hampshire, returns were carried out (Dennis et al., 2023). The study highlighted a range of issues that employers should consider in their response. Most participants reported a significant decrease in their confidence regarding their own abilities and their suitability for the job. Some reported a lack of motivation, anger, disappointment, job stress, job dissatisfaction and reduced commitment, as well as conflicted emotions regarding the constant risk and the impact of the job compared to the benefits, while some also indicated a desire to leave the force.

Others demonstrated an increase in hypervigilance-related cognitive tendencies towards suspicion, mistrust and negative expectations for the future, such as profiling people immediately and automatically, as well as anticipating the worst outcome from any situation. Some expressed an increase in safety-keeping behaviours such as planning escape routes, making sure there is adequate coverage and protection and avoiding situations requiring conflict, as well as an increase in physiological arousal (e.g., increased heart rate).

The findings of the study were shared across the Op Hampshire network, and forces were advised to consider introducing processes to monitor and provide closer supervisory and wellbeing support for repeat victims.

Leadership and Supervision

While a comprehensive and well-directed strategy is important, the ultimate success for a local Op Hampshire response relies on frontline delivery through first-line supervisors. The quality of first contact with victims is essential and is based around the concept of an initial post-assault wellbeing assessment which goes deeper than simply asking if someone is "okay."

The experiences drawn from police victim surveys, focus groups and anecdotes were used to develop post-assault wellbeing assessment guidance for supervisors which has been and continues to be promoted through Op Hampshire supervisor training sessions, presentations and published website guidance. This includes but is not limited to being supportively intrusive around not-so-obvious elements such as assessing repeat victimisation concerns, decompression needs, confidence and the capability and capacity to function.

Criminal Justice and the Assault on Emergency Workers Act

A sense of injustice can have a negative effect on the victim. The introduction of the Assault on Emergency Workers Act 2018 brought a range of potential improvements including a sentencing uplift and was launched with a strong supportive narrative. One of the key elements for Op Hampshire is identifying and implementing improvements in criminal justice processes. It is acknowledged that there are elements of housekeeping that will improve the chances of a successful prosecution and greater sentencing outcomes. However, improvements being sought require input and commitment from the entire criminal justice family.

The introduction of the Assault on Emergency Workers Act brought a significant and fresh focus on the issue of assaults on emergency workers. As the national Op Hampshire lead, I am often asked for advice or comment on individual cases. This can be difficult as all I can provide is opinion; I cannot mandate or direct policy, but I do my best to give an informed position based on experience. Over the years, I have been asked to comment on a number of specific case examples and criminal justice issues, whether they be charging decisions, discontinuances or sentencing outcomes. I am not, nor have I ever claimed to be, a criminal justice expert and I always apply caution in my responses as this area is often more complex and nuanced than we see at face value. However, from experience, it is worth providing some thoughts on elements of investigation and criminal justice.

I am often informed of cases where our colleagues do not feel that they have received the justice they deserve due to a sentencing outcome, disposal decision or compensation award. These can have a real impact on victims and in some cases lead to the question "what's the point"?

Being realistic, I understand how some colleagues can at times feel despondent. In part, we have been the victims of our own success. Expectations were raised following the launch of the Assault on Emergency Workers Act, with supportive comments on how assaults on emergency workers should be considered as assaults against society and therefore should be punished more severely. It coincided with the Protect the Protectors initiative and with an uplift in sentencing from the maximum six-month custody for the old Assault on a Constable (Section 89, Police Act) offence. The maximum sentence under the new act increased from 12 months to 2 years.

The introduction of the new act and sentencing uplift felt like real progress; in fact, it helped generate a lot of energy for Op Hampshire. It helped us encourage the reporting of assaults, but in fairness, I am not convinced that we have seen any significant increase in actual sentencing for assaults on police officers and staff. I base this on anecdotal accounts, as it is difficult to evidence without the ability to separate police victims from other emergency workers when looking at national sentencing data for Assault on Emergency Worker cases.

The important thing here is perseverance as the criminal justice system largely starts with us and we have to play our part to keep driving Op Hampshire forward. We must encourage the reporting of offences; to not do so masks the bigger picture and we need to keep building that evidence that articulates the realities of policing. It also potentially leaves the risk posed by the offender to go unaddressed.

We still need to ensure that our colleagues feel valued and supported by colleagues, supervisors and leaders; this is something we can absolutely and positively influence. That immediate support and aftercare, and that senior-level drive to build improvements, is still very much in play.

Reporting and investigating are the first steps, providing the very best evidence to support a prosecution. This means well-structured and detailed statements that clearly cover the essential points to prove, corroborating evidence like CCTV and body-worn video and taking the time to include a well-crafted victim impact or personal statement (VPS).

VPSs are integral to sentencing decisions. It is one thing to prove the offence and this is where a victim's evidence must be on point, but it equally applies to articulating impact. When we start to understand the harm, culpability and aggravating factors for assault offence sentencing, we can improve our chances of an improved outcome. Very often, there are factors in an assault case that do not get articulated in evidence. Some of them are so obvious that it is understandable why they might not be mentioned.

Some culpability factors that might be involved could include a defendant's intention to cause fear of serious harm, including disease transmission, a prolonged or persistent assault, strangulation, threatened or actual use of a weapon or weapon equivalent, and the leading role in group activity.

Harm factors may include the severity of injury and pain suffered or indeed the duration or longevity of any psychological harm or distress caused. The impact an assault has had on a colleague as a Police Officer or the impact it has had on their family life. How life might have changed on a day-to-day basis and any additional support you have required.

Potential Benefits

Anecdotal feedback from the PFEW and UNISON suggests that Operation Hampshire is widely accepted as one of the most positive and supportive initiatives launched in recent years. Aside from providing a framework that helps forces meet their obligations to employees under the Health and Safety at Work Act, it acknowledges the realities of frontline policing and provides realistic steps to improve the response to officer and staff assault. If implemented and managed effectively, it should provide some obvious benefits including:

- A workforce that feels valued, supported and cared for.
- Improved officer safety training methods based upon accurate data.
- Better justice outcomes from improved investigative/CJ processes.
- Increased workforce capacity, capability and resilience.
- Reduced incidence or length of abstraction attributable to assaults.

The Future

Momentum is key. We must keep Operation Hampshire on the agenda and continue to promote, advise, develop and explain how individuals can play their part.

The Operation Hampshire initiative has been running on a national level since 2021, through the National Police Wellbeing Service (NPWS). Forces have been provided with sufficient guidance and support from which to introduce meaningful strategies to improve their response to officer and staff assaults. Given the level of support and significant stakeholder backing, it should rightly be expected that forces now have and will maintain these processes with a reduced level of central direction. Essentially, this should by now be a wellbeing standard within every force.

The NPWS will continue to provide a central supporting role through the dedicated National Operation Hampshire Coordinator. This will continue to include subject-matter expert advice and knowledge-sharing opportunities.

The continued success of the initiative relies on the enthusiasm of forces. Some are clearly further ahead in their development than others, but engagement remains positive. The objective is to achieve consistency across the UK. Reflecting on the earlier introduction of Op Hampshire within the MPS, it is my genuine opinion that this is a long-term process which requires a persistent focus to keep it firmly on the agenda as a priority. This will ensure that processes are embedded as a standard for the long term and ultimately for the benefit of the men and women who risk their physical and mental wellbeing in serving the public.

References

Dennis, A., Davidson, L., Theodoropoulou, A., Carter, H., Amlôt, R., & Hesketh, I. (2023). "I don't want to be a victim again": The impact of repeat assault on police officers. *Frontiers in Psychology*, *14*. https://doi.org/10.3389/fpsyg.2023.1145944

Pang, M. S., & Pavlou, P. A. (2019). On information technology and the safety of police officers. *Decision Support Systems*, *127*, 113143.

9

STUDENT OFFICERS' WELLBEING

John Harrison

The Police Covenant: Heralding Better Healthcare for the Police

What Is the Police Covenant and Why Do We Have One?

At first glance, the term Police Covenant is unlikely to excite the interest of a police officer. Yes, it does include the word police. But covenant? What on earth has this got to do with operational policing and why should I be remotely interested in it? Lovers of Channel Four's Countdown will be familiar with the origin of words section, delivered by the wonderful Susie Dent, the programme's lexicographer. So, let's explore the word covenant. It originates from the Latin word convenire, which means to be suitable or to come together. It was first used in the 14th century in Middle English and comes from Anglo-French and the present participle of covenir, which means to be fitting.[1] As a noun, the word covenant means an agreement. In law, it means a formal agreement, contract, or promise in writing. The Police Covenant is a legal agreement about the well-being of police officers and police staff.

Ok, big deal? Don't we already have health and safety legislation that covers the police? Well, yes, we do. In the United Kingdom (UK) we have the Health and Safety at Work Act 1974, which places a statutory duty on all police forces to safeguard, as far as reasonably practicable, the health, safety, and welfare of employees.[2] In this context, police officers are considered to be employees. This overarching legislation, which enables the enactment of a host of health and safety regulations written to keep us safe at work, is very important. Breaches of health and safety legislation are criminal acts which can lead to the imposition of fines, or even imprisonment. Police Authorised Professional Practices (APP), policies, and procedures are written to comply with health and safety legislation as well as other legal requirements. Notwithstanding this, there is a wealth of evidence that wellbeing in the police is sub-optimal. Examples include the annual Pay and Morale survey carried out by the Police Federation of England and Wales (PFEW),[3] and the surveys of wellbeing conducted by the National Police Wellbeing Service (NPWS).[4] The most recent survey of members of the PFEW reports low levels of

DOI: 10.4324/9781003518860-10

wellbeing and concerns about mental ill health. The prevalence of feeling stressed, anxious, or having a low mood has increased from 77% in 2020 to 82% in 2023. Nearly half of respondents have sought help for their mental health from work, the NHS, or elsewhere. The 2023 NPWS found that wellbeing is a major issue for many individuals across the policing workforce. High levels of burnout and fatigue, anxiety, not being able to recover from stressful incidents, the negative impact of working shifts, difficulty recovering from high work demands through impaired rest days and poor sleep quality, and difficulty 'switching off' outside of working hours have been identified.

It is evident that we need more than a health and safety framework to achieve a culture of wellbeing in policing. If we think about Maslow's hierarchy of needs, wellbeing is built on satisfying our basic needs – something to drink and eat, being warm and dry – and ensuring that we live in a safe environment. If we add in a feeling of belonging and of being valued, we can develop our own sense of self-worth and an understanding of what we can be – self-actualisation.[5] The Police Covenant is an important step towards a culture of wellbeing in that it places in law the requirement that members of the police workforce, past and present, should not be disadvantaged as a consequence of their role. For the first time in UK legal history, the Secretary of State responsible for the police (the Home Secretary) must make a report to Parliament annually about wellbeing in the police.[6] This must be about the physical protection of the police, the support required by their families, and it must recognise the obligations of the police and the sacrifices that they make in carrying out their duty. The Home Secretary must state whether disadvantages have occurred and, if they have, what response will be made. There is a requirement to consult with appropriate stakeholders and the report must contain a summary of the views expressed. This will lead to a much clearer picture within Parliament of the state of police wellbeing and of the actions being taken to address any disadvantages.

How Will the Police Covenant Affect Healthcare for the Police?

The UK National Health Service (NHS) is legally responsible for the provision of healthcare to every citizen free at the point of delivery, apart from certain limited exceptions approved by Parliament. The NHS Constitution states that you have the right to access NHS services and you have the right to receive care and treatment that is appropriate to you, meets your needs, and reflects your preferences.[7] Unlike the Armed Forces, the police do not have a dedicated health service. This means that injuries or illnesses arising whilst serving are treated via a general practitioner or the nearest Accident and Emergency department. In essence, no special consideration is given to the health needs of the police. They are treated just like any member of the public.

Police Forces have occupational health (OH) departments. This is consistent with the approach taken by large employers. Doctors working in OH specialise in occupational medicine, which is an applied branch of mainstream medicine focusing on the relationship between work and health. The nursing equivalent is occupational health nursing, which is a nursing specialty requiring specialist training and accreditation by the Nursing and Midwifery Council. Both occupational medicine and occupational health nursing are preventative specialties. The focus on work and health addresses and seeks to accentuate the positive health benefits of employment and to mitigate any negative health impacts. Thus, there is a business, legal, and moral case for investing in OH departments.[8] The business case is that we need to have police officers who are deployable. This ensures that the Chief Constable can deliver crime plans agreed with Police and Crime Commissioners. There is a duty on any public sector organisation to deploy its resources efficiently and effectively. It has been estimated that mental ill health costs employers in the UK £56 billion per year. The legal case relates to the need to comply with statutory obligations (health and safety, employment, and equality legislation) and the civil law (contract and tort). The moral case is particularly strong in the police because we expect police officers and some police staff to subjugate their own needs on behalf of society. There is a psychological contract that is based on a *quid pro quo* understanding that the health and wellbeing of police personnel will be supported in return for social selflessness and, often, bravery.

An early priority of the Police Covenant was the development and implementation of police OH standards. Building on work that started in 2019 with the launch of Foundation Occupational Health Standards, the Police Covenant has encouraged further development and the creation of Enhanced and Advanced Occupational Standards. These were launched in 2023. They can be found on the National Police Wellbeing website.[9] The standards set out quality domains for OH services in the police. They ensure that the necessary trained personnel are employed and that the clinical facilities provided are appropriate. They ensure that appropriate service level agreements are in place that describe the scope and quality indicators for service delivery that will meet the needs of the police. They are benchmarks against which all police Forces can measure their state of development. This is assessed by His Majesty's Inspectorate of Constabulary Fire and Rescue Services (HMICFRS) during the PEEL assessments (Police efficiency, effectiveness, and legitimacy).[10]

However, police OH can only do so much. As preventative specialties, occupational medicine and occupational health nursing seek to prevent ill health occurring. They have important roles to play in the implementation of Force health and wellbeing strategies (see a national health and wellbeing strategy for policing). This covers the promotion of good health, the prevention of ill health, the early detection of ill health, and the subsequent intervention with the aim of restoring health and addressing the causes of that ill health. Because OH services are not treatment services, we rely on the NHS to provide treatment. This means we have to look at what treatment services are provided by the NHS that will meet the needs of the police and how to access them. Experience tells us that, currently, accessing non-emergency NHS services involves long waiting times. Even accessing emergency healthcare may be problematic because of delayed throughputs in NHS accident and emergency departments. This may be compounded by the experience of police officers who find themselves in the same hospital space as offenders. Work is ongoing, as a Police Covenant initiative, to review the health needs of the police and to explore how it might be tailored to meet the stated aims of the Covenant, that is that police officers and police staff are not disadvantaged because of the roles they perform. For example, we have seen already that mental ill health in the police is a concern. We need to ensure that the NHS is providing timely access to mental health services staffed by health professionals that have been trained to assess and treat police personnel. With respect to Accident and Emergency Departments, this means reviewing and revising care pathways that are cognisant of police-specific needs. Considerable success has been achieved in ensuring suitable and sufficient healthcare for military veterans when they transition from active service to civilian life. This has been driven by the Armed Forces Covenant. It is hoped, therefore, that similar success will occur now that the Police Covenant is a legal entity. The next section will consider how the Armed Forces Covenant has changed the way in which health is delivered for military veterans.

Lessons from the Armed Forces Covenant

The concept of a Military/Armed Forces (AF) covenant was introduced in the UK in 2000.[11] The concept is linked to the need for a "higher ethics" for a fighting organisation comprising personnel that operate throughout a "complex spectrum which embraces conflict prevention operations, conflict itself and post-conflict activities, all of them with joint, multi-national and inter agency dimensions, and under the scrutiny of government, society and the media at home and abroad". The concept of the covenant is that soldiers should expect fair treatment in return for making personal sacrifices. The issue of supporting injured soldiers came to a head, politically, in 2007, and led to the creation of a Military Covenant Commission.[12] The 2010 Murrison Report – "Fighting Fit" – identified 13 actions to address the need to support military personnel suffering from mental ill health, especially post-traumatic stress disorder (PTSD) and mild traumatic brain injury (mTBI).[13] A sister paper – "A Better Deal for Military Amputees" – also authored by Andrew Murrison in 2011, laid the foundations for national specialist commissioning of prosthetics and rehabilitation.[14]

The AF Covenant itself was published in 2010 and as well as enshrining the idea of fairness it also focused in particular on "no-disadvantage" and a "fair response to sacrifice".

- "Former members of the Armed Forces should expect the same level of support as any other citizen".
- (There should be) "No Disadvantage due to service in the provision and continuity of public services".

The creation of a national Armed Forces commissioning function in NHS England in 2013 gave a focus for assessing and responding to specific needs. Since then, a number of bespoke services have been developed to respond to areas of perceived disadvantage and/or specific service-related illness, injury, or conditions. These include:

- A veterans' trauma network comprising 12 NHS Veteran Trauma Centres and 4 specialist units, each with military and civilian medical experts, treats service-related physical health problems.
- Support for disabled veterans includes disablement service centres and a veterans' prosthetics panel funding high-quality prosthetic limbs.[15]
- Op Courage (see later) is the latest incarnation of an NHS specialist mental health service for military personnel due to leave the service, reservists, veterans, and their families. Thus, the combined physical health/mental health support of military personnel has become axiomatic.

Bespoke Clinical Services

In 2021, Op Courage was launched. This is the Veterans' Mental Health and Wellbeing Service. It provides specialist care and support for service leavers, reservists, veterans, and their families. It combined what had been separate mental health services offering treatment for conditions with different levels of complexity. Thus, there had been a service supporting the transition to civilian life (TILS), a complex mental health treatment service (CTS), and a veterans' mental health high intensity treatment service for people with life-threatening illnesses (HIS). These services were integrated so that they could be accessed at the most suitable level across seven regions of England (Different arrangements are available for personnel in Scotland, Wales, and Northern Ireland).

The following care is available:

- Intensive medical care and treatment for a crisis.
- Care and treatment for anyone displaying the early signs of mental health problems.
- Therapeutic treatment for more advanced mental health conditions and psychological trauma.
- Additional routes into other NHS services such as eating disorder services and "Improving access to psychological therapies (IAPT)".
- Assisting with wider health and wellbeing needs by working with charities and local organisations across housing, drug and alcohol misuse, finances, and more; the dual diagnosis assessment and treatments (along with other mental health, MH, comorbidities) are a key factor.
- Helping transition to civilian life by ensuring mental health care and support from the Defence Medical Services.

Of note, Operation Courage extends some support to families. Families may be involved in the care plan that is formulated for affected individuals.

The Veterans Trauma Network (VTN) is a network of ten NHS hospitals across England that provide specialist care for veterans with service-related injuries: Plymouth, Oxford, London (three centres), Birmingham, Nottingham, Liverpool, Leeds, and Middlesbrough. The VTN is run by healthcare professionals who are either veterans or serving personnel. The centres are co-located with Major Trauma Centres, so veterans have access to a full range of facilities. The VTN has been renamed the Veterans Physical Health and Wellbeing Service, or Op RESTORE. The new name is intended to make it easier for veterans to get help for their service-related physical health problems.[16]

A New Approach to Healthcare Commissioning

An important success for the Armed Forces Covenant was the inclusion in the NHS Long Term Plan of a commitment by NHS England to improve the health and wellbeing of the Armed Forces. The Armed Forces Covenant is embedded within the NHS Constitution.[17] The approach to healthcare commissioning for the Armed Forces, including military veterans, is set out in the document *Healthcare for the Armed Forces Community: A Forward View*.[18] A partnership agreement is in place between NHS England and the Ministry of Defence to support joint working that delivers the Armed Forces Covenant requirements and supports joint working between Defence Medical Services and the NHS.

Commissioning of healthcare for the Armed Forces has a statutory basis in the Health and Social Care Act 2012.[19] NHS England acknowledges the shared responsibility for healthcare provision for serving military personnel and the role of regional commissioners such as the Integrated Care Boards for (non-serving) personnel registered with an NHS GP – for families and veterans.[20] The role of integrated care systems, partnerships that bring together NHS organisations, local authorities, and others to take collective responsibility for planning services, improving health, and reducing health inequalities across geographical areas, means that commissioning of services is localised and holistic.[21]

There are 42 integrated care systems in England. Integrated care boards are responsible for planning and funding most NHS services in an area; integrated care partnerships are committees that bring together a broad set of system partners to develop a health and care strategy for the area. The health and care strategy must consider the needs arising out of the Armed Forces Covenant and the requisite funding channelled through integrated care boards. In the Armed Forces Act 2021, the Armed Forces Covenant was strengthened, requiring legal bodies, including NHS Commissioning Boards and Local Authorities, to have "due regard" for the needs of the armed forces community, as laid out in the Covenant.[22] In Wales, the Integrated Care Fund is a Welsh Government-funded preventative programme which aims to integrate and encourage collaborative working between social services, health, housing, and the third and independent sector to improve the lives of the most vulnerable people in Wales.[23] Seven Health Boards are responsible for planning and delivering NHS services in their areas, and there are three NHS Trusts.

Veterans-Friendly GP Practices

NHS England has also supported the accreditation of armed forces/veteran-friendly healthcare providers. A general practice (GP) accreditation scheme, commissioned by NHS England and delivered by the Royal College of General Practitioners (RCGP). The Military Veteran Aware Accreditation scheme was created to help GPs identify and treat veterans. The scheme aims to improve medical care and treatment for veterans, who may face additional challenges when they return to civilian life.[24] Practices can qualify for veteran-friendly status by offering extra support for ex-military personnel. Qualifying criteria are:

- They have a lead for veterans' issues within the surgery,
- They have a process to identify and flag veterans on their computer system,
- They undertake dedicated training and attend armed forces healthcare meetings,
- They increase understanding of the health needs of veterans amongst both clinical and administrative staff.

The requirements are not onerous. Practices ask new patients who are registering with the surgery whether they have ever served in the British Armed Forces. The answer is then coded on the GP computer system. There should be a clinical lead who commits to keeping up to date with the latest research and who advises colleagues on the requirements of the Armed Forces Covenant. Where practicable, s/he will undertake to see veterans when they consult the surgery for assistance.[25] The RCGP has set up a Veterans' Health Hub for GPs. It provides information to GPs considering registering for the accreditation scheme and includes supporting resources such as information about veterans' health, services and charities providing support to veterans and educational resources for GPs.[26] Over 3700 practices are now accredited.

A National Health and Wellbeing Strategy for Policing

We know that police work is challenging and that demands on physical, mental, and social health are part and parcel of the job. A wellbeing strategy, therefore, must encourage the development of a full understanding of the health stressors and their potential impact on the police family. Police forces must develop safe systems of work based on risk assessment and control. This is both a legal (health and safety) and a moral requirement. Systematic and individual resilience will be predicated on the elimination of risk, where possible, amelioration or mitigation of risk where practicable, and tolerance of risk with appropriate care pathways and capacity to deliver.

The Police environment creates health and wellbeing challenges. The "Front Line Review" published by the Home Office, in 2019, identified a range of issues impacting on wellbeing.[27] The following actions were committed to by Government:

BOX 9.1 THE FRONTLINE INNOVATION PROJECT

Achieving the right balance between meeting demand and supporting individuals.
Management of external demand.
Management of internal demand.
HMICFRS inspections and wellbeing – embedding wellbeing within day-to-day policing.
A national evaluation mechanism for wellbeing provision.

The evolving nature of operations and, at times, demanding working conditions can compromise health and wellbeing. The *Front-Line* Review identified the following factors that were perceived to influence the wellbeing of the workforce:[28]

BOX 9.2 'CHALLENGE' STRESSORS

- Organisational structures, operating models, and roles
- Change management
- Hours, shifts, rest days, leave, breaks, and commuting
- Work-life balance
- The ability to decompress
- Safety

'Hindrance' stressors

- Constraints to performance – bureaucracy, inadequate tools

Organisational climate and culture
Provision and adequacy of wellbeing support services – prevention and reaction

Added to this is the inherently dangerous and often physical nature of some police work. The amount of exposure to traumatic incidents is significant compared to that of the general population, which consequently impacts the mental health of those in certain policing roles.

A new national health and wellbeing strategy has been agreed that promotes good health through strong leadership and a culture of wellbeing. This is a tangible output of the Police Covenant. It aims to minimise the occurrence of ill health by raising awareness of organisational and lifestyle risks and enabling and empowering appropriate risk reduction. Wellbeing support will encompass prevention, early detection, and treatment of ill health to achieve optimal recovery. In addition, best practice rehabilitation will facilitate effective and timely return to full deployability and productivity. It will underpin individual and force resilience. The strategic vision is a culture – promoting health, protecting workplaces, and safeguarding the workforce – that will give all police personnel the ability to adapt, self-manage, and thrive in the face of work and life challenges. The aim is that policing will be the emergency service of choice by promoting inclusivity and diversity and giving opportunity for all. The mission is to create, promote, and maintain the conditions for the "Police Family" – police officers and police staff, employed or volunteers, and their families – to live healthy lifestyles in healthy environments, reducing injury, illness, and suicide as far as possible, to maximise wellbeing, work ability and a sense of belonging. This will support national initiatives to recruit and retain police officers and police staff.

Every police force in England and Wales is responsible for devising and implementing its own health and wellbeing strategy. The national strategy is intended to be a framework for forces to adopt when formulating their own strategies. A health and wellbeing Authorised Professional Practice (APP) has been developed. It is estimated that it will be launched in 2025. As an interim step, Workforce Prioritisation Guidance has been produced. This may be used to guide implementation as well as for benchmarking and audit purposes.

What Do We Mean by "Health"?

A new concept of health has been used in the health and wellbeing strategy. Understanding of health and wellbeing has been influenced by the World Health Organisation (WHO) definition. This describes health as the "state of complete physical, mental and social wellbeing and not merely the absence of disease or infirmity". This definition, which dates from 1948, has the advantage of its breadth of concept and ambition. In the twenty-first century, with changed population demographics, patterns of illness, and views on health, the need to define health differently has arisen. Inclusion of the word "complete" has been challenged on the grounds that the unintended consequence is that most people will be unhealthy most of the time. It encourages the medicalisation of society and opens the door to unnecessary medical screening. We now accept that good health is a composite of physical, mental, social, and spiritual wellbeing. Levels of these health components will fluctuate daily. This may be particularly true in the presence of a chronic illness.

The new definition of health used in the strategy is the ability to adapt and self-manage in the face of social, physical, and emotional challenges. This resonates in policing where adaptability and self-reliance are key attributes of police personnel. Thus, a healthy police population would have a high proportion of personnel who have the ability and capability to address the demands of policing and thrive. A further elaboration of this, with respect to the three domains, has been put forward. For physical health, it is the ability to mount a protective response to a physiological stress to reduce the potential for harm. For mental health, the "sense of coherence" has been described as giving capacity to cope and recover from psychological stress and prevent post-traumatic stress disorders. This is concerned with promoting comprehensibility, manageability, and meaningfulness in difficult situations. Social health is about being able to fulfil potential, meet obligations, retain independence, and participate in social activities, including work.[29] Huber's definition of health has been criticised as confusing health with behaviour. Within healthcare, the person-centred care model is being applied. This approach to care, which focuses on self-management, healthy behaviour, job retention, and desired quality of life, is more in line with current thinking and replaces the patient-centred care model.[30] In person-centred care, health and social care professionals work collaboratively with people who use services. Person-centred care supports people to develop the knowledge, skills, and confidence they need to more effectively manage and make informed decisions about their own health and health care.[31] Thus, at a force level, behaviours consistent with effective policing would seem to be an appropriate indicator of wellbeing. However, with respect to individual wellbeing, effective health self-efficacy and confidence in making healthy decisions to support personal work ability might be a preferable focus and marker of success.

With regard to the Police Covenant, the principles of person-centred care are helpful. The Health Foundation describes four principles. Care is:

- Personalised
- Coordinated
- Enabling
- Involves dignity, compassion, and respect.

The national framework for police-aware healthcare, described later in the chapter, is based on collaborative working between healthcare professionals to deliver personalised care. It advocates the need to understand everybody's individual health needs based on knowledge of their personal, work, and social circumstances. It recognises the importance of autonomy in healthcare decision-making but also the need to build self-efficacy. Care should be enabling. In policing terms, this might be enabling a return to work or helping someone to leave a Force feeling supported and with confidence to tackle what comes next. A culture of wellbeing must be based on treating people with dignity, compassion, and respect, which are core principles of police ethics.

Health and the Police: Five Delivery Areas

The national health and wellbeing strategy is action oriented. At the core of the model are five delivery areas.

- Join well
- Train well

- Work well
- Live well
- Leave well

Thus, there is a framework for focusing wellbeing initiatives on the entire "employment" journey.

Join Well

It goes without saying that we need to recruit the right people for policing. But what does that mean in practice? Policing encompasses a wide variety of roles. Pillar four of the Policing Vision 2030 sets an ambitious challenge for police forces. The vision is to achieve a talented, representative, and inclusive workforce that has the capabilities to meet future policing challenges.[32] 2030 might seem to be a long way off. However, in planning and change management terms it isn't. Policing must consider how it is going to attract and retain the workforce that it needs. This will be against a backdrop of a rapidly changing world of work. The McKinsey Global Institute reports that 1 in 16 workers may have to switch occupations by 2023.[33] Job growth will be concentrated in high-skill jobs, such as healthcare or science, technology, engineering, and mathematics – so-called STEM fields. Other jobs will be at risk because of automation and the use of robotics. The PwC *Workforce of the Future* report examines four distinct workforce scenarios based on surveys of more than 10,000 people representing different global economies.[34] Whilst the scenarios represent extremes of change reflecting the predominance of one of corporate integration, business fragmentation and entrepreneurialism, collectivism or individualism, there are clear messages to business leaders. We must act now. We must recognise that the future remains uncertain and be open to recognising multiple and evolving scenarios. The workforce focus will be people and not jobs/roles. We need to be prepared to nurture agility, adaptability, and re-skilling.

It is important that potential applicants to join the police are fully apprised of the demands of the role. Police officer applicants need to be fully aware of the physical and psychological demands that are likely to be placed on them, if successful. Pre-application awareness should include a general awareness of the functional demands and the relevance that underlying health conditions might have in the determination of suitability. An assessment of any current or past health conditions is part of the recruitment process. This is carried out in police OH departments. This is a detailed review of applicants' full medical history. The relevance of a health condition is risk-based and is made against a risk framework that includes:

- The ability to perform the functional requirements of the Public and Personal Safety Training (PPST) curriculum.
- The risk of sudden incapacitation due to a health condition.
- The ability to render regular and efficient service.

Fundamental to any OH assessment is the need to ensure that the health and safety of individuals, their colleagues, and the public are at the forefront of the consideration of suitability. The safety-critical nature of frontline policing roles means that discrimination against applicants with relevant health conditions and disabilities is lawful as a proportionate means of achieving a legitimate goal. However, each assessment is undertaken on an individual basis. The possibility of implementing reasonable workplace adjustments to offset any disability will always be considered. New guidance is being issued by the College of Policing to assist OH departments in the assessment of police officer applicants. It is expected to be launched in Spring 2025.

Train Well

The training and probationary period of a police constable's life in the police is an ideal time to introduce important aspects of wellbeing and to inculcate healthy behaviours which will stand him or her in good stead for their career. Raising awareness and developing an understanding of mental health should be a core part of the training curriculum. The acquisition of knowledge and skills at this stage will not only impact the long-term wellbeing of individual officers but also help them understand and manage the public. Policing is a 24/7 operation and so healthy behaviours, in general, are also important to help new recruits sustain a long career and leave policing in good health (see "Live Well" and "Leave Well").

Mental health stigma is an important barrier to promoting and maintaining good health. The overarching mission of the health and wellbeing strategy is to promote good mental health. The axiom "no health without mental health" was coined by a previous cross-governmental outcomes strategy.[35] This was a recognition that mental health is central to quality of life, productivity, and life ambitions, such as training and education and employment. The intention of the then government was to mainstream mental health such that there would be a parity of esteem between physical health and mental health services. In 2017, an independent review of mental health and employers was published.[36] *Thriving at Work* set out six mental health core standards for organisations including the production, implementation, and communication of a mental health at work plan, development of mental health awareness among employees, and encouraging open conversations about mental health and the support available for when employees are struggling. A key challenge for policing is to create a workplace culture where emotional intelligence and insight into emotional wellbeing is regarded as a professional strength. Asking for help is not demonstrating weakness. Many forces have mental health and wellbeing resources that include videos of people talking about their own mental health issues and how they have overcome them. The videos and animations section of the Oscar Kilo website contains a collection of "real stories" from police officers and police staff, as well as specially commissioned short films depicting life in the police.

Neurodiversity is a concept that is becoming understood within policing. We now understand the term neurodiversity to mean that brain differences are natural variations within populations. Each person has a brain that is unique to them.[37] Training and education in neurodiversity may be important in two ways:

- Supporting the police workforce. This includes improving awareness and understanding for individuals and ensuring that managers are able to provide the necessary support.

- Providing knowledge and skills for frontline officers to improve outcomes at incidents involving neurodivergent individuals.[38]

It is estimated that, for at least 20% of the adult population in the UK, differences in brain performance may mean that they are diagnosed with conditions such as dyslexia, being on the autistic scale, developmental coordination disorder (formerly known as dyspraxia), and attention deficit hyperactivity disorder (ADHD). Whilst these diagnostic categories may be regarded as neurological conditions, they are not illnesses. Such conditions may be associated with impairment in certain settings and environments and may constitute a workplace disability for which reasonable adjustments should be explored.[39] It should be recognised that there may be considerable benefits from having a neurodivergent workforce in policing. The variations in brain performance mean that there may be enhanced performance in areas important to policing, such as attention to detail, strong technical abilities, high levels of concentration and steadfastness, creativity, and the ability to view the bigger picture.

A formal diagnosis of a neurodiverse condition, such as autism or dyslexia, is not mandatory and should not delay recruitment decisions. The charity, The Autistic Society, advises that it is up to individuals whether they seek a diagnosis.[40] Professor Nancy Doyle argues that it should not be necessary to obtain a formal diagnosis of neurodiversity to secure reasonable workplace adjustments. The Equality Act defines disability in relation to functional impairment, not diagnosis. Professor Doyle highlights the difference between neurotypical cognitive scores, where the variation is relatively small, and those of neurodiverse individuals who have "spiky profiles". This means that there is a larger variation across the domains of cognitive function testing: some scores will be higher than neurotypical scores, some lower. It is argued that this spiky profile characterises neurodiverse people; diagnosis of specific conditions – e.g., dyslexia, DCD, ADHD – focuses on the most prominent deficits belying the fact that there is poor correlation between formal diagnosis and work performance. Rather than focus on obtaining formal diagnoses, police forces should assess the needs for workplace adjustments by simply asking neurodiverse applicants about their needs. They should structure such assessments with regard to the cognitive and behavioural functions of a frontline officer.

Work Well

The approach to working well is predicated on understanding workplace hazards and associated risks to health. Where risks cannot be avoided, we have to try to reduce them, as far as possible. We need to understand how workplace hazards might lead to ill health and set up health surveillance systems to identify adverse effects at the earliest opportunity. We can then take action to stop harmful exposures and treat illnesses, if required. This is analogous to the National Decision Model that is used throughout policing.[41] There is a legal and ethical framework guiding occupational health and safety. It should be evidence-based. Options for intervention will draw on organisational policies. The impact of interventions must be assessed, as part of the risk management cycle.

An obvious example of managing a workplace hazard may be seen in the rollout of Operation Hampshire.[42] This is concerned with assaults on police officers and staff. There is a general awareness that assaults occur. Indeed, some people may see this as "part of the job". However, it can never be acceptable to ask people to come to work and be assaulted. By collecting data, we can understand better the type of assaults that occur, when and why they occur, and to whom. This intelligence helps us to change the way we police, where necessary, and to ensure that police officers and police staff have the necessary training to minimise the likelihood of being assaulted. We also need to ensure that any victim of an assault receives appropriate care and treatment, both physical and psychological. Remember, the Police Covenant is about police officers and staff not being disadvantaged.

We have identified mental health at work as the number one health concern in policing. There are three priority areas in the strategy:

- Stress at work
- Trauma risk management
- Suicide

There is a legal requirement for police forces to carry out stress risk assessments. The UK Health and Safety Executive (HSE) has produced management standards against which stress risk assessments may be carried out. They relate to six areas of work design: demands, control, support, relationships, role, and change.[43] It is important that managers have the necessary competencies to identify and manage stress at work. Forces should avail themselves of the HSE Line Manager Competency Indicator Tool.[44] The tool has been designed to allow managers to assess their behaviours in relation to preventing and reducing stress at work. There are 12 headline competency areas to assess. A score of 75%, or less, highlights a need to develop the requisite competencies. Thinking about workplace stress in policing terms, reference to the identification of challenge and hindrance stressors in the "Front Line Review" might be helpful.[45]

Trauma risk management should now be a central component of all forces' mental health plans. Policing is arguably unique in that many of its roles involve almost daily exposure to psychological trauma. The UK's first survey to assess trauma management and working conditions in UK policing engaged with 18,175 officers and staff across the UK between October and December 2018. Headline findings set the UK's first Post-Traumatic Stress Disorder (PTSD) prevalence rate in policing at 1 in 5 and the world's first Complex PTSD (CPTSD) rate in a working population (12%).[46] The survey, funded by the Police Dependents' Trust, now Police Care UK, was published in Psychological Medicine in 2020.[47] It involved a 15-minute online survey based on the European Working Conditions Survey (EWCS) that included new questions about psychological hazards, trauma exposure and trauma impact in everyday policing. Notably, it included a new screen for CPTSD, the International Trauma Questionnaire (ITQ). The prevalence of PTSD, at 8%, was higher than the reported prevalence in the UK Armed Forces. Of concern was the finding of high levels of CPTSD for which optimal treatment is yet to be determined. This finding highlighted important differences in trauma exposure and its impact between the Armed Forces and the police. Frequent, sometimes daily, exposure to a wide range of psychological trauma in policing appears to increase the risk of the development of PTSD, with consequences for police occupational health services and for NHS mental health services. It should also be noted that the presence of hindrance factors is associated with an increased rate of PTSD and CPTSD symptoms.[48]

The International Classification of Diseases is a set of codes used by healthcare providers to classify and code diagnoses, symptoms, and procedures. It is maintained by the World Health Organisation and the National Centre for Health Statistics.[49] PTSD is defined in the ICD-11 diagnostic codes as a set of symptoms that may develop following exposure to an extremely threatening or horrific event or series of events. It is characterised by all of the following:

1. Re-experiencing the traumatic event or events in the present in the form of vivid intrusive memories, flashbacks, or nightmares. Re-experiencing may occur via one or multiple sensory modalities and is typically accompanied by strong or overwhelming emotions, particularly fear or horror, and strong physical sensations.
2. Avoidance of thoughts and memories of the event or events, or avoidance of activities, situations, or people reminiscent of the event(s).
3. Persistent perceptions of heightened current threat, for example as indicated by hypervigilance or an enhanced startle reaction to stimuli such as unexpected noises.[50]

CPTSD is a separate disorder that, in addition to the characteristics of PTSD, is typified by a sense of failure and worthlessness, inability to regulate emotions effectively, and disruption to personal relationships. Both disorders involve impairment of functioning.

The detection and management of PTSD has been informed by recent research. The Police Traumatic Events Checklist (PTEC) helps individuals and managers have conversations about psychological trauma and to assess its impact.[51] Individuals who are showing signs of being affected by PTSD should be referred to the force's OH department. This will enable a clinical assessment to be performed. Evidence of PTSD might be picked up by self-assessment, peer support, managers, or by health surveillance programmes. An example of the latter is the psychological surveillance programme, which is part of the NPWS Psychological and Trauma Risk Management Service.

We now have a national action plan for suicide prevention and postvention in England and Wales.[52] It recognises that death by suicide in the police workforce – people who are currently serving or who have served – deserves attention. It addresses a culture that prevents people from talking about suicide specifically, and about mental health in general. Suicide and deaths, due to poisoning where the coroner had insufficient information to make a determination, were the leading causes of death for both men and women aged between 20 and 34 years, up to 2018. The document is a seminal national action plan designed to coalesce ideas and action across the policing landscape. Whilst policing is not currently recognised as an occupation at risk by the Office for National Statistics, any suicide is a needless loss of life and causes great concern. A government policy paper has highlighted areas for forces to consider when developing services and interventions:

- Everyone should feel confident that they have the skills to be involved in preventing suicide.
- Mental health is intrinsically linked to and as important as physical health.

- No one should be excluded from suicide prevention efforts.
- Early intervention is vital.
- Those with lived experience should be involved in prevention activity.
- Strong collaboration is essential.
- Timely, quality evidence is fundamental.[53]

The action plan builds on a police consensus setting out the police service's commitment to suicide prevention.[54] The consensus has been agreed by the National Police Chiefs' Council (NPCC), Association of Police and Crime Commissioners (APCC), the Home Office, Unison, the Police Federation of England and Wales, and the Police Superintendents' Association.

Fatigue is a critically important factor for the development of mental ill health, as well as for undermining health and wellbeing generally. When we are sleep deprived, we don't think straight. We reach for stimulants, such as caffeine and sugary foods, which can further destabilise our sleep patterns, lead to weight gain, and increase the risks of ill health. Management of fatigue has been addressed by the HSE and forms part of the legal obligation to manage workplace risks.[55] It is noted that more than 3.5 million people are employed as shift workers in the UK across a variety of industry sectors, including the emergency services. Poorly designed shift working arrangements and long working hours that do not balance the demands of work with time for rest and recovery can result in fatigue, accidents, injuries, and ill health. Key principles in fatigue management include, but are not limited to:

- Fatigue needs to be managed like any other workplace hazard.
- It is important not to underestimate the effects of fatigue – accidents are more common on night shifts, after a succession of shifts, when shifts are long, and when there are inadequate breaks.
- Compliance with the Working Time Regulations alone is insufficient to manage the risks of fatigue.
- Problems with overtime and shift-swapping may indicate inadequate resource allocation and staffing levels.
- There is no single optimum shift system, and so a planned and systematic approach to assessing and managing risks can improve the health and safety of workers.
- There are many risk factors in shift schedule design which must be considered, including workload, work activity, shift timing, shift duration, the direction of shift rotation, and the number and duration of breaks during and between shifts.

The HSE has published guidance to employers on managing shift work.[56] Data has been collected both nationally and internationally to help understand the undesirable effects of shiftwork in policing.[57]

Live Well

The negative effects of shift work are pervasive. For most members of the police workforce, policing is a 24/7 lifestyle. Even for roles that are nominally 9–5 jobs personal resilience to mitigate work stressors requires attention to healthy behaviours. An evidence-based approach to behaviours supporting wellbeing is contained in a 2008 government report of the *Foresight Mental Capital and Wellbeing Project*.[58] Mental capital was defined as a person's cognitive and emotional resources. Mental wellbeing was defined as a dynamic state in which an individual is able to develop their potential, work productively and creatively, build strong and positive relationships with others, and contribute to their community. Both definitions are highly relevant to modern policing. A key message was that, if we are to prosper and thrive in our changing society and in an interconnected and competitive world, both our mental and material resources will be vital. This links closely to the definition of health chosen for the police health and wellbeing strategy. The Foresight Project commissioned a review to produce the wellbeing equivalent of the "five fruit and vegetables a day" slogan used to promote healthy eating. The actions are:

- Connect.
- Keep learning.
- Be active.
- Take notice.
- Give.

A useful mnemonic is CLANG.

Connect means connect with people around you, be it friends, family, work colleagues or people in your community. Keep learning refers to trying something new. It might be rediscovering an old interest or taking up something new, such as learning an instrument or a foreign language. In essence, it can be anything new that will be enjoyable, provide new knowledge of a skill and build self-confidence. Being active should be self-evident. However, be creative. It does not necessarily mean going to the gym. It can be getting into the habit of going for a walk, cycling, dancing, swimming, or gardening. It could be combined with the keep learning objective. Take notice means being curious as well as being in the moment. This should fit well with policing where curiosity is an important attribute. The message is to be aware of the world around you and to learn to savour the moment. Giving is about doing something nice for somebody. It could be as simple as smiling at colleagues, or even people in the street! Volunteering is common amongst the policing community.

Dr Phil Hammond extended the notion of CLANG to form CLANGERS – adding eat, relax, and sleep to the pneumonic.[59] A healthy and balanced diet is essential for our wellbeing, in both the short term and the long term. As biomechanical beings, we need to put the right fuel into the machine. It can really affect how we perform at work, our energy levels, and our mood. In addition, what we eat can have a massive impact on our long-term health and on how well we age. For more information, visit the Oscar Kilo website.[60] A recent link between our guts and our brains has been described. The enteric nervous system (ENS) is found in the lining of the gastrointestinal tract – from the oesophagus (food pipe from the mouth to the stomach) to the rectum.[61] Although not capable of rational thought, the ENS has been found to communicate with the brain and is responsible for a two-way interaction between mood and bowel disorders. Thus, mental ill health may be associated with bowel symptoms, such as constipation, diarrhoea, bloating, and pain. However, bowel disorders may trigger mental health conditions. There is also a complex interaction between gut nerve signals, gut hormones, and the gut microbiota – the millions of bacteria that live in the gut. The microbiota is concerned with nutrient extraction, metabolism, and immunity. The biosynthesis of bioactive molecules, such as vitamins, amino acids, and lipids, all depend on these microorganisms. They help to keep the lining of the gut healthy. Conversely, an unbalanced microbiota is associated with diseases such as cardiovascular disease, cancer, respiratory diseases, irritable bowel disorder, brain disorders (Parkinson's disease and Alzheimer's disease), and chronic kidney and liver diseases.[62]

There is international research that indicates that police officers are at an increased risk of cardiovascular disease.[63] [64] [65] In the United States, there is concern about the prevalence of metabolic syndrome amongst law enforcement officers as this is a risk factor for cardiovascular disease. Metabolic syndrome is a combination of insulin resistance (leading to high blood sugars), high blood pressure, being obese with a large waistline, and having unhealthy blood fats (high triglycerides and low levels of HDL).[66] Advice about how to check whether you have metabolic syndrome, and how to prevent it, may be found on the NHS website.[67] Note that you might have metabolic syndrome but not have any symptoms of the underlying changes.

Conclusion and Looking to the Future

This chapter has set out how the Police Covenant is influencing health and wellbeing in policing. It gives a legal imperative for police forces to consider their arrangements for supporting the police workforce in that there is a requirement that they should not be disadvantaged because of their roles. This is in addition to the health and safety legal framework that places a duty of care on all Chief Constables. Moving forward, it is likely that the Home Office will become more involved and demanding of Chief Constables to demonstrate how they are taking action in this regard.

Of course, they cannot do this on their own. The NHS will have to play its part. Police officers and police staff seek clinical advice and access to treatment through their GPs. We need doctors and other healthcare practitioners to be aware of their healthcare needs so that consultations factor in the health risks of being a member of the police workforce. In addition, we need the commitment of the Police Covenant to be considered when treatments are being prioritised according to clinical need. The aim, therefore, is to replicate the approach taken by the Armed Forces covenant with the creation of police-aware GP practices and memoranda of understanding with regards to the commissioning of police-aware healthcare services. Some progress has been made. Working with the Royal College of General Practitioners, online educational modules have been created to assist GPs gain a better understanding of police healthcare needs. A pilot of shaping local healthcare commissioning has just concluded details of which may be found on the Oscar Kilo website.[68] Building on a general duty of all Health Boards to reduce health inequalities, the demands of the Police Covenant provide leverage to engage with healthcare commissioners. Specific areas of interest are timely access to mental health services, especially with respect to the treatment of PTSD, and appropriate care pathways for police officers and staff who have cause to attend Accident and Emergency Departments for treatment.

The national health and wellbeing strategy is an important output from the Police Covenant. It collates a number of existing initiatives within an overarching framework and sets out a rationale for a holistic approach to workplace wellbeing. The workplace wellbeing model aligns the domains of the Blue Light Wellbeing Framework (BLWF), launched in 2017, with a cycle of prevention.[69] A third edition was launched in 2024.[70] It is a statement of intent containing a set of standards against which forces can benchmark themselves. The national health and wellbeing strategy has developed an action-orientated model that will assist forces in assessing their capability to deliver against the cycle of prevention. In addition, health and wellbeing priorities have been selected for attention in the five delivery areas. This evidence-based problem-solving approach applied nationally should be a driver of organisational change leading towards the culture of wellbeing that is envisaged.

Notes

1 Oxford Languages. *Oxford Languages and Google.* Accessed October 23, 2024. https://languages.oup.com/google.
2 Health and Safety at Work etc. Act 1974. Accessed October 23, 2024. https://www.legislation.gov.uk/ukpga/1974/37
3 Police Federation of England and Wales (PFEW). "Pay and Morale Survey." 2024. Accessed October 23, 2024. https://www.polfed.org/payandmorale
4 National Police Wellbeing Service (NPWS). *National Wellbeing Survey.* 2024. Accessed October 23, 2024. https://www.oscarkilo.org.uk/news/national-police-wellbeing-survey-2023-results Accessed 10/12/25.
5 Wikipedia. "Maslow's Hierarchy of Needs." October 22, 2024. Accessed October 23, 2024. https://en.wikipedia.org/wiki/Maslow%27s_hierarchy_of_needs
6 Police, Crime, Sentencing and Courts Act 2022.
7 Department of Health and Social Care (DHSC). "The NHS Constitution for England." August 17, 2023. Accessed October 24, 2024. https://www.gov.uk/government/publications/the-nhs-constitution-for-england
8 UK Government. "Occupational Health: Working Better." November 24, 2023. Accessed 24 October 2024. https://www.gov.uk/government/publications/occupational-health-working-better
9 NPWS. "Enhanced and Advanced Occupational Health Standards." 2024. Accessed 29 October 2024. https://www.oscarkilo.org.uk/services/clinical-governance-group/occupational-health/enhanced-and-advanced-occupational-health-standards Accessed December 10, 2025.
10 HMICFRS. "What Is PEEL?" October 8, 2024. Accessed October 29, 2024. https://hmicfrs.justiceinspectorates.gov.uk/peel-assessments/what-is-peel
11 *Soldiering – The Military Covenant*, Army Doctrine Publication, vol. 5 (London: The Stationery Office, February 2000). Accessed December 10, 2025. https://assets.publishing.service.gov.uk/media/5a7efc1ced915d74e6227b89/2000-ADPvol5_Soldiering_the_Military_Covenant_Ver2.pdf
12 Wikipedia. "Armed Forces Covenant." Accessed December 14, 2022. https://en.wikipedia.org/wiki/Armed_Forces_Covenant
13 Andrew Murrison. *Fighting Fit – A Mental Health Plan for Servicemen and Veterans* (London: Ministry of Defence, August 2010). Accessed December 14, 2022. https://assets.publishing.service.gov.uk/media/5a79ea73ed915d042206bf78/20101006_mental_health_Report.pdf

14 Andrew Murrison. *A Better Deal for Military Amputees* (London: Ministry of Defence, 2011). Accessed December 21, 2022. https://assets.publishing.service.gov.uk/government/uploads/system/uploads/attachment_data/file/215338/dh_130827.pdf
15 NHS. "Veterans, Service Leavers, and Non-Mobilised Reservists." Accessed December 22, 2022. https://www.nhs.uk/nhs-services/armed-forces-community/veterans-service-leavers-and-non-mobilised-reservists/.
16 Imperial College Healthcare NHS Trust. "Op RESTORE: The Veterans Physical Health and Wellbeing Service." 2024. Accessed October 29, 2024. https://www.imperial.nhs.uk/our-services/op%20restore
17 NHS England. "Armed Forces and Families Healthcare." Accessed October 29, 2024. https://www.england.nhs.uk/contact-us/privacy-notice/how-we-use-your-information/our-services/armed-forces-and-families-health-care/
18 NHS England. *Healthcare for the Armed Forces Community: A Forward View to 2022*. Accessed October 29, 2024. https://www.england.nhs.uk/publication/healthcare-for-the-armed-forces-community-a-forward-view/
19 Health and Social Care Act 2012. Accessed October 29, 2024. https://www.legislation.gov.uk/ukpga/2012/7/introduction
20 Ministry of Defence. "Serving Personnel, Mobilised Reservists, and a Few Families Are Registered with MoD GPs." Accessed October 29, 2024. https://committees.parliament.uk/writtenevidence/50548/pdf/
21 Anna Charles. "Integrated Care Systems Explained: Making Sense of Systems, Places and Neighbourhoods." The King's Fund. Accessed December 14, 2022. https://www.kingsfund.org.uk/insight-and-analysis/long-reads/integrated-care-systems-explained
22 Armed Forces Act 2021. UK Public General Acts 2021, c. 35. Accessed October 29, 2024. https://www.legislation.gov.uk/ukpga/2021/35
23 Welsh Government. *Integrated Care Fund Evaluation (Summary)*. March 2022. Accessed December 14, 2022. https://www.gov.wales/sites/default/files/statistics-and-research/2022-03/integrated-care-fund-evaluation_0.pdf
24 NHS England. "GP Practices Across the Country to Become 'Veteran Friendly.'" July 30, 2018. Accessed October 30, 2024. https://www.england.nhs.uk/2018/07/gp-practices-across-the-country-to-become-veteran-friendly/
25 Armed Forces Covenant. "Veteran-Friendly Accreditation for GP Practices." July 18, 2024. Accessed October 30, 2024. https://www.armedforcescovenant.gov.uk/case-study/veteran-friendly-accreditation-for-gp-practices/
26 Royal College of General Practitioners (RCGP). "Veterans' Health Hub." 2024. Accessed October 30, 2024. https://elearning.rcgp.org.uk/course/view.php?id=803.
27 The Home Office. *The Front Line Review: Recommendation Report*, p. 8. July 2019. Accessed October 30, 2024. https://assets.publishing.service.gov.uk/government/uploads/system/uploads/attachment_data/file/815791/FLR_Recommendations_report_sent_V2.pdf.
28 Peter Betts and Clare Farmer. *Home Office Police Front Line Review: Workshops with Police Officers and Police Staff – Summary Report* (Office for National Statistics, July 2019), p. 32. Accessed October 30, 2024. https://www.polfed.org/westmids/media/2621/08072019-ons_flr_fullreport_5july-08072019.pdf
29 Machteld Huber et al. "How Should We Define Health?," *BMJ* 343 (2011): d4163. https://pubmed.ncbi.nlm.nih.gov/29902944/
30 Essenburgh. "From a New Definition of Health Towards Person-Centred Care." April 20, 2021. Accessed October 30, 2024. https://www.essenburgh.com/en/from-a-new-definition-of-health-towards-person-centred-care/

31 The Health Foundation. *Person-centred Care Made Simple: What Everyone Should Know about Person-centred Care* (London: The Health Foundation, January 2016). Accessed October 30, 2024. https://www.health.org.uk/sites/default/files/PersonCentredCareMadeSimple.pdf.
32 Strategic Policing Partnership Board. *Policing Vision 2030*. March 31, 2023. Accessed December 12, 2024. https://assets.college.police.uk/s3fs-public/2023-03/Policing%20Vision%202030.pdf.
33 James Manyika. *What Is the Future of Work?* McKinsey & Company. January 2023. Accessed December 12, 2024. https://www.mckinsey.com/featured-insights/future-of-work/what-is-the-future-of-work.
34 PwC. *Workforce of the Future: The Competing Forces Shaping 2030*. Accessed December 12, 2024. https://www.pwc.com/sk/sk/inovacie/assets/workforce-of-the-future-the-competing-forces-shaping-2030-pwc.pdf.
35 UK Government. *No Health Without Mental Health: A Cross-Government Outcomes Strategy*. February 2, 2011. Accessed December 12, 2024. https://www.gov.uk/government/publications/no-health-without-mental-health-a-cross-government-outcomes-strategy.
36 UK Government. *Thriving at Work: The Stevenson/Farmer Review of Mental Health and Employers*. October 2017. Accessed December 12, 2024. https://www.gov.uk/government/publications/thriving-at-work-a-review-of-mental-health-and-employers.
37 The Brain Charity. *What Is Neurodiversity?* 2023. Accessed December 13, 2024. https://www.thebraincharity.org.uk/workplace-neurodiversity/.
38 Sarah Gardner. "Training Officers to Respond to Neurodivergent People," *Going Equipped* 5 (2022): 29–30. Accessed December 13, 2024. https://assets.college.police.uk/s3fs-public/2022-11/Going-equipped-Autumn-Winter-2022.pdf?v=1669046155.
39 UK Government. *Definition of Disability under the Equality Act 2010*. 2023. Accessed December 13, 2024. https://www.gov.uk/government/publications/definition-of-disability-under-the-act.
40 The National Autistic Society. *Pre-Diagnosis Support: A Guide for Adults Who Think They Might Be Autistic*. Accessed December 13, 2024. https://www.autism.org.uk/advice-and-guidance/topics/diagnosis/before-diagnosis/how-to-bring-up-that-you-think-someone-may-be-autistic.
41 College of Policing, *National Decision Model*. January 24, 2024. Accessed December 13, 2024. https://www.college.police.uk/app/national-decision-model/national-decision-model.
42 Oscar Kilo. "Operation Hampshire." 2024. Accessed December 13, 2024.
43 Health and Safety Executive (HSE). *What are the Management Standards?* 2024. Accessed December 13, 2024. https://www.hse.gov.uk/stress/standards/overview.htm.
44 Health and Safety Executive (HSE). *Line Manager Competency Indicator Tool*. 2024. Accessed December 13, 2024. https://www.hse.gov.uk/stress/mcit.htm.
45 The Home Office. *The Front Line Review: Recommendation Report*, 8. July 2019. Accessed December 13, 2024. https://www.gov.uk/government/publications/front-line-policing-review/front-line-review-recommendation-report.
46 University of Cambridge. *Establishing the Evidence Base: Policing – The Job & The Life Survey (2018)*. 2020. Accessed December 13, 2024. https://www.cam.ac.uk/files/inner-images/thejobthelife_findings.pdf.
47 Chris R. Brewin et al. "Posttraumatic Stress Disorder and Complex Posttraumatic Stress Disorder in UK Police Officers," *Psychological Medicine* 52, no. 2 (2020): 1287–1295. https://www.repository.cam.ac.uk/handle/1810/310067.

48 Brendan Burchell et al. "The Association Between Job Quality and the Incidence of PTSD Amongst Police Personnel," *Police Journal* 17 (2023): paac054. https://doi.org/10.1093/police/paac054/6717934
49 New Jersey Department of Health. *ICD Codes*. 2024. Accessed December 17, 2024.
50 ICD-11 for Mortality and Morbidity Statistics. *PTSD*. 2024. Accessed December 17, 2024. https://icd.who.int/devct11/icd11_mms/en/current.
51 Police Care UK. *What is PTEC?* 2024. Accessed December 17, 2024. https://www.policecare.org.uk/help/ptec/.
52 NPWS. *National Suicide Action Plan for Policing*. 2004. Accessed December 23, 2024. https://oscarkilo.org.uk/services/clinical-governance-group/suicide-prevention-and-postvention/national-suicide-action-plan-policing
53 Gov.UK. *Suicide Prevention in England: 5-Year Cross-Sector Strategy*. 11 September 2023. Accessed December 23, 2024. https://www.gov.uk/government/publications/suicide-prevention-strategy-for-england-2023-to-2028/suicide-prevention-in-england-5-year-cross-sector-strategy.
54 NPWS. *Working Together to Prevent Suicide in the Police*. 22 February 2022. Accessed December 23, 2024. https://www.oscarkilo.org.uk/news/working-together-prevent-suicide-police-service.
55 Health and Safety Executive (HSE). *Fatigue*. 2024. Accessed December 23, 2024. https://www.hse.gov.uk/humanfactors/topics/fatigue.htm.
56 Health and Safety Executive (HSE), *Managing Shiftwork: Health and Safety Guidance*. 2006. Accessed December 23, 2024. https://www.gov.uk/government/uploads/system/uploads/attachment_data/file/390908/hsg256_managing_shift_work.pdf.
57 NPWS. *Sleep and Fatigue Interventions*. 2024. Accessed December 23, https://www.oscarkilo.org.uk/services/healthy-living/sleep-and-fatigue-interventions/better-sleep-toolkit Accessed December 10, 2025.
58 The Government Office for Science. *Mental Capital and Wellbeing: Making the Most of Ourselves in the 21st Century. Final Project Report*, p. 316. October 2008. https://www.gov.uk/government/publications/mental-capital-and-wellbeing-making-the-most-of-ourselves-in-the-21st-century
59 Dr Phil Hammond. *Clangers For All, Every Day*. September 18, 2018. Accessed December 23, 2024. https://drphilhammond.com/blog/clangers-for-all-every-day/.
60 NPWS. *Nutrition for Wellbeing*. 2024. Accessed December 23, 2024. https://www.oscarkilo.org.uk/news/wellbeing-investigators-week-action-2025 Accessed December 10, 2025.
61 Johns Hopkins Medicine. *The Brain-Gut Connection*. 2024. Accessed December 23, 2024. https://www.hopkinsmedicine.org/health/wellness-and-prevention/the-brain-gut-connection.
62 Kaijian Hou et al. "Microbiota in Health and Diseases," *Nature* 7, no. 1 (2022): 135. https://doi.org/10.1038/s41392-022-00974-4.
63 J. Greeshma et al. "Cardiovascular Disease Risk Factor Prevalence Among Police Officials: Findings from a Cross-Sectional Study in Kerala, India," *Journal of Occupational Health* 66, no. 1 (2024). https://doi.org/10.1093/joccuh/uiae025.
64 Jongin Lee et al. "Risk of Cerebro-Cardiovascular Diseases in Police Officers and Firefighters: A Nationwide Retrospective Cohort Study," *Yonsei Medical Journal* 63, no. 6 (2022): 585–590. https://doi.org/10.3349/ymj.2022.63.6.585.
65 Franklin H. Zimmerman, "Cardiovascular Disease and Risk Factors in Law Enforcement Personnel: A Comprehensive Review," *Cardiology in Review* 20, no. 4 (2012): 159–166. https://doi.org/10.1097/CRD.0b013e318248d631.
66 Heart UK, *Metabolic Syndrome*. 2024. Accessed December 23, 2024. https://www.heartuk.org.uk/genetic-conditions/metabolic-syndrome.
67 NHS, *Metabolic Syndrome*. 2024. Accessed December 23, 2024. https://www.nhs.uk/conditions/metabolic-syndrome/.
68 NPWS. *Local Healthcare Engagement Resources*. 2024. Accessed December 23, 2024. https://www.oscarkilo.org.uk/local-healthcare-engagement-resources Accessed December 10, 2025.

69 College of Policing. *Blue Light Wellbeing Framework: Organisational Development and International Faculty*, p. 12. May 2017. https://production.oscarkilo.aws.college.police.uk/media/document/8455.
70 College of Policing. *Blue Light Wellbeing Framework*, 3rd Edition, p. 14. 2024. Accessed December 23, 2024. https://production.oscarkilo.aws.college.police.uk/blue-light-wellbeing-framework-blwf.

10

THE FAMILIES PROGRAMME

Claire Long

Introduction

This chapter is written by Claire Long, who has spent a lifetime in policing, largely with Police Mutual. The chapter is written in a non-academic style and is valuable as it tells the story of the work being done by the Police National Wellbeing Service to enhance the provision for families.

The Police Covenant Commitment to Families

The Police Covenant is very clear in its commitment to Police Families. According to the government,

> The covenant is a recognition by government, policing and society as a whole, acknowledging the sacrifices made by those who work or have previously worked in our police forces. It is intended to ensure that officers, staff, volunteers and their families are not disadvantaged as a result of their service in the police and seeks to mitigate the impact that this may have on day-to-day life. In practical terms the covenant will place a legal requirement on the government to report annually to Parliament on issues relating to police welfare, wellbeing and support aiming to improve the working experience of people in policing and help smooth the transition out of policing for police leavers provide support to the families of those working in policing.

For the families programme, the wording of the covenant was a starting point, but it didn't provide much to go on. Unlike the military, where much more is known about family life, police families are in some ways anonymous to the service; they live amongst us and are fully integrated into society. Apart from "next of kin" details on an HR form, very little is known about them.

DOI: 10.4324/9781003518860-11

The uniqueness of policing can be hard to live with. Every day we are dealing with emergencies, the unexpected and sometimes that results in family plans being thrown up in the air. Not to mention the worry and concern our families must have at times. The job of policing is very exposed through documentaries, crime series, the press and social media, resulting in families knowing only too well the dangers that their loved ones are facing. Policing can also significantly affect the officers and staff themselves, the impact of which is often felt at home.

The Covenant is not the only reason that the Families Programme exists. With or without the police covenant, recognising the vital role that families play in supporting officers and staff makes perfect business sense. Post-COVID, the world of employment has taken another step in terms of flexibility, increased working from home, flexible hours, with some firms abolishing "fixed hours" and "number of hours" worked altogether, rather focusing on deliverables and outcomes. It is hard for emergency services to compete when it has such contrasting demands. Policing is a 365/24-hour service, dealing with challenging incidents which impact both physically and mentally. Policing needs to attract and retain talent. Having a better understanding of police families and a family offer that is compelling will undoubtedly help in becoming an "Employer of Choice".

What Is a Family?

There is a quote which says something along the lines of "The bond that links your true family is not one of blood, but of respect and joy in each other's life." That sentiment definitely played a part in the thinking about what family meant in terms of this programme and how it was going to be positioned.

Families are often positioned as being something overwhelmingly important and positive. Across cultures, they have a certain structure/shape that is easily identifiable, sometimes separated by significant geographies. Family life is seen as something valuable and precious. Whilst the above is undoubtedly true for the vast majority, this programme wanted to acknowledge that families do come in all shapes and sizes and that you don't have to be a blood relation or a legal partner to be family. We also wanted to acknowledge that for some the word "family" can have a negative connotation due perhaps to abuse, neglect, dislike or conflict. For others, with families gone or absent, loneliness can be a very real problem.

There are times when you need to define what "family" means, if we were putting together a policy perhaps or working on something which had a legal aspect. This was not the case for this programme and so we deliberately did not give it a definition.

Returning to the "respect and joy in each other's life" seemed like a good place to start. It was up to each individual officer, staff member or volunteer to define family for themselves.

Understanding the Needs of Police Families

Until this point, there had been very little research into the impact of policing on police families and identifying what their needs were. This was a vital first step in helping shape the family support required by the Covenant.

NPWS commissioned research undertaken by Dr SJ Lennie from the Open University. It was called “Investigating Police Families’ Wellbeing and Support Needs”. Dr Lennie conducted a large-scale survey that engaged “non-police” family members, obtaining over 1400 responses. This was complemented by hosting four focus groups: three with “non-police” family members and one with serving officers. Four biographical interviews were also carried out with serving officers. Within this data, the study captured the perspectives of partners, parents, grandparents, adult children and serving officers. At the time of writing, it remains the largest study on wellbeing and support needs of police families in the UK.

As a police service, it would be arrogant to assume that police families are simply there to bend to the will of policing. That policing and the consequences of it will willingly be accommodated within the family unit. Families have a lot to contend with, with often two people working, busy careers, busy lives, caring responsibilities, children; the list goes on. There are also families where both parents work within the Police Service.

Sections of the final report made uncomfortable reading, detailing the day-to-day challenges that police families face and their plea for greater connection and recognition. The research highlighted how much police families contribute to policing through the support and sacrifices they make for those working in it.

> The police dominates every aspect of our lives in one or another, really …his job kind of dominates every aspect. So every decision we have to make or I make or make around the kids, its got to kind of run through his work and his shifts or his commitments and so on”.

This quote comes from our own research describing the unwritten assumption that policing somehow comes first in families when in reality many households are juggling two careers, with kids also having possible caring responsibilities.

We know from our work that when policing dominates the household in such a way this can and does lead to resentment towards the job. Leading this work we have had to be very mindful of this. It is arrogant to assume that as an employer your needs are always going to take precedence. Policing needs to be cognisant that one person’s job is only one factor that police families have to deal with, and they deal with a lot.

Similarly, police forces are under tremendous pressure, managing budgets and an ever-increasing demand, and if we really wanted the families’ work to get traction, we had to be sensitive to those existing pressures in our approach.

The research made a number of recommendations:

- Forces should connect more closely to their police families with targeted communications, including them in key events
- Creation of active family networks and safe spaces
- Psychological support for families
- Impacts on child mental health through having a serving police parent/s
- Childcare
- HR policies

The research findings were communicated to stakeholders across policing and within the NPWS governance structure to help build momentum. We now had a solid foundation on which to build the programme.

Defining Our Approach

The objectives for the families workstream were that families would:

1. Have a voice that is listened to and acted upon.
2. Be recognised for the valuable contribution they make to policing.
3. Feel informed about policing.
4. Be supported through a range of materials designed specifically for them.

From these objectives and taking into consideration our research, we formulated a plan.

Picking up on some of the themes of the research findings, we developed a range of resources that were targeted at families and focused on some of the challenges that they faced – nutrition, fitness, mental health awareness, sleep, communication, communication with children, financial education and managing shifts. The resources sit on the Oscar Kilo website and were promoted to forces so that they could also use these very specific resources, and NPWS promoted them heavily via social media.

Campaigning through social media was always going to form a large part of our work, given we did not know the people whom we were targeting and no easy road in. The idea of communicating to families solely via officers, staff and volunteers was not really that appealing, likening it to giving a child their school report to take home to their parents; there was always a chance that important communication would not land. It would also be contradictory to the research which told us that families wanted an independent direct relationship with the service.

Our campaigning started with the Thank You campaign – a film accompanied by a poem, which illustrated very clearly the limits put on family life by policing and the sacrifices made by family members. A sub-theme throughout the research is the lack of recognition generally for the police family experience, so we wanted to shout out a big thank you to police families everywhere.

We won't solve everything tomorrow, but one of the things we've heard is that a simple acknowledgement of how tough it can be really helps. It can mean people feel less alone and more seen. Saying that it can be difficult out loud is the start of change... that's where the "Thank you" campaign comes in. At the time of writing (December 2024), there have been over 66,000 views of the film. The feedback has been incredible, with some very high-profile sharing of the film. Some of the viewers have been moved to tears to finally see police family life depicted in an honest, unfiltered way.

Support for Police Children

Our research highlighted the impact that having a police parent can have on children within the family and suggested further research into this area. We know that this is a real concern, which is why we launched our "Once upon a time" campaign, to help policing families have important conversations with their children.

The Book Trust charity sets out why a bedtime story is so important for children – for literacy, vocabulary and imagination, as part of a good sleep routine and for bonding with caregivers.

It's not always possible for people working in policing to be around for a bedtime story. It's really important children understand why this might happen.

We focused on the beautifully written and illustrated Red Robber Raid children's book which gives families a chance to share a special bedtime story and explore together why a parent or carer might miss out on mealtimes, bedtimes or other family time.

We gave away 1000 books (although nearly 5000 families wanted them) and created activity packs based on Red Robber with word searches and dot-to-dots. To accompany the book, we sourced "Oscar, the dog", which was a soft toy that formed part of the story. An eBook was also developed with a voice-over by one of the NPWS team, and this is still available on our website for everyone to use.

There is much more we want to do in the children's space and have already commenced work with a child sleep coach to develop short informational videos which will help both parents and their children get a better night's sleep.

Police Family Network

A small network was created with forces who we knew were already doing a lot to engage with families. Collaboration is key to getting buy-in and to accelerating progress. By creating a family toolkit, we could combine ongoing initiatives with the research plus some implementation tips, developing a library of ideas that forces could pick up quickly and easily. The library could then expand as our work developed.

Our starting point was circa 20 really good suggestions as to how forces can deepen their connection with police families. Everything from family panels, to newsletters, to networks, to how families can protect themselves online, picking up on many of the research recommendations – and since we published on the OK website there are many more ideas coming forward.

There are two suggestions that have particular significance. The first is the creation of a policy hub. We have been working closely with the National Police Chief's Council Family working group who produce guidance on what should be included in exemplar family-related policies, and they gave us permission to share their work and hopefully extend its reach. Policy matters; it standardises how we do things and sets culture. Each police force develops its own set of family policies, and we aspire that they can all be benchmarked against the best. The policy hub helps them do just that.

The second suggestion was the development of a wellbeing booklet specifically for the families of officers and staff new joiners, based on a resource used by North Wales. The contents of the booklet are customisable; forces can add their own logos, messages from the Chief Constable and all of their local wellbeing resources. The booklet prepares families for what their loved ones may encounter as they join the service. It explains the job in more detail, explains what wellbeing is and how to spot signs of changes to mental health. This resource was a great starting point for forces to begin their communication with police families, which they can then build on throughout probation and beyond.

What Is Next?

We are still at the foothills of our family journey, and there is much more to do.

In the coming year, we will extend the police family network, opening it up to all 43 forces so that we can really benefit from all of the great work forces are doing to support police families everywhere.

We want to understand, appreciate and recognise all police families regardless of ethnicity or make-up and need to do further research to make this a reality.

An area of particular concern is the impact of police investigations on police families, and this work spans across several of our workstreams. We know that some forces are doing great work in this area and want to harness the learning so that we can develop a national wellbeing product.

Finally, we want to further extend some of the NPWS Wellbeing services to the police family, starting in areas of most urgent concern.

We knew from the outset that reaching out to police families would prove challenging and indeed that has been the case. Communication and engagement has been invaluable in the development of this workstream. Slowly but surely those anonymous family members who day in and day out support policing, making significant sacrifices are becoming known to us. Only then can we in turn listen to them, thank them and most importantly help them.

11

POLICE LEAVERS

Context, Impacts, and Support Initiatives

Ceri Jones and Stuart Noble

Introduction

This chapter explores the research on police leavers. We also explore leavers' resettlement support needs, drawing comparisons with the military model. The chapter is illustrated with quotes from the extensive research through interviews and surveys we have conducted with police leavers over the last several years.

Current and Historical Context

The numbers of police leaving the service in the UK police service are at record levels. In the year ending March 2023, a record 9,192 full-time equivalent (FTE) police officers left the 43 territorial police forces in England and Wales, marking a 6.6% leaver rate—the highest since records began in 2003 (Home Office, 2023). Voluntary resignations constituted 50% of departures, an increase from 42% in the previous year, indicating significant shifts away from traditional retirement exit. This surge in attrition highlights critical changes to police leaver trends.

Historically, police officers served approximately 30 years before retiring with a full pension. However, recent legislative changes, particularly the introduction of the 2015 Police Pension Scheme, have transformed this trajectory. The new scheme raised the normal pension age to 60, allowing flexible retirement options from the age of 55, albeit with actuarially reduced pensions (Institute for Government, 2023). These changes have significant implications, influencing financial planning and prompting officers to reconsider their career durations. Many current retirees wish to continue to work until the standard retirement age or beyond. Some retired police officers are recruited into civilian roles within the police service; others look for alternative employment in other industries, as this quote from a retiring officer illustrates.

> I plan to retire from being a police officer, then intend to seek further employment.

DOI: 10.4324/9781003518860-12

Newer recruitment models, including initiatives such as Police Now and direct entry pathways, have shifted career expectations, introducing the notion of policing as a shorter-term vocation. This evolving perception challenges traditional assumptions about lifetime service; some may plan earlier exits, pursuing careers beyond policing.

Research attributes rising attrition rates to occupational stress, organisational dissatisfaction, and psychological health concerns (Cockcroft et al., 2023). According to the Police Federation (2024), physical and psychological health challenges significantly influence decisions to leave policing prematurely, with some retiring through medical ill-health. Elliott-Davies (2018) emphasises organisational stressors such as workload, bureaucracy, and limited resources as dominant factors precipitating early departures. High workloads and a lack of resources can leave officers considering leaving earlier than planned (Jones & Noble, 2024). Here is an illustrative quote from a retiring officer:

> The job changed. I no longer felt like I was making a difference—endless paperwork, fewer resources, more scrutiny. It became impossible to do the work properly.

Impacts on Mental Health

Officers with approximately 30 years' service will have been exposed to an estimated 900 traumatic events in their careers (Rudofossi, 2009). The psychological implications of policing can be profound, with police officers frequently exposed to violent and traumatic incidents that can lead to post-traumatic stress disorder (PTSD) and other mental health problems (Violanti et al., 2018). Officers face a higher risk of exposure to violence and injury on the job than many other professions, which can lead to anxiety and other mental health problems (Regehr et al., 2019). Traumatic and violent event exposure can increase their susceptibility to stress-related disorders such as anxiety, depression, and post-traumatic stress disorder (PTSD) (Wang & Hesketh, 2012; Grandison et al., 2020). This, in turn, can influence individuals' decision to leave.

> I was exhausted. The pressures just didn't stop, and I found myself dreading each shift. It got to the point where I knew I had to leave for my own health.

Research from the US suggests retirement can have a negative impact on officers' mental health, with the majority of suicides at work occurring in the five years prior to retirement (Violanti et al., 2011). After retirement police veterans' rate of suicide is three times that of the general population (Violanti et al., 2013), with five years lower life expectancy (Brandl & Smith, 2013; Caudill & Peak, 2009).

Work-Life Balance

Family impacts are also significant. Police officers may experience stress related to family or relationship problems or other personal factors (Violanti et al., 2018). Although policing presents numerous challenges for family members, it can also yield positive outcomes. Police families often develop enhanced safety awareness and risk assessment skills, contributing to a secure home environment (King et al., 2023). Officers can serve as positive role models, exemplifying values such as integrity and civic responsibility, positively influencing family dynamics and children's ethical development (Mental Wealth Hub, 2023). Transitioning into retirement represents an opportunity for reconnection with family, often improving family relationships (Drew et al., 2024).

Theoretical Frameworks

Work identities significantly shape individuals' sense of self, offering insights into behaviour within police organisations (Alvesson et al., 2008). While research extensively covers police recruitment and socialisation, there is limited focus on the leaving process (Charman & Tyson, 2023). Alvesson et al. (2008) propose three identity perspectives: social identity, identity work, and identity regulation. Social identity theories effectively explain group dynamics within policing contexts (Charman, 2017; Bradford et al., 2014). However, identity work and identity regulation offer deeper insights into voluntary resignations.

Identity work involves maintaining coherent self-images by managing disruptions from major changes or crises, often leading to self-doubt (Alvesson & Willmott, 2002; Van Maanen, 2010). Identity regulation emphasises external structures shaping identities, highlighting individuals' limited control (Alvesson, 2010; Foucault, 1980). Misalignment between work and personal identities can intensify organisational pressures, prompting identity threats and role exit (Ramarajan & Reid, 2013; Petriglieri, 2011).

The Social Identity Model of Identity Change (SIMIC) provides additional insights into identity transitions when individuals leave organisations. SIMIC highlights that maintaining identity continuity and establishing new social groups are vital for psychological wellbeing during significant life transitions, such as retirement (Haslam et al., 2019; Jetten et al., 2014). In policing, deeply rooted professional identities within hierarchical structures amplify identity disruption upon leaving service. Without structured transition support, former officers may experience identity disorientation, stress, and social isolation (Cruwys et al., 2015). SIMIC's effectiveness has been demonstrated in contexts like military retirement, where interventions fostering new identities and social networks significantly reduced psychological distress (Kintzle & Castro, 2018). These interventions typically involve structured support programmes focusing on identity reconstruction, social skills development, and building new social connections. This could include initiatives such as pre-retirement planning, peer mentoring schemes, community engagement opportunities, and counselling services specifically addressing identity challenges.

Role exit theory (Ebaugh, 1988) outlines four phases: initial doubts, seeking alternatives, the turning point, and creating the ex-role. Initial doubts emerge from dissatisfaction or burnout, signalling potential exit (Ashforth, 2000). Early intervention during this phase is critical but often missed. Individuals explore alternatives before a turning point catalyses the exit process. Finally, transitioning involves identity loss and adopting a new self (Ebaugh, 1988; Goffman, 1959).

Police Leavers Identity and Sense of Self

Being a police officer is often cited as a vocational role. Police officers often exhibit strong values of public service and civic duty. Research indicates that the role identity and values inherent in police work can positively influence officers' professional conduct and personal development. A study by Filstad and Karp (2021) highlights that police leaders, acting as role models, significantly shape the behaviours and attitudes of their subordinates, reinforcing ethical standards and fostering a culture of integrity within the force, and officers can act as role models to the wider community.

The structured, hierarchical police environment fosters strong professional identities, which can be disrupted upon leaving the service (Patterson et al., 2001; Brandl & Smith, 2013). Many retiring officers report a profound sense of loss, compounded by diminished camaraderie and peer support networks, contributing to isolation and adverse mental health outcomes (Ruiz & Morrow, 2005). When lengthy, collegiate service bonds between officers are strong, the loss of membership from this group can be extremely difficult (Cameron & Griffiths, 2017). This is an example quote illustrating this concept from a retiring officer.

> We come to finish day and then we drop off the cliff, because there's been no transition period and you're working at this level and all of a sudden you drop. And for police officers specifically, you are, you then become Mr Somebody or Mrs Somebody. Because I've just met an ex-Chief Constable that I used to work for he was a Divisional Commander and it's interesting, because he said to me, oh will you book me in at the gate because I'm treated like a leper. But he's only Mr Suchabody, now isn't he.

For officers, high work commitments and strong role identity within the underpinning police culture promote solidarity and loyalty, but simultaneously isolate members from developing extensive, diverse social networks beyond the workplace. Reorienting and redefining individual identity when leaving can be difficult, particularly for male officers who identify more strongly with their work identity than female officers (Cameron & Griffiths, 2017).

Maintaining peer networks when leaving the service is an important element of identity continuity and can protect an individual's wellbeing and mental health. Policing peers are much more likely to access colleagues for support than internal structures such as occupational health and counselling services or external agencies such as GPs or mental health services. In policing, low social support from colleagues is a risk factor for adverse psychological outcomes (Sherwood et al., 2019). By contrast, strong social support networks moderate the impact of stressors and reduce depression and PTSD symptoms (Southwick et al., 2005). Access to peer support also creates opportunities to intervene before an individual struggles to cope and needs sickness absence (Whybrow et al., 2015) and in policing, growing evidence demonstrates peer support programmes' effectiveness in reducing psychological morbidity and reducing stigmatised views of seeking support (Watson & Andrew, 2018).

Resettlement and Support Initiatives

The UK Police Covenant represents formal governmental recognition of responsibilities towards police officers post-service, aiming to reduce disadvantages resulting from their service (Gov.uk, 2022). However, structured transitional support remains limited compared to other sectors, as this quote from a retiring officer illustrates.

> A lot of what we do is carry on working at this speed, we come to finish day and then we drop off the cliff, because there's been no transition period and you're working at this level and all of a sudden you drop.

There needs to be sufficient recognition, time, and structured support for individuals to make the transition from employment to leaving the service and to move through the recognised stages of that transition. Individuals who are able to move through their own process of decision-making adjust to their new lives more easily than those who cannot (Ebaugh, 1988).

Military Resettlement Programmes

Insights from military transition models emphasise the effectiveness of structured transition programmes, which provide extensive career guidance, vocational training, and resilience-building support two years before and after leaving service. While some veterans report challenges, such as poor job matches or irrelevant job-seeking activities (Jones et al., 2022), positive experiences highlight successful transitions facilitated by targeted coaching and employer engagement. The Armed Forces Covenant further enhances veterans' transitions by ensuring fair treatment and special support through initiatives like guaranteed job interviews, skills translation, and mentoring programmes (Becker et al., 2022). Given the parallels between military and police occupational cultures—characterised by strong group cohesion, defined roles, and distinct hierarchies—these support strategies may be relevant for policing contexts, emphasising the importance of proactive organisational support during transitional phases.

Police Resettlement Support

Structured police resettlement programmes and toolkits, such as those delivered by ourselves and the National Wellbeing and Policing Support (NWPS) Leavers Toolkit, offer comprehensive support and advice on a range of topics. These programmes typically feature psychoeducational material, resilience training, and career planning support, aiming to mitigate the psychological and social impacts commonly associated with retirement transitions. Effective resilience management during transition includes addressing mental health vulnerabilities, reducing stress, and preventing isolation, particularly among officers with trauma histories (Grandison et al., 2020).

Future career preparation is important in structured resettlement programmes as many police officers feel unsure how to translate policing skills into civilian job roles and industries and lack confidence in applying for other roles or navigating the job market, as this quote from a senior officer illustrates.

> Yeah, sometimes it's not your competence. It's who you're up against, you know, but it did, it did give me a stumble in my conference thinking. Ohh Christ, what I'm, you know, am I gonna be driving a van round Tesco delivery?

Practical career preparation, proactive job market engagement, and clear identification of transferable skills significantly reduce anxiety and facilitate smoother transitions (Calvo & Sarkisian, 2011). Structured interventions may also include peer support networks, vocational workshops, and tailored counselling, ensuring a comprehensive approach to retirement planning and career opportunities beyond policing (Ebaugh, 1988; Smith & True, 2014).

Conclusion

Rising police attrition rates reflect significant occupational stressors and evolving retirement pathways. The psychological, social, and practical impacts of retirement necessitate structured, comprehensive transition support. Recognising these challenges and systematically addressing them through evidence-based frameworks like SIMIC and targeted support initiatives is important to ensuring effective transitions for police officers, enhancing their psychological resilience, and promoting positive post-service outcomes. Further research and policy interventions are recommended to sustain the effectiveness of transition support structures in policing.

References

Alvesson, M. (2010). Self-doubters, strugglers, storytellers, surfers and others: Images of self-identities in organization studies. *Human Relations*, *63*(2), 193–217.

Alvesson, M., Ashcraft, K. L., & Thomas, R. (2008). Identity matters: Reflections on the construction of identity scholarship in organization studies. *Organization*, *15*(1), 5–28.

Alvesson, M., & Willmott, H. (2002). Identity regulation as organizational control: Producing the appropriate individual. *Journal of Management Studies*, *39*(5), 619–644.

Ashforth, B. E. (2000). *Role transitions in organizational life: An identity-based perspective.* Routledge.

Becker, C., Fisher, N., & Jones, A. (2022). Veteran employment and transitions: Understanding civilian employer knowledge gaps. *Journal of Military Studies*, *11*(2), 123–141.

Brandl, S. G., & Smith, B. W. (2013). An empirical examination of retirement from the Milwaukee Police Department: Implications for future retirements and retiree benefits. *Policing: An International Journal of Police Strategies & Management*, *36*(3), 497–513. https://doi.org/10.1108/PIJPSM-06-2013-0055

Bradford, B., Murphy, K., & Jackson, J. (2014). Officers as mirrors: Policing, procedural justice and the (re)production of social identity. *British Journal of Criminology*, *54*(4), 527–550.

Calvo, E., & Sarkisian, N. (2011). Retirement and well-being. *Annual Review of Gerontology and Geriatrics*, *31*(1), 132–163.

Cameron, K., & Griffiths, C. (2017). Police officer identity and the challenges of leaving the service. *Police Practice and Research*, *18*(6), 584–596. https://doi.org/10.1080/15614263.2017.1337713

Caudill, J. W., & Peak, K. J. (2009). Police suicide: Understanding the risk. *The Police Chief*, *76*(1), 40–46.

Charman, S. (2017). *Police socialisation, identity and culture: Becoming blue.* Palgrave Macmillan.

Charman, S., & Tyson, S. (2023). Policing transitions: The experience of leaving policing. *Policing and Society*, *33*(1), 1–17.

Cockcroft, T., Garthwaite, K., & Smith, S. (2023). Understanding early departures from the police service: The role of organisational and occupational stressors. *Policing and Society*, *33*(1), 45–62.

Cruwys, T., Haslam, S. A., Dingle, G. A., Haslam, C., & Jetten, J. (2015). Depression and social identity: An integrative review. *Personality and Social Psychology Review*, *19*(3), 215–238.

Drew, J. M., Sargeant, E., & Martin, S. (2024). Why do police consider leaving the profession?: The interplay between job demand stress, burnout, psychological distress, and commitment, Policing: *A Journal of Policy and Practice*, *18*, paae036. https://doi.org/10.1093/police/paae036.

Ebaugh, H. R. F. (1988). *Becoming an ex: The process of role exit*. University of Chicago Press.

Elliott-Davies, M. (2018). Police officer wellbeing: The importance of organisational support. *The Police Journal*, *91*(2), 143–157.

Filstad, C., & Karp, T. (2021). Police leadership as identity work: Role modelling and relational learning. *Policing and Society*, *31*(4), 460–476. https://doi.org/10.1080/10439463.2020.1714972

Foucault, M. (1980). *Power/knowledge: Selected interviews and other writings 1972–1977*. Pantheon Books.

Goffman, E. (1959). *The presentation of self in everyday life*. Doubleday.

Gov.uk. (2022). *Police Covenant*. Retrieved from https://www.gov.uk/government/publications/police-covenant

Grandison, G., Walsh, D., & Maguire, R. (2020). Police officer mental health: A systematic review. *Police Practice and Research*, *21*(6), 632–650.

Haslam, C., Jetten, J., Cruwys, T., Dingle, G., & Haslam, S. A. (2019). *The new psychology of health: Unlocking the social cure*. Routledge.

Home Office. (2023). *Police workforce England and Wales* . Available at: https://www.gov.uk/government/statistics/police-workforce-england-and-wales-31-march-2023/police-workforce-england-and-wales-31-march-2023 Accessed November 2, 2025.

Jetten, J., Haslam, C., Haslam, S. A., Dingle, G., & Jones, J. M. (2014). How groups affect our health and well-being: The path from theory to policy. *Social Issues and Policy Review*, *8*(1), 103–130.

Jones, K., Fisher, N., & Becker, C. (2022). Public employment services and veteran labour market inclusion. *British Journal of Employment Relations*, *60*(4), 927–949.

Jones, C., & Noble, S. (2024). Report to NPWS: Police Leavers Employment Gateway Pilot. Unpublished report. College of Policing National Police Wellbeing Service (NPWS).

King, L. et al. (2023). Family safety and risk awareness among police households. *Journal of Family Safety*, *4*(2), 112–127.

Kintzle, S., & Castro, C. A. (2018). Examining veteran transition to civilian life. *Military Psychology*, *30*(3), 202–212.

Mental Wealth Hub. (2023). *Police wellbeing: Family and social support*. Retrieved from https://www.mentalwealthhub.com

Patterson, M. C., Poole, A. D., Trew, K. J., & Harkin, N. (2001). The psychological and physical health of police officers retired recently from the Royal Ulster Constabulary. *The Irish Journal of Psychology*, *22*(1), 1–27.

Petriglieri, J. L. (2011). Under threat: Responses to and the consequences of threats to individuals' identities. *Academy of Management Review*, *36*(4), 641–662.

Ramarajan, L., & Reid, E. (2013). Shattering the myth of separate worlds: Negotiating nonwork identities at work. *Academy of Management Review*, *38*(4), 621–644.

Regehr, C., Carey, M. G., Wagner, S., Alden, L. E., Buys, N., Corneil, W., Fyfe, T., Teo, S., & White, M. (2019). Prevalence of PTSD, depression, and anxiety disorders in public safety personnel. *Canadian Journal of Psychiatry*, *64*(1), 54–64. https://doi.org/10.1177/0706743718814819

Rudofossi, D. (2009). A cop doc's guide to public safety complex trauma syndrome: Using five police personality styles. *International Journal of Emergency Mental Health*, *11*(3), 200.

Ruiz, J., & Morrow, E. (2005). Retiring the old centurion: Life after a career in policing—An exploratory study. *International Journal of Public Administration*, *28*(13–14), 1151–1186.

Sherwood, L., Rothwell, J., Froggatt, K., & Jordan, J. (2019). Occupational stress and coping in UK police officers: The role of social support. *Policing and Society*, *29*(1), 104–117. https://doi.org/10.1080/10439463.2017.1367716

Smith, L. N., & True, G. (2014). Military transition interventions: Promoting resilience and reintegration. *Journal of Military Psychology*, *26*(3), 135–147.

Southwick, S. M., Vythilingam, M., & Charney, D. S. (2005). The psychobiology of depression and resilience to stress: Implications for prevention and treatment. *Annual Review of Clinical Psychology*, *1*, 255–291. https://doi.org/10.1146/annurev.clinpsy.1.102803.143948

Van Maanen, J. (2010). Identity work and control in occupational communities. In S. B. Sitkin, L. B. Cardinal, & K. M. Bijlsma-Frankema (Eds.), *Organizational control* (pp. 111–166). Cambridge University Press.

Violanti, J. M., Charles, L. E., Hartley, T. A., Mnatsakanova, A., Andrew, M. E., & Burchfiel, C. M. (2011). Suicide in police work: Exploring potential contributing factors. *American Journal of Public Health*, *101*(12), 2202–2205. https://doi.org/10.2105/AJPH.2011.300308

Violanti, J. M., Owens, S. L., McCanlies, E., Fekedulegn, D., Andrew, M. E., & Lawler, J. (2013). Law enforcement suicide: A national analysis. *International Journal of Emergency Mental Health*, *15*(4), 289–297. https://doi.org/10.4172/1522-4821.1000138

Violanti, J. M., Mnatsakanova, A., Andrew, M. E., Allison, P., Gu, J. K., & Violanti, E. F. (2018). Police stressors and health: A state-of-the-art review. *Policing: An International Journal*, *41*(4), 642–656. https://doi.org/10.1108/PIJPSM-06-2016-0088

Wang, M., & Hesketh, B. (2012). Achieving well-being in retirement: Recommendations from 20 years of research. *SIOP White Paper Series*, *1*(1), 11–22.

Watson, L., & Andrew, G. (2018). Peer support in policing: The case for early intervention. *Occupational Medicine*, *68*(7), 480–485. https://doi.org/10.1093/occmed/kqy094

Whybrow, D., Jones, N., & Greenberg, N. (2015). Promoting organizational well-being: Tackling workplace stress and mental ill health. *Journal of Public Mental Health*, *14*(1), 47–56. https://doi.org/10.1108/JPMH-11-2014-0040

12

THE POLICING MIND

Does the Job Make the Brain or *the Brain Make the Job*?

Jessica K. Miller

Introduction

Policing is made up of people. People who seem to feel 'different' because of the job. The people (who are not *police* people) present police people *to other people* through the media and entertainment industry. These people change how people see the police. And somehow in all of this, the police are now almost not seen as people at all.

Which makes things challenging.

The 2020s have been harsh times to be in policing and with the news media's thirst and politicians' capacity to bring to light some dubious and unsavoury characters who once operated in the shadows of policing, it's hard to refocus on the reality of what it means to be in the police – a reality that is daily life for nearly a quarter of a million officers, staff and volunteers in the UK. Not understanding how these people live, think and contribute would be considered discriminatory, if being of the police family were a recognised protected characteristic.

Their story, our story, of life in policing is not always that enlightened or informed in the world of entertainment either (as engaging as much of this entertainment is for those *not* in the job). A repertoire of crime dramas from the 1970s through to the 2020s (from *Inspector Morse* and *Bergerac*, *The Sweeney* and *Filth* through to *Happy Valley*) so often default to caricatures of burnt-out, disillusioned cops with challenging behavioural traits, limited self-awareness and dysfunctional relationships, trapped in a limbo, facing retirement, wondering who they are supposed to be in a wider world that probably doesn't understand what they have experienced and isn't inclined to find out.

Spending time with thousands of officers and staff (their faces, ideas, responses) and having read tens of thousands of their stories (in words and numbers) has told me that the people of policing (our officers, staff, volunteers, supporters, friends and families) need not hide in the shadows – and nor are they caricatures. Research and testimony have given us some real wake-up calls in the 2020s about police mental health: unacceptable

DOI: 10.4324/9781003518860-13

rates of post-traumatic stress disorder, sickness absence, heartbreaking losses through suicide and a loss of meaning in what it means to police.

These things are what they are. And yet, we also see day in and day out that people in policing have incredibly adaptive brains, fierce motivations to protect others and relentless dynamism to deal with what the job, life (and quite frankly, the public) throws at them. Police officers, staff and volunteers rarely (if ever) have the time – or means – to be able to understand the reality of what their thinking means for their trajectory.

Who gives them the chance to see how their job shapes them, their brains and their sense of self? Likely no one.

But times are different now. We are in a position to change this.

Because we have science. And we have the capacity to steer our ultimate powerhouse: *the human brain.*

Why Science Has Already Rescued Us

Research from neuroscience and advanced reflective practice traditions clearly shows that policing may change us and our approach to life, but it's not as personal – nor as inevitable – as it may seem. There is objectivity. There is space to choose.

Science and technology now very aptly demonstrate for us that the human brain (including the policing brain) can rewire *simply because we tell it to.* We can use established techniques to increase our cognitive agility, and we can practice and refine how we process information and the experiences we have (wanted and unwanted).

What is more, this can help rewire physiologically, too, so that we can use our own bodies better for the jobs we do. We can realign to the demands of our jobs by becoming more skilful with our minds and bodies and by taking up the chances we are now being offered. It's just that maybe we haven't had a minute to stop and realise that.

More and more technology and sophisticated training interventions are being made available to policing all the time, through well-established and impressive organisations and evidence-based initiatives, big and small. From biometric surveillance to neuropsychological techniques, policing is upskilling to enable minds and bodies to reclaim their aptitude to manage the realities of a job like no other. The efficiencies are quantifiable, the potential for resilience unfathomable.

But it starts with taking a few minutes to take it in.

Policing the Brain

So, if science has the answers for how to increase resilience in policing, what's holding us back?

Why are there 43 (forces) different ways of engaging in this to different degrees? Why is there no standard approach, resourcing or funding? What stops policing from running with this?

Perhaps these are cultural, political (even navel-gazing existential) questions, answers to which may be mercurial, cyclical, dull or downright deflating. Some of us might like to dabble in all that. Some of us may also like to respond and *get on with something* (anything!).

We have an opportunity here to dip into some light insight into what might be making us tick. With this comes a tiny chance to *get going right now* and to make a little difference which edges us closer to what we want to see for policing – without waiting for something grand or some*one* grand to show up. But, for now, this is just a moment where your eyes are on a page and you have a chance to not be reacting to anything else. So, take this chapter as a win. Your chance to exert your right to either reflect or just take a few minutes out, staring at a page or a screen. (No one will know!)

Right. What is policing? What are the parameters we naturally work with?

We can acknowledge that there are components of policing that are at play in how we make decisions about looking after our minds (and how our minds work with our bodies). The secret to resilience is working *with* those components, just as they are.

- Policing is an institution of public service. It is outward-facing for the safety of others.
- Policing needs a power structure which involves compliance and order.
- Policing operates in an economy that depends on society wanting more than it has.
- Policing operates in realms that are not common ground for the majority of the general public, and working conditions mean that many officers and staff are single-crewed or working in shift patterns or terrains which are not conducive to sociability.
- Policing is about everyday threat management, typically engaging with those inflicting or experiencing suffering, and requires the use of force and control.
- Policing also comprises chronic emergency response, dynamism and time pressure.

Neuropsychology, medicine and contemplative traditions all seem to agree on what *good conditions* are to cultivate and improve mental health and trauma resilience. You may have already noticed that – ironically (or maybe blindingly obviously) – these conditions of what resilience needs are pretty much the opposite of what policing typifies.

Awkward

Brains and bodies need us to be smartly self-compassionate when required, to be open to new ways of thinking and to the reality that everything changes, to be able to rest in safety, satisfaction and a sense of being connected.

So, we need to up our game.

Braining the Police

It isn't neuroscience.

Ok, well maybe it is a bit, but it's mainly intuition: you know this stuff deep down.

There are some features about policing that make it somewhat challenging for the brain to get into a state of resilience and development. These features of policing aren't going anywhere. We have the human brain and we now know that these brains can really go places by adapting to their environment in skilful ways, under our direction. Some people call this 'self-directed neuroplasticity'. Others call it, 'waking the heck up and switching on'.

There is a wonderful phrase:

Brains evolve to fit their environment, not to make you happy.

Here, I think we finally have the chance in policing to do both: to adapt to our environment and also to be happy. But the two may be mutually exclusive at times, and we need to face that head-on. Always, the policing environment needs responding to, and other times, when we are not actively policing an emergency, we need to refuel the happiness bit. It will be a continuous commitment. One that should not be on the shoulders of individuals alone. It should be a commitment by teams, forces, the institution, and the wider society to honour: working in the field of human suffering (victims and perpetrators thereof) demands respect – and investment in the skillset needed in order to sustain it.

A fully functional industry should minimise the risk of individuals resigning themselves to the negative conditions of burnout, compassion fatigue, meaninglessness, insecurity, isolation and even shame. It is important to be realistic; accepting these things can be experienced now and then in policing (as they can in life outside of policing). That said, the institution, forces, teams, supervisors and peers all have a responsibility to reiterate on a daily basis that these conditions are a risk – not viable parameters for how we think and feel, for what we do with our lives or for how we see ourselves.

These conditions are not our 'lot' in life, simply because policing is a hard environment. Policing is a terrain in which our brains can operate. They can operate in a way which is fitting to the demands, but also in ways which are resilient to its impacts. It can operate under our steer in a way that counterbalances all that it needs to, to keep us strong and happy.

Here, we offer example approaches on how to steer the policing brain in ways that foster resilience. These are not instructions. They are invitations.

Some suggestions are things we can take on as individuals; some are things we can encourage or support others to deliver on. Once we read these, we have insight into how things can be better. What we do with fresh understanding is always down to us.

We can't un-read this, nor undo any insight – but we *can* choose to ignore it.

We're human.

We always have the choice to let evolution do its thing, letting our brains sleepwalk into a near masochistic domain where the job gets done (*ish*) to the sacrifice of our happiness (and sometimes to the sacrifice of those who care about us).

We always have theright to decline new ways of thinking and stick to what we default to.

If you keep doing what you've always done, you'll keep getting what you always got.

Getting Practical

Real resilience for policing brains in the UK today: some ideas…

Train Brains in Threat Management

Brains aren't supposed to live in constant threat mode, and we know that this damages the brain over time. Learning to regulate the threat response and switch to connection with others can be hugely impactful in *acute situations*, too, such as scene recovery in armed response. It can also help those viewing images or taking 999 calls to get tiny breaks in the midst of long shifts of exposure. Witnessing the change from threat mode to status to connection to alertness to threat mode (and so on) is sometimes all it takes to gain some control and a sense of resilience.

Make Common Ground Out of Trauma Exposure

Traumatic incidents are *already the known terrain* of everyday policing. Yet, the damage they cause isn't actually about the incident (most of the time). Much of the time, damage arises because the incidents are unprocessed, unspoken of, isolating ill-equipped individuals, reducing their resilience and damaging their trust in the organisation. The most critical step towards individual, team and force resilience is recognising the exposure as everyday AND as abhorrent as it is. This is very possible. Use visuals, common language and open communications to be honest about the nature of the work you do with others. No one is asking any team, force or institution to ignore the threat they are made to respond to. We are just asking for recognition that sometimes the threat can shape us in return if we don't manage it. A simple acknowledgement that the job hurts, and we *know,* can go far to restore trust, meaning and respect. These are the building blocks of resilience on the front line.

Integrate Healthy Processing of the Abnormal or Challenging Experiences

Unprocessed trauma (in the *healthiest* of officers) has been proven to impair their situational awareness, engagement and attention and ability to regulate social tolerance. These things are kind of important in policing, are they not? Processing trauma need not be an ambitious psychological, emotional, gut-wrenching feat. It can be as simple as saying to a colleague, "*Well, that was pretty rough, wasn't it? What the heck?*" By normalising the need to get perspective and make sense of something bizarre, intense, abhorrent or sad, we are kick-starting our brains' natural capacity to file such experiences reliably and safely. Debriefs, a cup of tea, or a structured breather is all it takes to allow a brain to address the impact, put it in perspective, feel connection to others and move on.

> If we get used to doing this, we are much more likely to notice those more unique experiences that are just 'too much' and which require more engagement and professional support. Noticing this and acting early increases our efficiency in resilience as individuals, families, units, teams and forces.
>
> Up-skill the body in releasing tension, resetting and priming again.

We don't necessarily need intricate biometric surveillance technology to tell us when our bodies are holding stress from being activated; we just need to tune in. Technology really inspires us to do that these days, but we can do that ourselves too.

Policing can become very focused on cognition, decision-making, planning and communication, and we can easily dissociate from what our body is telling us as we try to 'just keep going'. Training in body self-awareness isn't what we are used to in frontline jobs. We are used to bodies just doing what we tell them to do – and we rarely help them afterwards because there is usually another job waiting, a family member needing us or sleep is calling. Because of this, prompts to check in with our body need to be deliberate, obvious and accessible.

One example might be engaging in a quick, simple one-minute routine of breathing and moving position, accessing (or even just imagining) nature and re-regulating and scanning our body's points of tension. All these scientifically proven techniques are offered in abundance online.

The challenge for those in policing is allowing ourselves to engage in them. Working gently with the body in this way will need to become part of a shift's duty, part of any policing day and an acceptable part of the culture and rhetoric of what it is to police. As long as self-care and body regulation are seen as an indulgence (rather than a common-sense physical requirement) our brains will not devote the mental effort needed. Without a deliberate shift towards body regulation, officers, staff and volunteers will likely sustain an increasingly accepted trajectory of chronic illness and disorder (such as hypertension, MSK issues, body image issues, addiction and susceptibility to injury). This has no place in the resilience we all deserve.

Recognise the Homebase and See the Whole Human

A policing brain typically wakes up at home and travels in to work in policing and returns afterwards. The policing brain has also usually developed in a home environment through childhood and adolescence and has lived a life and learned to adjust to life using the lessons learned in home, school and the social world. How brains deal with the challenges of policing necessarily depends on their experiences before a career (and even their experiences immediately before a shift). Life outside of policing has a place in our resilience and can set a baseline of stress tolerance for any given time period.

We also know that when individuals have to deal with the dichotomy of *personal versus police* life, this can be harmful. (Research shows that in forces where officers and staff report being unable to take one or two hours off work for a family crisis, levels of trauma impact in those forces are twice those of forces where that option is more feasible). This means something. Yet, so many mental health 'offers' in police forces (and other third sector organisations) deter officers and staff from even discussing home or personal issues when facing problems at work for which they need help. Refusing the brain access to all its experience is denying it the permission to use all its resources to achieve resilience.

When we learn *not to be afraid* that life can get us into habits of thought that sometimes need a little steer and attention, then we unlock the capacity for real change, optimum performance and authentic wellbeing. Accepting the whole human gives us resource. It doesn't deplete.

Act Now on Working Conditions That You Influence (and Admit That We All Do)

How we are with each other and how we invest in the work environment matters greatly. Police working environments have been a bone of contention this decade as police standards and culture have been called to account in the media, government and in forces across the UK. So much so, that the scale of the challenge can seem overwhelming. Yet, recent research has offered us some insight into how we can deal with some challenges head-on.

Trauma research has identified factors in the workplace that can be addressed with a good chance of reducing clinical prevalence of trauma disorder. These factors include: increasing a sense of meaningfulness, recognising the reality of everyday trauma exposure, investing in line manager supervisions and dealing with issues such as sexual harassment. We also know that management issues can be an aggravating factor in trauma exposure tolerance and that situations such as being under investigation have been associated with higher suicide risk in policing. By ensuring that working environments are honest about trauma exposure, attend to supervisions, are respectful of gender sensitivities and are cognisant of moral injury and what it feels like to be under investigative scrutiny, we already know that forces can naturally increase resilience. If we can do so proactively with younger generations of new recruits, this may serve us well for longer than we think. Having these factors at the forefront of our minds as we go about our daily lives in and around policing may actually constitute the cultural shift that sceptics profess is impossible.

Choose the Smallest Change: ~~"Butterfly wings"~~ Neurons, Chemicals, Guts and Feeling Good

There is a (somewhat cutesy) metaphor about butterfly wings and tsunamis out there that (I think) makes some point about a tiny movement making a huge change. There are other adages about legendary figures (Mother Teresa as one, perhaps Spider-Man as another) who say that sometimes we can't do great things, but small things with great love. These sayings can be very nice for some people. Inspiring.

As a rather cynical and brutal scientist, I prefer to explain why small changes and wholesome intentions are good in a *different way*.

When we want things to be *different* in life, to feel better, our brains and bodies become very subtly activated, giving us all sorts of instructions (instructions which we are not always consciously aware we are receiving). We tend to react automatically.

When we want change, we all respond differently.

Some of us with more female hormones than others naturally get quite a nice infusion of feel-good chemicals when someone we love does something very *small* for us (albeit usually something which involves a demonstration of empathy). Some of us with more male hormones or traits tend to save up energy to focus on big things that have impact and fix things. In power structures and institutions with a renowned 'culture', there can be a tendency to default change to the responsibility of 'the powers that be' and for some religious traditions, even 'him upstairs'. Some folks will wait for big change to happen by someone else, somewhere else, at another time.

So, what does all this mean for change in policing?

Policing is arguably a male-dominated environment with a perceived culture. Small wins and little gestures can seem so inconsequential. There is a lot to fix out there!

Yet, the brain *really* does benefit from a simple reward of feeling something different has gone well. Brains love novelty and they rarely get to feel satisfied – especially when in a daily environment where we respond to a relentless alarm and a message to correct something that is not going well.

By choosing just one small change in working with the policing brain better, we are instantaneously offering our minds some balm and some nourishment, encouragement to keep going. We are not waiting for anything to *change*; we are not waiting for or demanding *more resources*, for *new leadership*, for *someone (anyone!)* to appear from nowhere and help us out. A small, simple change that *we ourselves instigate* is a quiet nod to the brain and body that '*we've got this*'. This small change may just be a turning point to lifelong and expansive resilience.

So, give it a go.

Find the smallest change you can make and enjoy it.

Academia. Policing. You.

Whether we are a self-conscious academic working hard not to be seen as precious or an officer concerned their intellect is not respected, we are all part of a police family because we are here, reading this text. Because of that, *we all have a chance.*

Be part of the conversation, develop a common language, educate the public on its understanding of the job. Be the person who keeps an eye out for others and who speaks up with insight – and if you can't point towards it yourself, smile and make space for those you know who can.

It's true.

We've got this.

13

WHAT DO WE MEAN WHEN WE USE THE WORD TRAUMA?

Zoe Davenport

Medical jargon has entered our everyday language more and more thanks to information being more available via the internet and social media, and social changes that mean we feel more comfortable discussing illnesses and health issues, such as cancer, which only a decade ago was still a fairly taboo subject. This is a positive change, particularly in relation to mental health. Being more open about our mental health has helped to reduce stigma and normalise people's experiences, as well as make access to mental health support easier. However, incorporating certain diagnostic terms into everyday language has skewed or changed the meaning of certain terms such as 'OCD' or 'bipolar'.

Trauma is another term whose meaning has been watered down by everyday use to describe less serious events such as a favourite show being cancelled or the rising cost of a sandwich, but what does the term really mean and what does it mean in relation to policing and other roles within the justice system?

There are two sides to trauma: one is the event or experience, and the other is how it affects us.

A traumatic incident is something out of the ordinary, an extraordinary event rather than something that happens every day such as a serious car accident or violent assault.

The other side of trauma is the series of reactions that we might experience following an incident like this, which can affect how we feel and behave. We often refer to these as trauma symptoms.

Everyone will react differently to a traumatic incident; what might affect me might not affect you and vice versa, or it might affect us both but differently. There's no right or wrong way to respond. Symptoms can vary from person to person too, but here is a list of some common ones:

- Feeling jumpy or on edge.
- Loss or change of appetite.
- Having dreams or nightmares about the incident and struggling to sleep.

DOI: 10.4324/9781003518860-14

- Feeling angry or excessively sad about what has happened.
- Difficulty concentrating.
- Thinking about the incident or having flashbacks or recurring images.

For the most part, when we experience a traumatic event, we can process what has happened and move on with little or no emotional impact, even if to begin with we have felt shocked or sad, and it's important to remember that having an emotional response to an upsetting or frightening event is entirely normal and it's what makes us human. It's also what makes (or will make) you good at your job. However, on some occasions we might struggle to resolve how we feel about the incident for a variety of different reasons, and we might experience trauma symptoms for a few weeks or months which may affect our jobs or relationships.

If this happens, it's important to get help.

We discuss where and how to get help at the end of this chapter.

The (Neuro) Science Bit

We often think of trauma and other mental health as 'all in the mind' and separate from physical injury, but psychological trauma is biological, and understanding this can help with feelings of shame or judgement of others and ourselves. A basic understanding of the biology of our brains and why we feel and think things following a trauma can help to identify our symptoms, make sense of how we feel and assist others with theirs.

Our brains are designed with an inbuilt mechanism that responds to danger. When triggered, this system results in a response called 'fight or flight'; you've probably heard of this.

Fight or flight (also known as fight, flight, freeze, appease) is the automatic response that is hardwired into us to help us respond to danger in the best way to keep us safe according to the threat.

When we see or hear something that we perceive as a threat, our brains process this information and send signals around the body to make changes to help us respond, such us widening our pupils to take in as much visual information as possible. The hormone adrenaline raises our heart rate, which in turn pumps blood around the body faster and the hormone cortisol helps to release glucose into our bodies to give us energy.

Freeze or appease (also sometimes known as freeze or fawn) again work to protect us against a threat by lowering the risk of conflict or keeping us still to avoid the passing threat. People who experience these responses often feel ashamed that they didn't put up a fight, but it's important to remember that we don't control our reactions; we are pre-programmed to respond in certain ways. If you or someone you know is struggling with their response to a traumatic situation, it can be helpful to talk this through with a professional who can help you to make sense of your feelings.

Trauma in Policing

Policing is not like other jobs. Becoming a police officer can offer a wealth of opportunities and experiences; however, unlike other jobs, there are certain risks. These risks vary from the physical to the psychological and emotional. There is now greater understanding of the impact of policing on officers and staff than ever before, resulting in huge improvements to the support on offer from forces and other agencies.

The average person might experience 3–4 traumatic incidents in their lifetime. For police officers, that number rises to 400–600 (Avon and Somerset Police Federation, 2019).

Earlier on in the chapter, we talked about trauma being an extraordinary event, the kind of thing that most people experience rarely. You could also describe this as a very bad day for someone.

The core of police work is responding to those bad days, whether it's on blues and twos as an emergency or later when they come to report a crime, which is why the figure for traumatic events that officers experience is so much higher than for those outside of policing and other emergency services.

As a police officer or someone who works in the criminal justice system, you turn towards what others turn away from. This means that you will see and hear things that other people don't.

At first, this can seem daunting; many officers will recall attending their first scene of a sudden death or death message. However, it is a privilege to be the person that others turn to in their moment of distress, and with the right tools and support, you can have a fantastic career.

Due to the nature of police work, officers have higher rates of post-traumatic stress disorder compared to the general public. The rates for officers are one in five compared to the general population, which is around four in every hundred. Despite these statistics, it is still very rare and getting help early if you experience the symptoms listed above can help speed up the healing process.

Many officers are reluctant to share stories of their day with partners or family to avoid upsetting them or 'contaminating' home life, but it's important to have people that you can talk to whether it's a supervisor or colleague in your team, or a friend that you met during training. Sharing those experiences with people who understand can make a huge difference.

Secondary Trauma

Secondary trauma is sometimes also referred to as Vicarious trauma. Secondary trauma differs from primary trauma in that secondary trauma occurs when we are exposed to other people's experiences of a traumatic incident. We don't need to experience the incident directly, but hearing multiple accounts of a distressing experience can impact us. This is a particular risk for those working with child and adult victims of emotional, sexual and physical abuse, call handlers who deal with continued distressed members of the public or anyone whose work involves reading or viewing traumatic content such as interview transcripts or videos.

Secondary trauma affects us differently to primary trauma too, in that, rather than a single shocking event, there are a series of seemingly less impactful experiences that slowly build up over time until we feel overwhelmed.

The easiest way to understand secondary trauma is to think of the compassion we feel towards victims, for example, as being like a jar of pennies. If we give a penny to each person, or story that makes us feel sad or angry, eventually we run out of pennies and are left with an empty jar. In this way, we can use up our empathy or compassion for others if we are constantly exposed to sadness and distress without a break.

The symptoms of secondary trauma also differ to those resulting from an incident. Secondary trauma symptoms can be harder to stop, are less immediate and are often things that we brush off as tiredness.

However, if left untreated, secondary trauma symptoms can develop into something more serious such as depression, so it's important to know the signs:

- Finding it hard to be empathetic or care about victims, feeling cut off or shut down.
- Feeling exhausted even after a good night's sleep or disrupted sleep or difficulty dropping off.
- Loss of appetite.
- Feeling easily irritated or having low tolerance, tearful or angry.
- Feeling hopeless or apathetic, pessimistic or cynical; a loss of interest in things.
- An increase in illnesses like colds or viruses, cold sores etc.
- Difficulty concentrating, struggling to make decisions.
- Overthinking or fixated thinking about victims' stories.

Some people may find themselves becoming emotionally overinvested in a victim, caring too much or crossing boundaries such as maintaining contact after a case has closed.

For many people, changes to sleep patterns are usually a sign; this might just be a short-term reaction to momentary stress, but be aware of how you are feeling, and if you notice a continuation of the symptoms above, make sure you get some help.

Taking regular breaks, time off away from work or moving to a new department can help to protect you from secondary trauma.

Myth Busting

There are many myths about trauma; cutting the facts from the fiction can reduce stigma and fear about what is a normal response. Knowing the facts means that we can educate those around us too, making the conversation about trauma and mental health less frightening. The use of facts and figures regarding those who experience trauma minimises incorrect beliefs.

Everyone Who Experiences Trauma Will Get PTSD

This isn't true. Most people who experience a traumatic event will recover by themselves or with help.

Only Soldiers Get PTSD

Our understanding of trauma and PTSD comes from research undertaken with military personnel from the First, Second and Vietnam wars who were exhibiting certain behaviours. We only began to understand trauma via this research, meaning that this disorder has historically been linked to soldiers and war. However, PTSD is not limited to those who have experienced combat. Anyone who has experienced a traumatic event can develop PTSD although most people don't.

You Can't Get Over Trauma

Yes you can! With the right support such as therapy, medication or a combination of both, many people go on to lead lives unaffected by their experiences. The key is getting help as soon as you recognise symptoms or feel that something isn't quite right. Knowing yourself, having a good foundation of self-care and knowing the signs to look out for are the keys to recovery.

It's never too late to get help; if even the incident was months or years ago, the right support can help recovery.

Trauma Is a Sign of Weakness

This is totally untrue and can be very damaging. Trauma is a response to an extraordinary experience, one that we cannot control. Acknowledging trauma and asking for help is best for you and those around you. The more we acknowledge and respond to trauma and other mental health issues, the more we are helping to reduce stigma, normalise mental ill health and educate each other.

You Only Get PTSD if Your Life Has Been Threatened

People experience trauma and develop PTSD following a variety of experiences, not only following a threat to life. There are no rules around who can and can't experience trauma.

You Can Just Think Your Way Out of It

Unfortunately, some people still think that mental ill health, whether its depression, anxiety or trauma, is a choice, and that people can just snap out of it. We know that this just isn't true, and these types of comments can make us feel guilty or ashamed. If someone is making unhelpful comments like these, find someone else to talk to; there are many other people who are understanding and can help.

Post-Traumatic Growth

Whilst much of the conversation around trauma can feel negative and worrying, there is new evidence and understanding emerging from research on trauma which shows that many people can grow and learn from a traumatic experience. Obviously, there are some caveats to this; there are some experiences which can be hard to reframe positively. However, sometimes a traumatic experience can help us understand our strengths, help us to develop emotionally and psychologically by developing a new level of resilience, change our outlook on life or improve our relationships by giving us a renewed view of what's important. It can even give us a more positive outlook on the world, especially following incidents such as those that require strangers to help each other as an example.

Post-traumatic growth can occur following therapy, but this is necessary. Not everyone will experience post-traumatic growth, and not every experience will result in it, but it's important to know that good can come from difficult experiences.

Getting Help

Asking for help can be difficult; knowing where to go and who to speak to (and what to say) can be confusing. Information regarding the types of treatment available, how to access them and what to say when you get there can make this process easier.

Talking therapies such as counselling can be helpful by providing a safe space where you can talk about the incident and how it made you feel. Counselling is a non-judgemental space, where you are free to discuss subjects that you may feel able to discuss with friends or family. Most therapists who work in and around policing have a good understanding of trauma and understand the kind of things that you might deal with in the course of your job.

In addition to counselling, there are specialist therapies that are designed specifically to help with trauma. Eye Movement Desensitisation and Reprocessing is a type of therapy that sometimes uses moving light or eye movements to help you reframe your experience into something less impactful.

You might have heard of Cognitive Behavioural Therapy, which is a type of structured therapy that is used with difficulties such as eating disorders or anxiety. Trauma-Focused CBT uses techniques to help process and manage trauma symptoms, and ultimately reduce them to enable people to return to normal life.

Occupational Health

Your employer will have in-house systems in place to help you. It's important that you understand what's on offer and how to access the services of your OH department. Whilst it can be worrying when asking for help from your employer, it is important to remember that they have a duty of care, and by seeking help you will help them to understand how you job can affect people thereby providing the right support.

GP

Your GP is a first step to getting help. They will be able to advise you on treatment options including specialist therapies such as EMDR or Trauma-Focused CBT, as well as medication. Waiting times for talking therapies can be longer than for other services, so it might be useful to consider additional options.

In order to provide you with the right care, it's important that you provide your GP with as much information as you can. Remember that they are there to help and are trained to listen, so try not to feel embarrassed. If you are worried about what to say, it can be helpful to write out what you need to tell them before your appointment. You can take these notes with you, and if you struggle in the appointment, you can pass them to your GP to read.

Medication

Medication for mental health can sound scary, and often people are worried that medication will change them or that they will become addicted. Medication can be helpful to manage symptoms that might be making day-to-day life difficult, such as reducing anxiety or tearfulness, enabling you to carry out day-to-day tasks and do the things that will help your treatment, such as going to counselling. Modern medication is not addictive and is often only needed for short periods of time.

If your GP recommends medication, they will be able to answer any questions or concerns that you might have.

Other Services

There are many charities and other services offering information and support for those who have experienced trauma as a result of their work. Some might provide specialist therapies, information for you and your family and have phone lines that you can call to get help.

These are some organisations that might be useful; however, there will be others available in your area:

MIND – Information on mental health, counselling services and advocacy www.mind.org.uk

CALM – Suicide prevention, information on causes of depression and anxiety www.thecalmzone.net

Police Care UK – The UK police support charity that provides advice and counselling www.policecare.org.uk

Oscar Kilo – Training, information and advice on staying well for police and police staff www.oscarkilo.org.uk

BACP – The British Association of Counsellors and Psychotherapists – information on all types of therapy, how to find a therapist and a list of registered therapists across the UK www.bacp.co.uk

UKCP – UK Council for Psychotherapy – information on therapy and directory of psychotherapists www.psychotherapy.org.uk

Counselling Directory – Information on mental health and UK-based therapists searchable by location or issue www.counselling-directory.org.uk

One in Four – counselling and support for survivors of child sexual abuse, violence and trauma www.oneinfour.org.uk

Switchboard – for LGBTQIA+ people needing support www.switchboard.lgbt

BAATN – Counselling for and by Black, African and Asian communities www.baatn.org.uk

Reference

Avon and Somerset Police Federation. (2019). *Capture data on traumatic incidents*. Retrieved October 2024. https://www.polfed.org/avonsom/news/news-articles/capture-data-on-traumatic-incidents/

14

SOCIAL EMBEDDEDNESS AND THE POLICE

The Foundations of Resilience for Police Officers

Gareth Stubbs

Introduction

Situating Social Embeddedness in the Policing Context

The role of social support in policing is not new. Foundational studies into police socialisation (Charman, 2017; Fielding, 1988; Skolnick, 2010; Van Maanen, 1973) have long recognised that the police role is not just a job, but an immersive identity built through peer interaction, group acceptance, and tacit cultural exchange. While this body of literature has explored the impact of group dynamics and cultural norms on police behaviour, less attention has been paid to how social embeddedness prior to and during the early phases of police work may influence officer wellbeing.

Social embeddedness refers to the ways individuals are connected to others within a social network and the degree to which these connections provide instrumental, emotional, and normative support. It is a concept that has gained increasing traction in labour market sociology (Granovetter, 1973, 1985, 1988), but remains under-utilised in police wellbeing literature. Recent empirical studies (Hesketh & Stubbs, 2024a, 2024b; Stubbs & Tong, 2024) suggests that new police recruits with strong social ties to existing officers receive both instrumental support (e.g., coaching, application assistance) and emotional support, leading to a smoother transition into the profession and stronger early identity alignment with the police role.

In contrast, officers entering the profession without such social ties – which can often be those from under-represented groups – report higher levels of anxiety, detachment, and precarity during recruitment and early service. These disparities in social support, while rarely framed in wellbeing terms, are increasingly relevant in an era where recruitment, retention, and officer mental health are all under critical review (Hesketh, 2015; Phythian et al., 2023; Purba & Demou, 2019).

This chapter integrates the literature on social embeddedness, organisational resilience, and policing to propose a more unified model of officer wellbeing that incorporates

DOI: 10.4324/9781003518860-15

pre-service and early service social context as foundational. Drawing on recent research, it argues that the strength and nature of an officer's social network can meaningfully impact their experience of policing from the outset, with implications for wellbeing, performance, and misconduct exposure.

Social Support, Resilience, and the Decay of the Social in Policing

Social support has long been recognised as a critical element of resilience in high-stakes occupations (Cooper et al., 2001; Rees et al., 2015). In policing, where daily work can entail moral injury, institutional contradiction, and public hostility, this support is an intrinsic component of a healthy workforce. Without it, the psychological cost of service rises sharply.

Jackman et al. (2020), in their study of an English police force, found that social support – especially when provided by peers – was positively associated with psychological wellbeing. Officers who perceived strong informal support from colleagues and family were significantly more resilient across multiple domains. Crucially, formal organisational support was not as predictive of wellbeing, underscoring the primacy of interpersonal connection over bureaucratic provision.

Support networks also enable the performance of what Caza et al. (2018) and Brown (2015) describe as identity work – the labour of reconciling personal values with institutional norms, especially under conditions of ethical strain. Policing requires officers to consistently manage contradiction: the performance of justice within unjust systems, the projection of strength under emotional strain, and the upholding of law amid moral ambiguity. In addition to this, Van Maanen (2010) notes, identity work in policing is not only continual but socially regulated; officers come to understand, perform, and sustain their professional identity through peer interactions that reinforce acceptable norms and emotional responses. Without robust social support, officers therefore bear these tensions alone, potentially increasing vulnerability to moral fatigue and burnout.

Traditionally, policing offered rich ground for informal bonding. Shared rituals, ranging from team sports to station-based gatherings, served not only as decompression mechanisms but also as subtle enforcers of cultural cohesion and emotional sharing (Waddington, 1999). However, the decline of these practices is now well documented. Austerity measures, remote supervision, cultural reform initiatives, and the digitalisation of work have all contributed to the centralisation of police stations (Hesketh & Stubbs, 2024a; Millie et al., 2024), and the removal of smaller, more intimate spaces for bonding amongst officers.

Recent analyses of police station closures have focused primarily on impacts to crime rates and response logistics (Blesse & Diegmann, 2018, 2022), yet the internal social consequences of these changes are less often discussed (Millie et al., 2024). As Loader and Mulcahy (2003) note, police buildings carry symbolic and relational weight – they anchor both public legitimacy and internal culture. While new stations may still offer refreshment areas or shared spaces, these are typically large, impersonal, and transitory in nature, offering little of the familiarity or containment that once allowed for genuine decompression and peer bonding. Waddington's (1999) conception of 'canteen culture' reminds us that it is not just proximity that matters, but the kind of space: smaller, routine gathering zones allowed officers to share informal knowledge, negotiate contradictions, and regulate each other's emotional responses. In their absence, the performance of identity work becomes more brittle, and the relational grounding needed for moral resilience may be harder to find.

For new recruits, this erosion may be especially harmful. Those with pre-existing ties to policing, via family or community, often access unshared communication codes, receive moral calibration through proximity, and experience smoother identity alignment (Stubbs & Tong, 2024). Those without such links discuss emotional distance and a lack of support through social embeddedness in their early service (Hesketh & Stubbs, 2024a).

The implications are clear: Social support is not equally distributed, and its decay through changes in the previous twenty years may disproportionately affect those most in need of it. The withdrawal of the 'social' from policing may not merely represent a cultural loss; it could be a structural weakening of the resilience architecture that officers rely on to survive, adapt, and serve.

Implications for the Individual and the Organisation

The decline of social embeddedness in policing is not just a historical trend; it is a live and active force shaping the emotional and ethical experience of officers today. For the individual officer, the implications are both immediate and cumulative. The absence of strong, trust-based peer networks leaves new recruits with few safe places to process emotional exposure, test the moral contours of their work, or simply decompress. The result is not always dramatic, but it may become cumulatively corrosive over time; without emotional scaffolding, identity coherence becomes harder to sustain. Officers may increasingly rely on surface-level coping, develop cynicism as a defensive posture, or begin to emotionally disengage from both the role and the communities they serve.

Where social connection is weak, so too is moral regulation. As Van Maanen (2010) and Waddington (1999) have argued, peer cultures in policing are central to the transmission of informal norms and the reinforcement of behavioural boundaries. This informal regulation is not always benign, but it does serve as a constant feedback mechanism, shaping what is seen as tolerable, commendable, or professionally shameful. When physical and social fragmentation reduces the frequency and intimacy of these peer encounters, this regulatory function may become diluted. Officers may find themselves isolated not just emotionally, but ethically, less likely to speak up, seek support, or challenge problematic behaviour.

In addition to this change in place/social regulation, the positive action agenda has rightly focused on increasing diversity and representation within the police; a long-overdue corrective to institutional homogeneity. It is possible that it may also have disrupted the very recruitment networks that historically sustained some elements of officer resilience. In previous eras, recruitment often occurred through tight-knit familial or local social ties: the sibling of a constable, the son of a community figure, or a trusted neighbour recommended by an officer already in service (Stubbs et al., 2023). These networks, while undeniably exclusionary in some respects, also carried with them an embedded resilience architecture, shared moral reference points, inherited cultural understanding, and ready-made peer scaffolding. Emerging data from our work suggests that as these organic pipelines have been displaced, many new recruits now enter policing with fewer pre-existing connections, less cultural capital, and less immediate access to emotional support. This is not an argument against reform, but it is a reminder that representation must be accompanied by structured efforts to rebuild the informal networks that once supported officers after hours, off the record, and under pressure. At present, this dynamic remains largely unexamined in the literature.

For the organisation, these shifts pose potential risks. First, retention. Officers who feel alienated, unsupported, or out of place are more likely to leave the service (Tyson & Charman, 2023). As Hesketh and Stubbs (2024a) discuss, those with limited social access or lacking a policing background can report a sense of misalignment during early service. This may contribute to under-represented candidates being more likely to exit within the early part of their career. Second, performance. Social cohesion has long been linked to trust, mutual accountability, and team-based operational effectiveness. When social cohesion weakens, communication may suffer and mistakes proliferate. One could argue that this could be the result of lower levels of intimate identity work. Third, misconduct. While often framed as individual pathology, forms of unethical conduct may flourish in contexts where social norms are more ambiguous, peer intervention is rare, and officers operate with a sense of professional dislocation.

There is also a reputational implication. Public trust in policing is not built solely through strategic communications or institutional reform; it is embodied daily in the way officers carry themselves, relate to others, and speak about their role. Officers who feel internally fragmented, unsupported, or emotionally adrift are less likely to project the kind of legitimacy that policing increasingly depends on. This is supported by the literature on self-legitimacy (Tankebe, 2019; Tankebe & Meško, 2015) which suggests that officers with confident and coherent self-concept may, in turn, make improved operational decisions.

In sum, the erosion of social embeddedness carries layered consequences. It risks isolating the individual, fragmenting the collective, and weakening the very cultural threads that bind a policing organisation together. As we look to build resilience in modern policing, social connection must not be treated as optional or nostalgic. It is a structural necessity.

Recommendations for Promoting Opportunity and Wellbeing

The erosion of social embeddedness in policing is not inevitable; it is a result of political, structural, cultural, and managerial choices. Restoring the social fabric of the service requires action at the political, individual, and organisational levels. What follows are targeted recommendations aimed at rebuilding the relational infrastructure that underpins resilience, belonging, and performance.

Any serious conversation about rebuilding social support in policing must begin with an acknowledgement of its political context – especially with regards to the recent changes in the UK. The erosion of social embeddedness is not an organic shift; it is the downstream effect of governmental decisions. Austerity measures, while politically framed as economic necessity, have systematically stripped away the physical and social infrastructure that once underpinned officer resilience. Likewise, the rise of New Public Management (Diefenbach, 2009; Gruening, 2001) has introduced a culture of quantification that values what can be measured, while neglecting what may truly matter:

relational trust, informal support, and emotional cohesion. These aspects are not luxuries; they are the invisible architecture of healthy survival in frontline work. And while it is undoubtedly difficult to measure social support in traditional KPI terms, this is no excuse for its erasure. We must be wary of Chesterton's Fence; the informal rituals, clubs, and communal practices that once surrounded policing existed for a reason. They emerged not by chance, but as organic responses to occupational need. To remove them without understanding their purpose is to create a brittle institution, one increasingly reliant on individuals to carry burdens that were once shared.

Potential Improvements at the Organisational Level

Design for Connection, Not Just Function

Modern police estates are often built for efficiency and security, but rarely for sociability. Planners should be encouraged to design stations and hubs that include deliberately small, quiet spaces for peer interaction and decompression. These may seem peripheral, but they serve as essential sites for informal bonding and emotional regulation.

Rebuild Peer Networks for New Recruits

With the decline of organic recruitment networks, there is a growing need to consciously cultivate new ones. Structured peer mentoring, cohort-based onboarding, and embedded socialisation programmes should be prioritised (Hesketh & Stubbs, 2024a). These systems must not only teach protocol, but also facilitate trust and vulnerability among officers.

Rethink Wellbeing Strategy

Too often, wellbeing initiatives can become individualised, offering yoga sessions, apps, or employee assistance programme referrals. While valuable, they rarely address the social architecture of wellbeing. Policies should invest in group-based support, facilitated team reflection, and peer-led debriefing structures that reflect how officers actually cope: relationally, informally, and through shared meaning-making.

Acknowledge the Cultural Costs of Reform

Diversity initiatives must continue, but they should be accompanied by efforts to create new cultural anchors that enable belonging for all. If positive action disrupts legacy pathways into the job, organisations must not only open the gates, but also lay foundations for community and cultural fluency once inside.

Track Embeddedness, Not Just Attrition

Current metrics of success often focus on how many officers stay or leave. But deeper insights could be gained by tracking perceptions of social support, identity alignment, and team belonging – especially in the first two years of service. These are early indicators of resilience and may be solid predictors of performance over time.

For the Individual Officer

Seek Mentorship – Formally or Informally

New officers should be encouraged to actively seek out trusted mentors or peers, particularly those willing to share moral reasoning and emotional transparency. The absence of organic networks makes this a vital contribution to self-preservation.

Use the Canteen, Even If You Don't Need Coffee

Shared presence matters. Officers can contribute to a healthier workplace culture by participating in group spaces, checking in on peers, and modelling openness, even though in practice these actions may be subtle. Waddington describes this beautifully in his essay on canteen culture (1999).

Challenge Isolation as a Red Flag

Officers who find themselves increasingly isolated should treat this not as a personal weakness but as a risk indicator. Reach out, debrief, connect. Emotional regulation in policing is a social act, not an individual burden.

Protect Each Other's Vulnerability

Perhaps most importantly, officers can help sustain the profession by protecting and normalising emotional expression among colleagues. Whether through humour, honesty, or shared silence, resilience is rarely built alone.

The recommendations outlined above are intended not as radical departures from current practice, but as reasoned proposals to re-centre a foundational component of occupational resilience. While the structure and demands of policing continue to evolve, the role of social embeddedness as a buffer against psychological strain, a mechanism for informal regulation, and a source of identity cohesion, remains significant. The evidence discussed suggests that its decline may be contributing to issues of retention, performance, and wellbeing. Accordingly, efforts to strengthen these relational networks should be approached with the same rigour afforded to other strategic reforms. While resource constraints and measurement challenges persist, overlooking the social dimensions of policing risks further disconnection between officers and the environments in which they work. A more systematic approach to embedding social support within both policy and practice may help mitigate this, contributing to a more sustainable and coherent policing model.

A Future Research Agenda: Rebalancing the Lens

Over the past several decades, policing research has been heavily shaped by a critical paradigm, rightly focused on addressing institutional failures, power asymmetries, and systemic harm. This body of work has been essential in holding policing to account and ensuring that marginalised voices are heard. Studies of procedural injustice, racialised violence, and organisational misconduct have rightly occupied central space in the literature. However, the dominance of this critical agenda has also meant that other areas of police experience, particularly those involving intra-organisational resilience and social cohesion, have remained significantly underexplored.

There has been, for example, minimal empirical focus on the role of police sport and recreation as mechanisms of social bonding. The social capital generated through these informal practices, and their role in sustaining resilience and moral regulation, has rarely been examined in contemporary research. Similarly, the strength and configuration of officers' social networks, both inside and outside the workplace, have not been the subject of sustained study. While anecdotal accounts and qualitative fragments exist, we lack a systematic, evidence-based understanding of what constitutes the average officer's support network, how it evolves over time, and how it correlates with psychological health or ethical performance.

This is not a call for uncritical celebration of police culture, nor a retreat from necessary critique. Rather, it is a recognition that the social fabric of policing may itself be a factor in long-term institutional functioning. As previous sections have demonstrated, social embeddedness is associated with improved decision-making, increased stress tolerance, and reduced likelihood of burnout. These outcomes are not only beneficial to individual officers; they are likely to produce downstream gains in public service, institutional trust, and operational integrity. In short, supporting the internal health of police organisations may, over time, enhance the public's experience of justice.

To move forward, the following research avenues are proposed:

Recommendations for Future Research

Mapping Social Support Structures

Large-scale qualitative and quantitative studies should be conducted to explore the configuration, strength, and utility of police officers' social networks. This could include longitudinal tracking of peer, familial, and community ties from pre-service through mid-career.

Ethnographies of Social Life in Policing

There is a need for updated, embedded ethnographic research that documents the everyday social practices of policing, including informal spaces, rituals, and relationships. This would allow a richer understanding of cultural maintenance, emotional support, and team dynamics.

The Role of Police Sport and Informal Associations

Police sport and club culture, once a central component of service life, warrants reinvestigation. Research might examine its historical role in cohesion, its current status, and its potential as a future resource for wellbeing and inclusivity.

Comparative International Work

Different jurisdictions have taken different paths in terms of organisational structure, community integration, and welfare support. Comparative research may reveal valuable insights about models of embeddedness and their effect on officer wellbeing and public outcomes.

Measuring Social Embeddedness as a Performance Predictor

Finally, methodological advances are needed to operationalise social embeddedness, not as a vague construct, but as a measurable predictor of decision quality, ethical conduct, and emotional resilience. It is possible that encouraging the right sort of social belonging in police organisations provides immediate and long-term benefits for both the officers and victims alike.

Conclusion

This chapter has examined the concept of social embeddedness as a critical yet underexplored dimension of police resilience. Drawing on an interdisciplinary foundation that integrates organisational theory, identity work, and the sociology of labour markets, it has argued that social ties, particularly those formed prior to and during early service, can serve as structural buffers against the psychological and moral demands of frontline policing. As traditional support structures decline due to political, managerial, and spatial transformations, the resulting fragmentation may have profound implications for officer wellbeing, institutional cohesion, and public trust. While calls for reform and professionalisation remain vital, they must be complemented by a reinvestment in the informal, relational, and culturally situated aspects of police life. In short, resilience in policing cannot be cultivated through policy alone; it must also be lived, experienced, and shared. Future research, policy development, and organisational planning must therefore recognise the relational infrastructure of policing as integral to both its ethical foundation and operational success.

References

Blesse, S., & Diegmann, A. (2018). Police reorganization and crime: Evidence from police station closures. *SSRN Electronic Journal*, 18–044. https://doi.org/10.2139/ssrn.3272123

Blesse, S., & Diegmann, A. (2022). The place-based effects of police stations on crime: Evidence from station closures. *Journal of Public Economics*, *207*, 104605. https://doi.org/10.1016/j.jpubeco.2022.104605

Brown, A. D. (2015). Identities and identity work in organizations. *International Journal of Management Reviews*, *17*(1), 20–40. https://doi.org/10.1111/IJMR.12035

Caza, B. B., Vough, H., & Puranik, H. (2018). Identity work in organizations and occupations: Definitions, theories, and pathways forward. *Journal of Organizational Behavior*, *39*(7), 889–910. https://doi.org/10.1002/JOB.2318

Charman, S. (2017). *Police socialisation, identity and culture: Becoming blue* (Vol. 1). Palgrave Macmillan Cham.

Cooper, C., Dewe, P., & O'Driscoll, M. (2001). Organizational stress: A review and critique of theory, research, and applications. *Organizational Stress: A Review and Critique of Theory, Research, and Applications*. https://doi.org/10.4135/9781452231235

Diefenbach, T. (2009). New public management in public sector organizations: The dark sides of managerialistic "enlightenment." *Public Administration*, *87*(4), 892–909. https://doi.org/10.June1111/j.1467-9299.2009.01766.x

Fielding, N. (1988). *Joining forces*. Tavistock.

Granovetter, M. (1973). The strength of weak ties. *American Journal of Sociology*, *78*(6), 1360–1380. https://doi.org/10.1086/225469

Granovetter, M. (1985). Economic action and social structure: The problem of embeddedness. *American Journal of Sociology*, *91*(3), 481–510. https://doi.org/10.1086/228311

Granovetter, M. (1988). The sociological and economic approaches to labor market analysis. In G. Farkas & P. England (Eds.), *Industries, firms, and jobs* (pp. 187–216). Springer US. https://doi.org/10.1007/978-1-4899-3536-6_9

Gruening, G. (2001). Origin and theoretical basis of new public management. *International Public Management Journal*, *4*(1), 1–25. https://doi.org/10.1016/S1096-7494(01)00041-1

Hesketh, I. (2015). *Wellbeing blues: Environment, leadership and resilience in the police service* [Lancaster University]. http://eprints.lancs.ac.uk/77771/

Hesketh, I., & Stubbs, G. (2024a). Police recruitment and positive action: The social building blocks of service. *International Journal of Police Science & Management*, *27*(1), 31–42. https://doi.org/10.1177/14613557241248312

Hesketh, I., & Stubbs, G. (2024b). Positive action paradox in UK police recruitment: A critical perspective. *The Police Journal: Theory, Practice and Principles*, *97*(2), 315–335. https://doi.org/10.1177/0032258X231172030

Jackman, P. C., Henderson, H., Clay, G., & Coussens, A. H. (2020). The relationship between psychological wellbeing, social support, and personality in an English police force. *International Journal of Police Science and Management*, *22*(2), 183–193. https://doi.org/10.1177/1461355720907620

Loader, I., & Mulcahy, A. (2003). *Policing and the condition of England: Memory, politics and culture*. Oxford University Press. https://doi.org/10.1093/acprof:oso/9780198299066.001.0001

Millie, A., Ralph, L., Rowe, M., & Jones, M. (2024). Police station meaning, closure and (in) visibility. *Policing and Society*, *34*(5), 403–416. https://doi.org/10.1080/10439463.2023.2293004

Phythian, R., Birdsall, N., Kirby, S., Cooper, E., Posner, Z., & Boulton, L. (2023). Organisational and individual perspectives of police wellbeing in England and Wales. *Police Journal*, *96*(1), 128–152. https://doi.org/10.1177/0032258X211052250

Purba, A., & Demou, E. (2019). The relationship between organisational stressors and mental wellbeing within police officers: A systematic review. *BMC Public Health*, *19*(1), 1286. https://doi.org/10.1186/S12889-019-7609-0

Rees, C. S., Breen, L. J., Cusack, L., & Hegney, D. (2015). Understanding individual resilience in the workplace: The international collaboration of workforce resilience model. *Frontiers in Psychology*, 6, 73. https://doi.org/10.3389/FPSYG.2015.00073/FULL

Skolnick, J. (2010). A sketch of the policeman's working personality. In S. K. Rice & M. White (Eds.), *Race, ethnicity and policing: New and essential* (pp. 15–32). NYU Press.

Stubbs, G., Ben Ayed Elkaroui, E., & Harny, I. (2023). Understanding the nature of social embeddedness in police recruitment in England and Wales. *The Police Journal: Theory, Practice and Principles, 97*(4), 615–633. https://doi.org/10.1177/0032258X231202122

Stubbs, G., & Tong, S. (2024). The "haves and have-nots" of social support during police recruitment: Why the playing field is anything but level. *Policing and Society*, *34*(3), 1–17. https://doi.org/10.1080/10439463.2024.2317313

Tankebe, J. (2019). In their own eyes: An empirical examination of police self-legitimacy. *International Journal of Comparative and Applied Criminal Justice*, *43*(2), 99–116. https://doi.org/10.1080/01924036.2018.1487870

Tankebe, J., & Meško, G. (2015). Police self-legitimacy, use of force, and pro-organizational behavior in Slovenia. In G. Meško & J. Tankebe (Eds.), *Trust and legitimacy in criminal justice: European perspectives* (pp. 261–277). Springer. https://doi.org/10.1007/978-3-319-09813-5_12

Tyson, J., & Charman, S. (2023). Leaving the table: Organisational (in)justice and the relationship with police officer retention. *Criminology and Criminal Justice, 25*(4), 1016–1032. https://doi.org/10.1177/17488958231191648

Van Maanen, J. (1973). Observations on the making of policemen. *Human Organization*, *32*(4), 407–418. https://doi.org/10.17730/humo.32.4.13h7x81187mh8km8

Van Maanen, J. (2010). Identity work and control in occupational communities. In Sim B. Sitkin et al. (Eds.), *Organizational control* (pp. 111–166). Cambridge University Press. https://doi.org/10.1017/CBO9780511777899.006

Waddington, P. (1999). Police (canteen) sub-culture. An appreciation. *British Journal of Criminology*, *39*(2), 287–309. http://bjc.oxfordjournals.org/content/39/2/287.short

15

OCCUPATIONAL HEALTH IN POLICING

Liz Eades

This chapter examines the role and purpose of an occupational health service in police forces. It sets out the principles of governance and how the aims of occupational health are totally aligned to the aims of national police forces. It describes how an effective occupational health service contributes to the smooth functioning of a police force, providing benefits to the organisation and the individuals that work within it.

What Is Occupational Health?

Occupational health (OH) is a preventative clinical specialty branch of healthcare that is all about health and work. It has two main concerns: how work affects health and how health affects work.

How Work Affects Health

There are just over 33.2 million people at work in the UK (July 2024) in many thousands of workplaces and situations. These workplaces can present numerous challenges and risks to a person's health from physical risks such as working with machinery and chemicals to psychological risks such as stress and pressure. There is legislation to protect people at work and address workplace health and safety, such as the Health and Safety at Work Act.[1]

How Health Affects Work

The second concern of OH is the effect that a person's health has on their work. People may commence a job with a pre-existing health condition, experience changes in their health or sustain an injury over the course of their working lives, and these will need to be assessed, managed and possibly adjusted for as their working lives progress.

DOI: 10.4324/9781003518860-16

Why Occupational Health?

Occupational health is instrumental in the protection of workers in any workplace setting. Everyone who goes to work wants to be safe and healthy at work. People who go into policing do so because they wish to provide a service to the public. Managers want their workforce to be as effective and efficient as possible to enable them to meet their organisational targets. People are more productive if they are happy and healthy at work. It has been shown that working and having an occupation is good for long-term health.[2]

Managing health and safety in policing is more complex than in other occupations and workplaces as police officers cannot always avoid risky situations. Having an occupational health service in policing is key to helping officers and their managers navigate the challenges, both physical and psychological.[3]

The predominant aims of an occupational health function, in any organisation, are to:

- Prevent ill health resulting directly from the work being undertaken.
- Provide health advice in relation to work-related health matters.
- Provide advice and activities that mitigate the risks arising from the effects of work on health.
- Advise managers and workers in relation to fitness to work.
- Recommend adaptations and suitability to work.
- Support and/or lead health prevention and/or health promotion activities.
- Act as public health specialists.

The role of OH is one of health protection and ill health prevention, assisting the organisation in enabling its people to perform at the highest level and to sustain that performance.

Who Does Occupational Health?

An OH service is made up of a number of different personnel, clinical and non-clinical. In policing, OH services are mainly carried out by doctors and nurses. They are usually doctors and nurses who, after general training, have undertaken further specialist professional training and qualifications and are specialists in health at work. The doctors may be called "the force Medical Advisor or Officer" (FMA/FMO). Nurses may be called "Occupational Health (nurse) Advisors" (OHA or OHNA). You may also meet clinic/practice nurses or occupational health technicians who carry out some clinical work under supervision. Some services also employ physiotherapists and counsellors or provide access to these services. The service may be managed by a senior OHA or FMA or a non-clinical manager. There is usually an administration team who assist with the running of the department.

The service in your force may be provided by directly employed police staff or by an external provider who supplies people to staff the service.

No matter how the service is provided, all the personnel who provide the service are not only bound by the policing code of ethics but also, in the case of clinical personnel, their own regulatory codes of ethics and confidentiality. Doctors, nurses and other allied health professionals such as physios and counsellors have professional bodies that regulate their practice. Everyone connected with OH, such as the admin team, will also have to adhere to codes of confidentiality. See more below.

What Does Occupational Health Do?

On the surface, an OH department looks very much like a GP surgery; however, in fact, what OH does is very different. OH does not replicate the functions of a GP. A visit to the GP is often prompted by a health concern; the GP may diagnose a health condition and provide a prescription for medication or a referral for investigations or to see a specialist. A GP service is part of Primary Care in the NHS. Occupational health in policing is not an NHS service; it is privately sourced and funded by police forces. The purpose of OH is not for diagnosis and treatment as in GP practice; equally, OH does not provide emergency treatment services like those provided by walk-in minor injury clinics or emergency departments. The functions of OH are very specialised, as detailed below:

Occupational health is a specialist independent advisory department that provides a range of services that are available to everyone in a police force.

Principles underpinning Occupational health provision are:

- Equitable – Reasonable, treating everyone equally
- Accessible – Ease of access and approachable
- Impartial – Objective, unbiased and fair

They work with a range of stakeholders such as the senior management teams, line managers and supervisors, the Human Resources department, workforce/union representatives, the Health and Safety team and the Wellbeing team, as well as officers and staff at all levels.

Main Activities of Occupational Health

A brief overview of the activities of OH:

- Advising the organisation about health risks and effects
  - Occupational health are subject-matter experts in health and the workplace. They understand risk, impacts on health and, importantly, how to reduce risk and negative impacts. They will also seek to understand the particular health needs of the organisation.
- Health protection and surveillance relating to physical and psychological risks at work
  - This is about monitoring health in relation to the risks of the job and ensuring that all the control measures in place are working so that health is protected. For example, people working in a noisy environment will have protection for their hearing and regular hearing tests will also be carried out by OH to make sure that the hearing protection is doing its job and hearing is not adversely affected.

  - Role risk assessment to establish monitoring programmes of not only physical but also psychological health surveillance.
  - Health surveillance is very specific to health risks in a workplace and is only done for those who need it. Some health surveillance is required by law.[4]
- Providing advice about health issues at work to managers and individuals. Assisting with absence and/or health management
  - Individuals may be referred to OH for advice, with the goal of helping managers and individuals to manage their health issues at work. Advice can also be provided on readiness for return to work or the need for rehabilitation during sickness-related absence. OH may carry out consultations, provide reports and provide guidance on workplace adjustments. There may be onward referrals to specialists for further advice or support. OH will manage cases from beginning to whatever conclusion is reached.
- Promoting good health
  - Prevention of ill health and the promotion of good health is at the heart of OH, which will introduce proactive initiatives addressing not only physical health but also mental health and wellbeing.
  - Organisations are becoming increasingly aware of the need to promote health and wellbeing at work, particularly mental health. OH work with any colleagues specialising in fostering wellbeing.
  - Integrating mental health programmes into work wellbeing programmes
  - Developing wellbeing strategies
- Education and training
  - Health and wellbeing are key elements of organisational planning. They have a place in many training situations, including induction courses for new student police officers and staff. They are also often addressed in managerial and leadership courses.
  - OH can, through training and education, encourage and empower staff and managers to support good health and wellbeing as a necessary part of attaining the organisation's goals.
- Using data to identify health trends and potentially optimise health outcomes
  - Analysing data on a large or small scale can highlight key wellbeing issues and trends; it may also provide insights into the cause and effect of other workforce issues.
  - Wellbeing analysis including OH trends can be crucial in developing a positive and healthy work environment. By understanding employee wellbeing, potential issues can be identified and targeted programmes and interventions initiated.
- Managing health information within the force
  - Keeping complete records is an integral function of an OH service. Records must be maintained to standards which meet legal, regulatory compliance and professional practice requirements.
  - Everyone in the force will have an OH record as it begins with recruitment assessments. The information contained within is personal, sensitive medical information. The OH service will have a written procedure detailing how they manage

information to achieve compliance with all the requirements above. See the section on "Consent and Confidentiality".

- Evidence-based practice
  - OH professionals must base their advice and intervention on evidence based in science. This should be used in balance with their expertise and knowledge of the organisation's preferences and needs as well as individual aspects.
  - Research in occupational health and diseases is constantly evolving, providing practitioners with the evidence and information they need to apply this in their own workforce, thus ensuring they provide the most current information.

What Occupational Health Means for You

Policing is subject to a number of health risks both physical and psychological that have to be understood and managed. Occupational health plays a part at every stage of a policing career journey from start to finish. At recruitment, an OH clinical assessment will take place to ensure that every recruit coming into policing is fit to do the requirements of the roles (with, in some cases, adjustments that may be necessary). It is important that OH has the complete picture of an individual's health so as to be able, with consent, to advise management and ensure the right adjustments are in place. As careers develop and progress, with different roles taken on, periodic OH assessment and health checks or monitoring may be needed to ensure that good health is maintained and early signs of problems identified. There are a number of roles in policing that require a specific check by OH, which may be a health interview or some clinical tests, depending on the role. Some specialist roles, like firearms, require officers to be fit to a defined standard to do the roles, such as good hearing and eyesight as well as physical fitness. They also need to be psychologically "well". They will have regular checks to be able to maintain their firearms licence.

If the health status of an officer or member of staff changes, if they develop a health condition or sustain an injury, it is important that an early referral to OH is made, so that managers and individuals can be advised on the best way to assist and manage their situation in the workplace. If a person is on extended sick leave, a referral to OH will help all parties to navigate through this period with the best possible outcome. Unfortunately, some policing careers have to be terminated early because of ill health or injury and OH will be part of this along with HR and line managers to ensure that the process is carried out in an appropriate and timely manner. On the more positive side, the OH team are often seen when they are out and about doing a variety of activities such as site visits and workplace attachments, vaccinations, health and wellbeing initiatives and "Ministry of Transport" (MOT) health checks. Occupational health may be involved in health education and training at several points during an officer's police career, giving talks to new recruits and presentations to work groups about specific health or wellbeing issues in that group.

There is usually information about what the force's OH team does and what this means for individuals on the intranet.

Confidentiality and Consent

No matter what or how OH delivers its service, the professional accountability of the OH practitioner is paramount. The duty of confidentiality is enshrined in all codes of medical ethics, including those of these professional bodies: The Nursing and Midwifery Council (NMC), The General Medical Council (GMC) and The Health and Care Professions Council (HCPC).[5] This includes making sure that people are informed about how and why their information is used and making sure it is only shared appropriately (ref principles of practice module). What does this mean?

If a person is referred into OH, they should be given information and understand the process, to be able to give informed consent to the OH consultation and the provision of a report to management. At consultation with OH there will be discussion about the content of a report to management. Sometimes OH may need to obtain further medical information from a GP or specialist: this can only be obtained with consent and individuals can view any reports about them before they are sent to OH. When OH write a management report, this is always independent and advisory to assist in the management of the individual, either at work or on return to work. The report will not contain any unnecessary medical details/diagnoses. Everyone has the right to view their report before it is sent to management and they can ask for factual errors to be amended; however, individuals cannot ask for the OH opinion to be changed.

Occupational Health in a Policing Context

Good occupational health practice begins with understanding the health needs of the organisation, importantly in the context of the legal framework that applies to the police.[6]

Policing is subject to specific regulations and is indeed a high health risk profession, and managing health and safety in policing is complex. Occupational health is an integral part of police operational effectiveness. The main objective of OH in policing is "enabling the front line to be effective in protecting the general public".

As well as being outward-facing in its service to the public, a force must also look inward to its workforce to ensure that they can perform their duties to the public in an optimal way; good health and wellbeing are essential to operational effectiveness.

It is important that chief officers have access to expert OH advice on emerging general health and public health issues that may affect the workforce, understanding the risk profiles and control measures. OH will monitor the policing and health/research environment to identify emerging health trends and issues.

The involvement of police in major incidents is inevitable and the involvement of OH and the integration into the operational procedures of a major incident is important. OH will support the health and wellbeing of police personnel involved directly or indirectly. This could be in the form of immediate practical health advice as well as longer-term interventions and follow-up.[7]

Everyone is different and human factors or ergonomics in policing are important to consider. This, in essence, is the study of how to design or modify the work environment to fit the needs of police personnel, rather than the other way around. The aim is to reduce the risk of injury and work-limiting discomfort. There are many examples in policing where this can be applied such as prolonged sitting in patrol cars, the wearing of body armour and belts, as well as operational and office-based tasks. This is where a truly multidisciplinary approach can be used in OH by the inclusion of physiotherapists, ergonomists and occupational therapists to look at workplace design and equipment as well as advising on posture and physical wellness programmes.

College of Policing, NPWS and Occupational Health

When the National Police Wellbeing Service was launched in 2019, a suite of measures was developed to promote and support wellbeing at work, which included occupational health subject-matter experts as part of the Wellbeing at Work delivery workstream. The function of the OH team in NPWS is to guide, inform and support OH services in policing with the aim of supporting national policing objectives.

It was recognised at an early stage that chief officers need to be assured that the occupational health service in their force is appropriate, good quality and fit for purpose. In addition, they need to be reassured that investment in occupational health will not only address organisational goals but also ensure compliance with legislation, meeting the challenges of the national wellbeing agenda. It is also important to facilitate that everyone in police services understands the role of occupational health in supporting their health needs, knows how to access occupational health and is confident that the clinical services offered to them are quality assured, consistent and underpinned by the best available evidence.

Therefore, the primary objective of the OH team within NPWS was to develop national occupational health standards, which were first published in 2019.[8]

Occupational Health Standards

The ultimate aim of the OH standards is to provide continuous improvement and consistency in occupational health services across policing in England and Wales. OH services need to be able to demonstrate that they are following the guiding principles: equitable, accessible and impartial.

The OH standards have been developed in three parts:

1. Foundation
2. Enhanced
3. Advanced

Foundation Level

These standards have six main areas:

a) Business Probity – this means conducting services with integrity and financial propriety.
b) Information Governance – this means properly maintaining clinical records and client confidentiality.

c) People – this means having competent clinical staff with the appropriate clinical governance.
d) Facilities and Equipment – this means providing facilities and equipment that are safe and appropriate for the services provided.
e) Relationships with the Organisation – this means engaging and interacting with the organisation regarding assessing health needs.
f) Relationships with Workers – this means engaging with everyone employed within the force to ensure that fairness, respect and involvement are promoted and maintained.

With foundation level standards in place, the two additional standards will provide opportunities for OH services to develop beyond the transactional, reactive services to proactivity and potential growth. It is expected that forces will move towards the enhanced standards (extending and adding) initially and, at the same time, consider how they might move into new areas that are ultimately visionary and transformative (advanced standards).

Since the publication of the standards, forces have been working towards achieving these. They are guided and supported by the NPWS OH team.

Further Work of NPWS OH Team

The Occupational Health Practitioner Network

The OH Practitioner Network was launched in 2022 and is committed to improving the provision of OH in policing and improving the health of those who work in the police, with the wider business benefits of an enhanced service to the public. Membership of the Network is open to everyone who works in OH in policing. There are regular meetings, training workshops and special interest groups.

Network Strategic Aims

1. Act as the voice of occupational health professionals who work in policing to communicate, inform and influence national developments.
2. Exchange information and knowledge across the Network for the purpose of developing the quality of police OH Services and the development of best practice.
3. Share specialist knowledge between the Network's professional groups to help inform the NPWS and its strategic aims.

The Network has a place on the Oscar Kilo website (oscarkilo.org.uk) and a members-specific area which contains a good practice library of guidance, information and templates to assist OH practitioners in developing and improving their services.

There are also several special interest groups running within the wider Network to enable particular groups to come together to support, share and promote best practice in their particular field of OH practice. These groups include managers of OH, physicians, technicians, physios and mental health nurses.

Occupational Health Principles of Practice e-Learning Modules

Modules have been developed to create training for new and existing occupational health clinicians who work in policing. The courses provide a basis (foundation level) for improved, sector-specific clinical practice. Delegates will improve their understanding of the health risks in policing and develop sector-specific practical principles to apply to practice.

Occupational Health Operating Models

There is no "one-size-fits-all" model for occupational health provision. Additionally, there is no statutory requirement for an employer to have OH provision. Nonetheless, doing so, particularly in high health risk employment such as policing, makes good business sense and meets some of the obligations of employers, as outlined within the scope of statutory provision such as the Health and Safety at Work Act.[9]

There is no one definitive model of how an organisation should establish and deliver its OH service. There are indeed various drivers mostly associated with:

- Organisation size
- Type of work carried out
- Risks
- Financial considerations

The Targeted Operating Models developed by NPWS aim to set out a framework of "best practice" for Police Forces in England and Wales and guides through, what can be described as a core, basic service, through to an enhanced or well-developed multidisciplinary team function. The recommended approaches link back to the Foundation and Enhanced and Advanced OH Standards for Police OH.

The NPWS has become well regarded and established within the policing community. The OH team working within the wider NPWS team demonstrates how OH can interface effectively with the wider wellbeing provision in police forces to both underpin and enhance performance and resilience.[10]

Conclusion

This chapter has explained the specialised role of occupational health: what it means, what it does and how it works in the context of policing. Also, what OH provides for an individual throughout their policing career. However, one's health, occupational or otherwise, is essentially one's own responsibility. The occupational health service exists to support members of the force operating at the peak of their performance; however, the service can only be effective if officers, staff and their managers take responsibility for this too and recognise those occasions when the support of OH is necessary and desirable.

Notes

1 The Police (Health and Safety) Act 1997 and Health & Safety at Work Act 1974.
2 World Health Organization & Burton, Joan. (2010). WHO healthy workplace framework and model: background and supporting literature and practices.
3 Striking the balance between operational and health and safety duties in the Police Service Health and Safety Executive 2009.
4 Health and Safety Executive. Health surveillance overview 2024.
5 Nursing and Midwifery Council – Code of Ethics (2022)
Faculty of Occupational Medicine – Ethics Guidance (2018)
Health Care Professionals Council – Standards of conduct, performance and ethics (2016).
6 Occupational Health and Wellbeing for British Policing, Harrison 2024.
7 NPWS Police Wellbeing: A staged approach when dealing with major incidents June 2020.
8 Foundation Occupational health Standards for Police Forces. National Police Wellbeing Service 2019.
9 The Police (Health and Safety) Act 1997 and Health and Safety at Work Act 1974.
10 Occupational Health and Wellbeing for British policing, Harrison 2024.

16

HOME-BASED WAYS OF WORKING

Charlotte E Hall, Samantha K Brooks,
Neil Greenberg, and Dale Weston

Introduction

On January 30, 2020, the World Health Organization (WHO) declared a "public health emergency of international concern" in response to an outbreak of a novel coronavirus, later named COVID-19. By March 11, 2020, the WHO officially classified the situation as a global pandemic.[1] Consequently, the UK Government implemented various behavioural strategies to mitigate the spread of COVID-19. Initially emphasising handwashing, these measures quickly escalated to stricter restrictions, limiting the public's ability to leave their homes except under specific circumstances. These included shopping for essential items as infrequently as possible, engaging in one daily exercise activity, seeking medical care, or providing support to vulnerable individuals.[2]

From March 16, 2020, the public was advised to "start working from home where possible".[3] As a result, nearly half of the UK workforce transitioned to remote working by April 2020.[4] Generally, prior to the COVID-19 pandemic, the literature surrounding working from home was mixed – as working in this way was deemed beneficial to some (e.g., due to the elimination of commuting time[5]), and challenging to others (e.g., due to blurred boundaries between work and home life[6]). More specific COVID-19 focused research also reports similar findings,[7] with many different factors seemingly able to impact employees' experiences when working from home.[8]

Due to the national "work from home" instruction, homeworking became commonplace for many UK police officers and staff.[9] This chapter reports on literature concerning the impact of working from home, both in the police force specifically, and more generally, in order to draw practical conclusions and recommendations for future practice. Firstly, we discuss the working from home arrangement as documented in pre-COVID-19 pandemic literature in reference to staff outcomes, followed by discussion of the COVID-19 pandemic in the same context. Commonly noted barriers and facilitators to effective homeworking across wider literature are then reviewed. Lastly, we draw

DOI: 10.4324/9781003518860-17

from discussions within this chapter to create a series of recommendations for the future of home-based working within the UK police force.

Definitions

For the purpose of this chapter, we have defined "police staff" to include both uniformed officers and non-operational civilian staff. As for working from home, it is necessary to note that the definition of a *home worker* often varies amongst literature and research – particularly within pre-pandemic literature. In fact, the definition of working from home has been described as a continuum[10] with many terms (e.g., but not limited to, "homeworking", "teleworking", "remote working", "telecommuting", "flexible working") being used interchangeably.[10] Therefore, for the purpose of this chapter, we have chosen to use a broad definition of *adults carrying out desk-based work from their own homes.*

Pre-COVID-19 Homeworking

Prior to the COVID-19 pandemic, homeworking was considered a growing trend, though it remained relatively uncommon. Research indicates that only about 5% of the general UK working population chose to work from home at the time.[11] Those able to work from home pre-pandemic were predominantly self-employed individuals, those in highly skilled and professional roles, people with higher qualifications, and individuals of higher social status and older age groups.[11, 12] Geographically, homeworking was more prevalent in London, the South East, and the South West than in other parts of the UK.[13, 14]

Of course, working from home was also limited to certain occupations. For example, roles in industries such as manufacturing, construction, hospitality, and food services required employees to work on-site.[11] Approximately, 60% of pre-pandemic home workers were concentrated in a relatively small range of occupational fields, such as information and communication, professional, technical, and administrative fields.[12, 14] Only 26% of police staff report they were able to sometimes work from home prior to the COVID-19 pandemic, with just 2% reporting they could work from home most of the time.[15] Furthermore, there were reports of ambivalence towards flexible working practices,[16] particularly in relation to uniformed officers (vs police staff).

Research into the benefits and drawbacks of working from home prior to the COVID-19 pandemic was mixed (i.e., in that it appeared to be a benefit to some, and a drawback to others). For many, it was often viewed positively, with benefits such as greater autonomy, the elimination of commuting, and fewer workplace distractions.[5, 17, 18] Studies also reported higher job satisfaction,[19] increased flexibility,[20] improved productivity,[21, 22] and reduced stress levels[23] among homeworking populations. Nonetheless, potential downsides were also identified. Homeworking could lead to longer working hours as individuals balanced paid work with household responsibilities.[19, 22] Employees often faced challenges in maintaining boundaries between work and home life, leading to difficulties such as multitasking, parental overload, and exposure to household distractions.[6, 22, 24] Perceived reduced visibility compared to on-site workers sometimes resulted in feelings of diminished recognition by managers and colleagues, along with concerns about limited supervisor support and restricted opportunities for promotion or professional development.[22,25,26] Moreover, some employees experienced isolation while working from home[17,26,27] and poorer mental health outcomes compared to those working in traditional office settings.[28,29]

Altogether, while the overall proportion of the UK workforce opting to work from home pre-pandemic was relatively small,[11] a comparably large proportion of police staff reported having the potential to work from home.[15] While we know broadly about the benefits and drawbacks associated with homeworking generally pre-pandemic, to the authors' knowledge, there is no research that has explicitly explored the experiences of working from home in the context of the police force.

COVID-19 Homeworking

As noted previously, the COVID-19 pandemic brought upon a range of social changes for the UK public, including importantly the instruction to work from home if at all possible. As a result, nearly half of the UK workforce transitioned to remote working by April 2020,[4] in comparison to a meagre 5% prior to the pandemic.[11] This vast transition also encompassed the UK police force, as within the lockdown period, 40% of police staff reported to work completely from home, with a further 16% doing so partially.[15]

COVID-19 focused literature on the impact of working from home corroborates with pre-pandemic literature, in that the experience of homeworking varied considerably between individuals. For example, a systematic review seeking to detail the relationship between working from home, mental health, and productivity during the COVID-19 pandemic found considerable variation in outcome (i.e., mixed findings in relation to both mental health and productivity) and concluded with the suggestion of a complex association with many mediating and moderating factors at play.[7] However, in relation to mental health, the associations were typically more negative than positive – suggesting that homeworking as a choice is considered largely beneficial which is in keeping with pre-pandemic research; however, when homeworking was instead mandatory, rather than by choice, there is potential that it may have a more negative association for certain individuals and occupations over others.[7]

As a result, it remains important to establish barriers and facilitators towards working from home, taking an occupation-specific approach where possible, to allow organisations or employers to take actions to improve the future experience of employees working in the same way. The following section discusses available research focused on the experiences of the UK police force working from home during the COVID-19 pandemic.

What Does the Research Say about Police Working from Home?

As discussed in the preceding section, the COVID-19 pandemic prompted a significant shift in working practices. Approximately 40% of police personnel transitioned to working from home, and over half (57%) of office-based police staff worked completely from home. One in six police staff engaged in frontline roles remained at work compared to 52% of their police officer colleagues.[30] In general, available reports suggest many forces adapted quickly to working any time, any place, anywhere.[9] For example, the vast majority of staff who were deemed to be at risk due to COVID-19 (e.g., due to shielding, isolating, or being considered high risk) were allowed to work from home.[9] Similarly, in forces where tasks could only be completed in the workplace, staff were often able to rotate between working from home and in the office. However, it is important to note that this approach was not consistent, with reports of a few forces not encouraging homeworking, nor allowing the arrangement to be openly available for their staff.[9] In these cases, all members of the workforce in these forces were considered key workers and had to attend their workplaces unless assessed as vulnerable.

Despite a vast majority of COVID-19 research focusing on key workers, which of course included uniformed police officers and staff, research specifically addressing the pandemic's impact on this occupation remains relatively limited. Similarly, little is known about the experiences of police working from home prior to the COVID-19 pandemic: this may be because it was relatively rare for police to work from home previously,[31] and so it has attracted little research attention.

What evidence there is shows that the COVID-19 pandemic exacerbated existing stressors, introducing new challenges that further strained already overburdened police staff.[15] The national lockdowns and associated restrictions led to increased workloads and elevated levels of stress among officers and staff, with nearly 55% of police personnel reporting heightened stress during this period.[15] Similarly, a study exploring the experiences of police staff working from home during lockdown in the United Kingdom[31] found that 42% (of 473 respondents) reported that their work became more difficult during lockdown. A significant factor in the increase in stress and difficulty of work is reported to be the additional domestic responsibilities faced by many police employees (i.e., dual role of caring and working responsibilities). The necessity of homeschooling and caregiving, compounded by pandemic-related uncertainty, left many staff members feeling emotionally drained and fatigued.[15] Some expressed guilt at prioritising work over the needs of children and elderly relatives.[31] The competing demands of work, childcare, and home responsibilities were particularly challenging for female staff.[15, 30, 32–34]

The flexibility of working from home was generally well received, with relevant research reporting improvements in work-life balance and productivity for police officers.[32] However, the transition was not without challenges. Maintaining team cohesion, lacking IT infrastructure, and managing blurred boundaries between work and home life were considered ongoing challenges.[32] The shift to using Microsoft Teams to communicate with colleagues and the loss of in-person social interactions meant that relationship-building was difficult, and many also reported that the shift to Teams increased the number of unnecessary meetings that were arranged.[33] Additionally, adapting to doing parts of the job from home was challenging for some, with established processes needing to be quickly adapted (such as taking witness statements by telephone).[33] For many, the lack of physical separation between professional and personal spaces made it difficult to disconnect from work: the competing demands of occupational responsibilities and domestic roles with no separation by physical boundaries led to blurred lines between work and home.[35] The findings emphasise the importance of proactive, most likely practical, strategies to support resilience and wellbeing among police staff, particularly during times of heightened stress. Examples of such approaches might include ensuring good access to childcare facilities, consideration of the provision of care for other vulnerable family members, and financial support, all with the aim of ensuring that police staff remain psychologically well, and therefore operationally effective.

Despite the challenges associated with working from home, a number of benefits have also been reported across the police literature. These include the lack of commuting, being able to work in a quiet space away from noise and distractions, improved work-life balance and fewer distractions, leading to greater productivity.[15, 30, 32] Many police staff working from home expressed a preference for retaining flexible and virtual working practices beyond the pandemic[31] These arrangements were seen as contributing to greater efficiency and improved work-life balance.[31, 32] To capitalise on these benefits, police forces should embrace the development of strategies that address the complexities of flexible working while ensuring equity among staff. It would be unfortunate to require staff to come into the office when homeworking is possible, just as it would be unfortunate to require only to work from home when doing so would restrict individuals from social or other opportunities that coming into the office might provide.

Summary

In conclusion, the pandemic highlighted both the potential and the limitations of flexible working arrangements for police forces. By addressing the noted challenges (e.g., blurred boundaries) and by fostering a supportive organisational culture, police forces can better adapt to evolving work practices while safeguarding the wellbeing of their workforce.

As it stands at the time of writing, there is a lack of evidence to support the development of an intervention that addresses these specific challenges in the context of the police force. However, recently, the authors of this chapter completed a three-year PhD research project (led by Charlotte Hall, and supervised by Prof Neil Greenberg, Dr Samantha K Brooks, and Dr Dale Weston) which focused on exploring the experiences of homeworking response-focused civil servants during the COVID-19 pandemic. These workers too experienced a rapid change to their ways of working (i.e., a transition from office working to homeworking), and due to contributing directly to the COVID-19 pandemic response, also experienced a shift in working priorities, an increase in workload and pace. Therefore, like those in the police force asked to work from home, UK response-focused civil servants were also at high risk of the combined demands of working from home and contributing to frontline response.

Various research papers are available as a result of this research project, including: systematic reviews of homeworking experience more generally;[7, 8] quantitative methods to ascertain factors associated with poor mental health whilst working from home in UK civil servants;[36] qualitative methods to explore the experience of working from home in UK civil servants;[37, 38] and a Delphi study working with subject-matter experts (i.e., in occupational health, mental health and UK Government employees) to derive a series of practical and actionable recommendations for the future of working from home in the Civil Service context.[39] Therefore, the following sections reflect on these findings, alongside more general research surrounding working from home, and relevant police-specific insights where possible.

Common Factors Impacting Working from Home Experience

The adoption of working from home practices, particularly during the COVID-19 pandemic, has highlighted both benefits and challenges across different occupational contexts, including policing. This section synthesises the limited police-specific findings with broader research on working from home (including that of response-focused civil servants as previously disclosed) to explore potential key barriers and facilitators to effective homeworking.

Working Environment

Research suggests that staff working from home, including those in the police force, faced challenges due to inadequate IT support, slow internet, and unsuitable home office setups.[8, 32] A lack of suitable space and equipment and issues with Wi-Fi were noted across research as common challenges. This aligns with increased findings of physical discomfort, such as back and neck pain, in homeworkers; often stemming from insufficiently ergonomic homeworking equipment and workstations.[8]

Flexibility

The flexibility of working from home allows for potentially improved integration of work and personal life, a benefit particularly evident among those with caregiving responsibilities. For police staff, this facilitated childcare during school closures due to being at home,[31, 32] while more general research highlights reduced work–family conflict when alternating between office and home days.[8]

Blurred Boundaries

Both police officers and others working from home found boundaries between work and home life somewhat difficult to manage. The absence of physical boundaries between work locations often led to extended work hours and hindered the ability to switch off after work.[32] Furthermore, the natural breaks from work which are commonplace within many organisational settings, such as informal interactions with colleagues, formal breaks, and commuting (i.e., natural buffers in an office setting) were often missed by those working from home.[8, 37, 38]

Distractions

Working from home during the COVID-19 pandemic was associated with an intensification of workloads[38] and increased presenteeism, where some employees continued working despite illness.[8] Police-specific research highlighted the potential challenges to staff's mental health of successive virtual meetings,[33] which added to the sense of extended work hours and fewer breaks. These demands, alongside the lack of commuting time, often led to prolonged working hours.[32] This finding was in keeping with more general research which indicated that employees were working longer hours at home, with fewer opportunities for informal social interactions or natural breaks.[8]

However, despite these challenges, both police-specific and broader research also pointed to the potential benefits of working from home in terms of productivity.[8, 32, 37]

Evidence suggests that, in some cases, the reduced likelihood of being distracted in the home environment provided employees with greater autonomy and control over their work processes, which aided productivity.[38] Studies show that this autonomy, combined with the flexibility of remote work, aided staff, particularly for those balancing work with caregiving or other domestic responsibilities.[32] For many, the ability to better manage personal tasks while fulfilling professional duties led to an overall sense of increased efficiency and satisfaction.[8]

Cost Impact

Working from home clearly eliminates commuting costs and time, which enabled employees to redirect these resources towards personal and professional priorities.[37] Police-specific findings align with broader research in police staff benefiting financially.[32] However, within police contexts, frontline officers expressed frustration over the inequity of working from home and having to physically come to work.[32]

Health Concerns and Physical Inactivity

Both police officers and general homeworkers reported an increase in sedentary behaviour and physical health issues while working from home.[8, 32] Inadequate furnishings, such as poorly designed desks and chairs, led to musculoskeletal problems, while prolonged screen time resulted in eye strain.[8, 32] Additionally, weight gain and reduced physical fitness were common complaints among homeworkers. However, some studies also noted a positive shift in eating habits among certain homeworkers, with healthier dietary choices (e.g., making own lunches) due to increased time at home.[8]

The impact of working from home on mental health was mixed. While many workers experienced less stress, others faced heightened anxiety, depression, and burnout, particularly when dealing with role conflicts or inadequate managerial support.[7, 8] For police officers, additional stressors included concerns about family safety, as well as feelings of guilt over reduced productivity when shielding or dealing with illness.[32] Despite these challenges, both police-specific and broader research reported that, for many, the overall impact of working from home was beneficial for mental health.[7, 8, 32]

Social Support

A significant barrier in police and general contexts was the loss of face-to-face interaction, resulting in feelings of isolation and loneliness.[8, 32, 37, 38] This impacted morale, team cohesion, and access to supervision. While some individuals preferred solitude,[8] many highlighted the need for hybrid models to maintain social and professional connections.[8, 32, 37, 38]

Summary

Overall, while homeworking offers substantial benefits, such as flexibility, productivity, and work-life balance, it also presents challenges that require organisational attention. For police forces specifically, ensuring fairer access to working from home, providing robust IT support, suitable IT equipment, and addressing mental health needs of their employees are necessary steps to take.

What Can Employers/Organisations Do to Help Police Working from Home?

Research surrounding working from home highlights both benefits and drawbacks to working from home and highlights consistently mixed findings in experience, making it essential to avoid drawing blanket conclusions when seeking to support employees. Despite mixed findings, using the material presented in this chapter, alongside reflections on the experiences of those in similar contexts (i.e., response-focused civil servants), a series of recommendations for the future of working from home within the UK police force are discussed below.

Equipment and Provisions

A common issue highlighted by research was a lack of suitable working equipment and training for employees working from home.[8, 32] This is unsurprising given the immediate, unplanned and widespread move to working from home during the COVID-19 pandemic. However, going forward, it is essential that employers provide their staff with the appropriate equipment and training to ensure they can work safely and comfortably from home. Workplace safety and comfort can be easily appraised in the office, but it is more difficult to assess employees' homes. It is therefore recommended that the use of online assessments of home office ergonomics is used to identify potential problems. Where problems are identified, troubleshooting advice should be provided, alongside potential provision of correct furniture and equipment from employers when it is financially viable to do so.

Healthy Working Practices

Working from home adjusts usual day-to-day working practices, for example by the removal of commuting time, lack of informal social interactions and distractions, or limitations around social break-taking behaviour. Findings suggest that employees were less likely to be taking adequate breaks whilst working from home and this has implications for the health and wellbeing of employees (i.e., increased sedentary behaviour, eye strain).[8, 32] Employers and employees should recognise that taking regular breaks from all work is helpful; however, ensuring workers take breaks is more difficult when homeworking. Employers and managers should seek to assure employees that they should be taking breaks in line with organisational policy whilst working from home; for ease, this could be communicated through emails, newsletters, or during team meetings or catch-ups. It may be that incentivising physical activity for homeworkers (e.g. use of reward for physical activity apps or encouraging staff to join collective physical activity challenges each month) could be helpful with this.

Address Health and Wellbeing

Where possible, we suggest that managers should lead by example, demonstrating healthy behaviours that encourage employees to approach homeworking with the same discipline as office-based work. This includes taking regular breaks, taking annual and sickness leave when needed, and avoiding prolonged sedentary behaviour. To address challenges such as physical inactivity, ergonomic issues, and mental health concerns, organisations could offer virtual fitness programmes/incentives as highlighted above, educate employees on setting up ergonomic home offices, and provide access to mental health resources, including counselling and wellness apps. Such initiatives may help foster a culture of wellbeing and productivity in remote work environments. Ensuring that home workers are encouraged to come into the office from time to time for meetings and inviting them to work social events may also be helpful.

Prioritise Mental Health Interventions

Policing work is known to be a high-stress occupation and the transition to working from home introduces specific challenges that have the potential to exacerbate stress and hinder team cohesion.[15] To address these concerns, organisations should consider how best to bolster social support for workers who do not routinely work in close physical proximity to colleagues. Potentially useful approaches include the use of peer support groups which may enable officers to share their remote work experiences and learn from one another. Peer support groups also may help bolster social support which has been repeatedly shown to protect mental health. Training managers to recognise signs of stress or burnout within their teams and increasing access to psychological support services tailored to the specific demands of policing are also likely to be helpful steps in maintaining a good staff of staff mental health and resilience.

Remote working can also disrupt social interactions among colleagues, leading to feelings of isolation and loneliness. To mitigate these effects, managers should adopt strategies to enhance team cohesion and connectivity. Informal weekly debriefs, team catch-up sessions, and optional virtual social events (e.g., quizzes or coffee roulette) can provide opportunities for connection. For new employees, integration into their roles and teams is essential; this can be facilitated through one-on-one introductions, group activities, and rapport-building exercises.

Proactive measures, such as promoting non-mandatory social opportunities, scheduling regular virtual team meetings, and leveraging collaborative tools for real-time interaction, can help maintain morale and reduce isolation. Additionally, occasional in-person teambuilding activities can strengthen relationships and foster a sense of belonging, ensuring that working from home does not compromise the cohesion and connectivity essential to effective policing.

Address Perceptions of Inequity

Managers must recognise the inherent differences between working from home and office-based roles, incorporating these distinctions into role planning and engagement strategies. Homeworking, especially when undertaken full-time, can raise concerns about career progression and access to work opportunities.[8] To alleviate such apprehensions, managers should prioritise dedicated discussions with employees about their career goals, progression pathways, and future opportunities. At the same time, organisations must address the feelings of exclusion or inequity that may arise among frontline workers who cannot work remotely.[32] Here, it is about making sure that employee needs can be met where possible. As in essence, it should be recognised that there will likely always be a part, at least for uniformed officers, that requires one to be present in the workplace/on duty. Introducing compensatory benefits (e.g., additional leave days; assistance with travel to work costs) may help promote a sense of fairness, while communicating the value of on-site workers in organisational success. Furthermore, promoting equity and inclusivity across all roles and demographics requires transparent criteria for determining eligibility to work remotely, with these being regularly reviewed. Additionally, conducting employee surveys to assess perceptions of fairness can provide valuable insights for refining strategies. By fostering open dialogues about workplace equity, organisations can better understand and address concerns, creating a more balanced and supportive working environment for all employees.

Flexible Working Practices

The experience of working from home varies between individuals. For some, homeworking is beneficial and results in positive outcomes, whereas for others, outcomes are more negative.[8, 32] Where possible, employers and managers should seek to converse with homeworking employees on a case-by-case basis to allow them to express concerns about their working arrangement or if they are facing any challenges that may hinder their work. During the COVID-19 pandemic, the change to working from home was rapid and left many feeling unprepared to work in this way (e.g.,[39]) – providing the opportunity for employees to communicate openly and honestly about issues (e.g., childcare, others working in the same household) provides the opportunity for managers to understand employee circumstances.

Implementing flexible working policies requires employers and managers to respect individual preferences and circumstances. This is deemed particularly important following extended periods of remote work, such as we saw during the COVID-19 pandemic. Case-by-case discussions between supervisors and employees can facilitate informed decisions about how to optimise working arrangements, considering factors such as living situations and work preferences. Allowing people in more administrative roles to work remotely, or flexibly, where feasible, creating rotating schedules for hybrid work among non-frontline staff, and clearly defining tasks suitable for remote completion are key strategies. Such policies enhance work-life balance, support employee wellbeing, and align organisational practices with the diverse needs of the workforce.

Conclusions and Looking to the Future

The evolution of working from home practices, accelerated by the COVID-19 pandemic, has reshaped organisational operations and highlighted the potential for flexible work arrangements across sectors. Prior to the pandemic, homeworking was a growing but limited practice, primarily accessible to individuals in highly skilled professions or specific administrative roles. However, the pandemic shifted this dynamic, as nearly half of the UK workforce, including around 40% of the UK police force, transitioned to remote working. This sudden shift revealed both the benefits and challenges associated with working from home, offering valuable insights for its future implementation.

Research shows that working from home can lead to improved work-life balance, reduced stress from commuting, and increased flexibility, enhancing productivity and employee satisfaction. These benefits are particularly relevant in high-stress environments like policing, where employees often face emotional and physical exhaustion. Flexible work arrangements during the pandemic enabled many police staff to manage domestic responsibilities while remaining able to contribute effectively to their roles. However, these advantages were not universal. Disparities in opportunities to work from home, inadequate resources, and the blurring of work–home boundaries created significant challenges. For many, feelings of isolation, struggling team cohesion, and physical health issues due to poor ergonomic setups were notable drawbacks.

In policing specifically, the pandemic underscored the need for equitable and inclusive homeworking policies. The frontline nature of policing meant that many officers were unable to work remotely, leading to perceptions of unfairness and conflict. On the other hand, police forces demonstrated their ability to integrate flexible working practices effectively, with many employees expressing a desire to retain hybrid or remote work options post-pandemic. This aligns with broader research indicating that hybrid models offer an optimal balance, allowing employees to benefit from both the autonomy of remote work and the social interaction of in-person collaboration.

Moving forward, organisations, including police forces, must focus on optimising the benefits of and addressing the barriers to effective homeworking. Investments in technology, ergonomic resources, and comprehensive mental health initiatives will allow for staff to work from home both safely and comfortably. Additionally, fostering a culture of fairness and inclusivity will help mitigate feelings of unfairness, particularly for those unable to work remotely. Clear communication, regular feedback mechanisms, and transparent policies will ensure that working from home is efficient and practical.

Ultimately, the pandemic has demonstrated that working from home is not a one-size-fits-all solution. Success depends on thoughtful implementation, tailored to the unique needs of different roles and individuals. By learning from experiences during the COVID-19 pandemic, organisations can create a sustainable, flexible working framework that supports employee wellbeing, enhances productivity, and strengthens resilience against future disruptions. For policing, integrating these principles will not only improve workforce morale but also ensure the continued delivery of essential public services in an evolving professional landscape.

References

1. World Health Organization. WHO Director-General's opening remarks at the media briefing on COVID-19. 11 March 2020 [Accessed 1 April 2024]. Available from: https://www.who.int/director-general/speeches/detail/who-director-general-s-opening-remarks-at-the-media-briefing-on-covid-19---11-march-2020.
2. UK Government. Staying at home and away from others (social distancing). 2020. https://www.gov.uk.
3. Prime Minister's statement on coronavirus (COVID-19). 2020 [updated 16th March 2020. Accessed 1 February]. Available from: https://www.gov.uk/government/speeches/pm-address-to-the-nation-on-coronavirus-23-march-2020.

4. Coronavirus and homeworking in the UK. April 2020 [Internet]. Available from: https://www.ons.gov.uk/employmentandlabourmarket/peopleinwork/employmentandemployeetypes/bulletins/coronavirusandhomeworkingintheuk/april2020.
5. Kelliher, C, Anderson D. Doing more with less? Flexible working practices and the intensification of work. *Human Relations.* 2010; 63(1): 83–106.
6. Matusik SF, Mickel AE. Embracing or embattled by converged mobile devices? Users' experiences with a contemporary connectivity technology. *Human Relations.* 2011; 64(8): 1001–30.
7. Hall CE, Davidson L, Brooks SK, Greenberg N, Weston D. The relationship between homeworking during COVID-19 and both, mental health, and productivity: A systematic review. *BMC Psychology.* 2023; 11(1): 188.
8. Hall CE, Brooks SK, Mills F, Greenberg N, Weston D. Experiences of working from home: Umbrella review. *Journal of Occupational Health.* 2024; 66(1): uiad013.
9. His Majesty's Inspectorate of Constabulary and Fire & Rescue Service. Policing in the pandemic-the police response to the Coronavirus pandemic during 2020. HMICFRS London; 2021.
10. Athanasiadou C, Theriou G. Telework: Systematic literature review and future research agenda. *Heliyon.* 2021; 7(10).
11. Reuschke D, Felstead A. Homeworking in the UK: Before and during the 2020 lockdown. *WISERD Report*, 2020. https://wiserd.ac.uk/publications/homeworking-ukand-during-2020-lockdown
12. Silver H. Working from home: Before and after the pandemic. *Contexts.* 2023; 22(1): 66–70.
13. Hobbs A. *The impact of remote and flexible working arrangements.* UK Parliament. 2021.
14. Mutebi N, Hobbs A. *The impact of remote and hybrid working on workers and organisations.* UK Parliament. 2022.
15. Fleming J, Brown J. Staffing the force: Police staff in England and Wales' experiences of working through a COVID-19 lockdown. *Police Practice and Research.* 2022; 23(2): 236–53.
16. Dick P, Hyde R. Line manager involvement in work-life balance and career development: Can't manage, won't manage? *British Journal of Guidance & Counselling.* 2006; 34(3): 345–64.
17. DeSanctis G. Attitudes toward telecommuting: Implications for work-at-home programs. *Information & Management.* 1984; 7(3): 133–9.
18. Kurkland NB, Bailey DE. The advantages and challenges of working here, there, anywhere, and anytime. *Organizational Dynamics.* 1999; 28(2): 53–68.
19. Wheatley D. Good to be home? Time-use and satisfaction levels among home-based teleworkers. *New Technology, Work and Employment.* 2012; 27(3): 224–41.
20. Hjorthol R, Nossum Å. Teleworking: A reduction in travel or just increased flexibility? *Journal of eWorking.* 2008; 2(1).
21. Hill EJ, Ferris M, Märtinson V. Does it matter where you work? A comparison of how three work venues (traditional office, virtual office, and home office) influence aspects of work and personal/family life. *Journal of Vocational Behavior.* 2003; 63(2): 220–41.
22. Hill EJ, Miller BC, Weiner SP, Colihan J. Influences of the virtual office on aspects of work and work/life balance. *Personnel Psychology.* 1998; 51(3): 667–83.
23. Raghuram S, Wiesenfeld B. Work-nonwork conflict and job stress among virtual workers. *Human Resource Management.* 2004; 43(2–3): 259–77.
24. Golden T. Altering the effects of work and family conflict on exhaustion: Telework during traditional and nontraditional work hours. *Journal of Business and Psychology.* 2012; 27: 255–69.
25. Richards A, Convery S, O'Mahony M, Caulfield B. Pre and post Covid preferences for working from home. *Travel Behaviour and Society.* 2024; 34: 100679.
26. Cooper CD, Kurland NB. Telecommuting, professional isolation, and employee development in public and private organizations. *Journal of Organizational Behavior: The International*

Journal of Industrial, Occupational and Organizational Psychology and Behavior. 2002; 23(4): 511–32.

27. Bailey DE, Kurland NB. A review of telework research: Findings, new directions, and lessons for the study of modern work. *Journal of Organizational Behavior: The International Journal of Industrial, Occupational and Organizational Psychology and Behavior.* 2002; 23(4): 383–400.
28. Mann S, Holdsworth L. The psychological impact of teleworking: Stress, emotions and health. *New Technology, Work and Employment.* 2003; 18(3): 196–211.
29. Hager FW. Links between telecommuting, social support and mental well-being among teleworkers: A literature review. *International Journal of Business & Management.* 2018; 6(2): 36–58.
30. Brown J, Fleming J. Exploration of individual and work-related impacts on police officers and police staff working in support or front-line roles during the UK's first COVID lockdown. *The Police Journal.* 2022; 95(1): 50–72.
31. Fleming J, Brown J. Policewomen's experiences of working during lockdown: Results of a survey with officers from England and Wales. *Policing: A Journal of Policy and Practice.* 2021; 15(3): 1977–92.
32. Newiss G, Charman S, Ilett C, Bennett S, Ghaemmaghami A, Smith P, Inkpen R. Taking the strain? Police well-being in the COVID-19 era. *The Police Journal.* 2022; 95(1): 88–108.
33. Roach J, Curran L, Cartwright A, McCarthy R. A study of police personnel wellbeing in England and Wales whilst working during the COVID-19 pandemic. *Policing and Society.* 2024; 35(6): 773–794.
34. Frenkel MO, Giessing L, Egger-Lampl S, Hutter V, Oudejans RR, Kleygrewe L, et al. The impact of the COVID-19 pandemic on European police officers: Stress, demands, and coping resources. *Journal of Criminal Justice.* 2021; 72: 101756.
35. Rowe M, Davis C, Ramshaw P. Managing impressions: Performance and identity in police leadership in the pandemic. *Policing and Society.* 2024; 35(3): 345–360.
36. Hall CE, Brooks SK, Potts HW, Greenberg N, Weston D. Rates of, and factors associated with, common mental disorders in homeworking UK Government response employees' during COVID-19: A cross-sectional survey and secondary data analysis. *BMC Psychology.* 2024; 12(1): 429.
37. Hall CE, Brooks SK, Greenberg N, Weston D. UK Government COVID-19 response employees' perceptions on working from home: Content analysis of open-ended survey questions. *Journal of Occupational and Environmental Medicine.* 2023; 66(12): e661–e667.
38. C. E. Hall SKB, N. Greenberg and D. Weston. "We're all in the same storm, but not all of us are in the same boat": Qualitative exploration of UK response-focused civil servants experiences of working from home during COVID-19. *BMC Public Health.* 2025; 25: 289.
39. C. E. Hall SKB, N. Greenberg and D. Weston. Recommendations to support the mental health and wellbeing of response-focused Civil Servants asked to work from home during public health emergencies in the United Kingdom: A Delphi study. Under review.

17

SUPPORTING SUSTAINABLE WELLBEING IN POLICING

The Power of Effective Communication and Engagement

Jenna Flanagan

Introduction

Context: The Policing Environment

Policing is inherently one of the most demanding professions, characterised by high stakes, unpredictable challenges, and exposure to potentially traumatic situations. Many of those working in policing frequently face long shifts, high-pressure decision-making, and a relentless cycle of incidents that require immediate and effective responses. This high-stress environment not only strains physical stamina but significantly impacts mental health. The constant pressure can lead to chronic stress, burnout, and, in severe cases, anxiety, depression, and post-traumatic stress disorder (PTSD). Over time, these issues contribute to diminished job satisfaction, reduced productivity, and higher rates of absenteeism, leaveism, or staff turnover.

However, roles in policing are varied and it's not just frontline officers or detectives, for example, who are exposed to trauma or high-stress situations. Police staff, including call handlers, crime scene investigators, and business support roles, experience different challenges. Call handlers, for instance, deal with the emotional toll of managing emergency calls and distressed individuals, often without closure on the outcomes. Crime scene investigators are exposed to potentially distressing environments, balancing meticulous forensic work with emotional resilience. Police communicators, such as Press Officers, are often called out to scenes of major incidents, exposed to distressing information, and provide support to bereaved families and victims of crime facing media attention in a high-pressure/high-demand environment. Other business support roles, while not directly exposed to trauma, can face high workloads, resource constraints, and the pressure to support frontline operations. These roles contribute to organisational burnout and stress in their own ways, highlighting the diverse nature of wellbeing challenges across the policing workforce.

DOI: 10.4324/9781003518860-18

The impact of these stressors is not confined to individual officers or staff. The ripple effects can undermine team cohesion, strain leadership relationships, and affect the broader organisational culture. In such an environment, creating resilience and supporting the mental and physical wellbeing of all staff is not just beneficial—it is essential for sustainable, effective policing.

The Need for Wellbeing Initiatives

To counter these challenges, employee wellbeing must be prioritised within policing organisations. Effective wellbeing programmes are designed to address both the immediate and long-term health needs of officers and staff, enhancing their capacity to manage stress and maintain mental health. Beyond the practical benefits, investing in wellbeing creates a culture of care, strengthening trust and morale within the organisation. For such initiatives to succeed, communication and engagement play a pivotal role. Clear, empathetic communication ensures that wellbeing programmes are not only understood, but embraced. Likewise, creating active engagement ensures that all staff feel valued and heard, motivating them to participate fully in these initiatives.

Recent findings highlight why effective, empathetic, and genuine communication is especially critical in the context of policing wellbeing. The 2023 National Police Wellbeing Survey, conducted by Oscar Kilo, the National Police Wellbeing Service, revealed that while many officers find their work meaningful, they face high workloads and emotionally demanding situations. Despite these challenges, there remains a reluctance to seek organisational support due to fears of stigma, breaches of confidentiality, and potential career repercussions. Similarly, the Police Federation of England and Wales' Pay and Morale Survey 2023 found that 58% of officers reported low morale, with many feeling undervalued by both the government and their employer. This dissatisfaction can deter officers and staff from accessing available support services, as they may perceive a lack of genuine care from their organisation.

These findings underscore the importance of creating trust through communication that is empathetic, transparent, and genuine. Effective communication can address concerns, reduce stigma, and create an environment where seeking support is normalised and encouraged.

The Role of Communication and Engagement in Wellbeing

This chapter aims to explore how communication and engagement can be leveraged to implement and support effective wellbeing strategies within policing organisations. While numerous wellbeing programmes may exist, their success often hinges on how well they are communicated and received. Communication in this context must extend beyond mere information sharing; it must be personal, empathetic, and responsive to the lived experiences of officers and staff.

A critical aspect of ensuring communication resonates with individuals is understanding behaviour change theories. Theories such as the Transtheoretical Model (stages of change), the Capability, Opportunity, and Motivation (COM-B) Model, and Social

Cognitive Theory emphasise that individuals must perceive a message as relevant and supportive to prompt action. For a communication strategy to be effective, it must connect on a personal level—speaking to the emotional and psychological needs of staff across diverse roles and backgrounds. Messages that are empathetic, transparent, and engaging help bridge the gap between awareness and action, encouraging individuals to take steps towards improving their wellbeing.

Engagement, on the other hand, must move beyond passive acknowledgement and encourage active participation, feedback, and ownership from all members of the organisation. This includes creating a sense of co-production where initiatives are designed "for staff, by staff," building trust and confidence and reinforcing the message that their wellbeing is valued and prioritised.

Understanding and implementing these principles requires an approach that blends practical experience with proven communication strategies and insights from behaviour change models. This chapter will provide insights into the core elements of effective communication and engagement that drive successful wellbeing initiatives, drawing from examples and lessons within the UK public sector and policing specifically.

A Broader Perspective on Communication

Innovative and practical communication practices must underpin all these efforts. Communication in an organisation does not solely rest with a designated communications team; it is a collective responsibility. At every level, staff must embody organisational values and embrace their role as communicators. Whether through formal campaigns or everyday interactions, the ethos of compassion, trust, and innovation in communication must be visible. Recognising this shared responsibility ensures that the organisation's culture is consistently reinforced, creating an environment where wellbeing is a shared priority.

Overview of the Chapter's Content

This chapter will delve into some key elements of communication and engagement as they pertain to wellbeing in policing in the following sections:

1. Understanding wellbeing in policing through a communications lens.
2. Role of communication in creating the right environment.
3. Engagement strategies for sustainable wellbeing.
4. From strategy to practice: implementing communication and engagement plans.
5. Challenges and considerations.
6. Conclusion.

By the end of this chapter, readers will have a comprehensive understanding of how communication and engagement can be the linchpin for effective, sustainable wellbeing initiatives in policing. This knowledge will equip anybody reading it with the insights needed to create healthier, more resilient teams and organisations.

Section One—Understanding Wellbeing in Policing through Communication

Challenges in Policing: The Personal Impact

Policing roles come with unique and varied stressors that affect mental and physical wellbeing. From uniformed officers and staff responding to life-threatening situations, detectives and civilian staff investigating serious and violent crime, to call handlers managing distressing emergency calls, the nature of the work often exposes individuals to significant psychological strain. High workloads, long hours, exposure to traumatic incidents, and the emotional demands of supporting the public create a backdrop of chronic stress. Meanwhile, those in support roles face different, but equally pressing, challenges, such as heavy administrative loads and pressures to meet organisational demands with limited resources. Some support roles are also exposed to distressing or traumatic information or situations which must not be dismissed.

The cumulative impact of these stressors is profound. Officers and staff alike may face burnout, anxiety, or post-traumatic stress disorder (PTSD), which not only diminishes their own health but also affects team cohesion and organisational performance. Effective communication plays a pivotal role in identifying and addressing these stressors. Regular check-ins, open-door policies, and peer support programmes help create an environment where individuals feel heard and supported, breaking down barriers to seeking help.

There are examples of effective peer support programmes to be found in police forces around the country—many of which follow the model set out by Oscar Kilo, the National Police Wellbeing Service.

The Importance of Wellbeing: Speaking to the Heart

Wellbeing is not just a personal concern; it is a critical organisational priority. Healthy, supported employees are more engaged, productive, and committed, leading to better retention rates and improved public service. However, achieving this requires more than transactional communication. Leaders must speak to the hearts of their teams, demonstrating empathy and understanding.

For example, campaigns that integrate storytelling—sharing real experiences from staff who have benefited from wellbeing initiatives—help build trust and relatability. Such approaches show that the organisation values its people as individuals, not just as employees, and create a culture of care.

Leaders who model empathy in their communication not only strengthen morale but also inspire others to do the same, creating a ripple effect throughout the organisation. But it has to be genuine, and leaders must "walk the walk"—not just "talk the talk."

Current State of Wellbeing Initiatives: A Communication Perspective

Effective communication underpins the success of wellbeing programmes in policing. While many organisations offer resources such as counselling, peer support groups, and trauma risk management, or intervention programmes, the way these initiatives are communicated can make or break their impact.

For instance, campaigns driven by authentic storytelling and clear messaging—such as those emphasising confidentiality and ease of access—help reduce the stigma often associated with seeking help. Behavioural insights, such as those suggested in the College of Policing's "Culture change through communications" guide, show that communication campaigns are most effective when they:

- **Align Messaging with Values**: Messages must resonate with the shared mission and ethos of policing, such as protecting and supporting communities.
- **Engage Diverse Audiences**: Communication must reflect the varied experiences and needs of all staff, from frontline officers to administrative teams.
- **Promote Inclusivity**: Using input from underrepresented voices ensures initiatives are relevant and relatable to all members of the organisation.

Some policing organisations have successfully used communication campaigns to increase engagement with wellbeing programmes. For example, targeted campaigns using peer testimonials and leadership endorsements have been shown to boost participation in mental health support services. However, challenges remain, such as the need for better two-way communication and personalised messaging.

Strengths and Areas for Improvement

While many wellbeing programmes demonstrate promising results, there are areas where communication strategies could improve:

- **Feedback Mechanisms**: Introducing structured feedback loops allows staff to voice their opinions on existing programmes, helping refine and tailor offerings.
- **Consistency in Leadership Messaging**: Senior leaders must consistently communicate their commitment to wellbeing, demonstrating it through their actions and words.
- **Storytelling and Transparency**: Campaigns should use storytelling to reduce stigma and show the tangible benefits of support services, while ensuring transparency about what initiatives entail.

Successful examples from other public sector organisations, such as the NHS and some local government organisations, highlight how regular updates, recognition of staff achievements, and visible leadership support can amplify engagement. For example, NHS organisations have used a mix of virtual and face-to-face forums to communicate wellbeing initiatives, creating a sense of accessibility and inclusion.

Practical Communication Strategies for Police Wellbeing

Drawing lessons from the College of Policing's "Culture change through communication" guide and NHS communication case studies, the following approaches can enhance the impact of wellbeing initiatives:

1. Empathy as the Foundation: Ensure communication is empathetic and human-centred, acknowledging the challenges staff face and offering genuine support.

2. Behavioural Insights: Use behavioural science techniques to craft messages that resonate emotionally and encourage action, such as using peer testimonials to reduce stigma.
3. Diverse Channels: Utilise a mix of communication methods (e.g., email, staff forums, peer networks) to ensure messages reach all staff effectively.
4. Inclusive Planning: Actively involve staff in the design of wellbeing initiatives, creating co-produced solutions that reflect their needs and experiences.
5. Measurement and Adaptation: Use data from staff surveys, feedback sessions, and participation rates to measure the effectiveness of communication campaigns and refine strategies over time.

Section Two—The Role of Communication in Creating the Right Environment

Creating the right environment for wellbeing in policing requires communication strategies that prioritise psychological safety, create two-way dialogue, and address organisational and personal challenges. Communication is not limited to traditional methods or the responsibility of a communications team. Instead, it happens at all levels of an organisation, every day, and is fundamental to shaping a culture where staff feel supported and valued.

Internal and External Communication Strategies

Effective communication in policing must encompass both internal and external approaches. Internally, organisations need clear and consistent messaging to staff about available wellbeing resources and the values that underpin these initiatives. Externally, collaboration with stakeholders, including the public and partner agencies, helps reinforce a shared commitment to supporting police wellbeing.

- **Internal Strategies**: These include regular briefings, intranet updates, and engaging visual campaigns that reinforce the organisation's commitment to mental health and wellbeing. Leaders play a critical role in modelling open communication and promoting the values of support and care.
- **External Strategies**: Partnerships with external organisations such as charities or public health agencies help to align messaging and amplify the reach of wellbeing initiatives. For example, campaigns co-created with organisations like Samaritans can emphasise shared values of confidentiality and trust.

Empathetic and Human-Centred Communication

Policing is a high-pressure profession where staff often operate under emotional and physical strain. Messages that acknowledge these challenges demonstrate empathy and create trust. Leaders who openly recognise the difficulties faced by their teams are more likely to build rapport and engagement.

Example: Internal communication campaigns that highlight real-life stories of officers who successfully navigated mental health challenges humanise wellbeing programmes and encourage participation.

Transparent and Honest Messaging

Transparency about what support is available, how it works, and how confidentiality is maintained is essential to build trust. Many officers may hesitate to access wellbeing programmes due to fears about confidentiality or career repercussions. Clear, upfront communication addressing these concerns can remove barriers.

Example: Providing detailed FAQs or anonymous testimonials about how participation in Occupational Health, counselling, or therapy services remains confidential can ease staff apprehensions.

Two-Way Communication with Clarity and Transparency

In policing, communication must be a two-way process where leaders not only share information but also actively listen and respond to feedback. Clarity and transparency are essential for building trust, especially around sensitive topics like mental health.

- **Clarity**: Messages about wellbeing initiatives must be straightforward, accessible, and tailored to diverse staff needs. Jargon or overly complex language can create confusion, reducing engagement.
- **Transparency**: Transparency about the purpose, processes, and outcomes of wellbeing programmes reassures staff. For example, clearly explaining confidentiality protocols can alleviate fears about using mental health resources.

Two-way communication mechanisms, such as anonymous feedback tools or open forums, encourage staff to voice their concerns and contribute ideas. This approach empowers staff to feel heard and involved in shaping wellbeing initiatives. But they must be truly anonymous or de-identified in order to keep that trust.

It's important to note here that within policing particularly, there is an automatic distrust, or cynicism of many corporate initiatives, surveys, or support resources provided, so the key elements of clarity, transparency and being relevant are absolutely critical.

Addressing Organisational Challenges: Hierarchy and Bureaucracy

The hierarchical and bureaucratic structures in policing can pose significant barriers to open communication. Staff newer in service may feel intimidated or fear repercussions for raising concerns, while senior leaders may inadvertently create distance through formal processes.

- **Flattening Hierarchies**: Leaders can create a more approachable culture by having open-door policies, hosting informal forums or "tea and talk" sessions, where staff at all levels can share experiences and ideas without fear of judgement.
- **Streamlining Bureaucracy**: Simplifying processes for accessing wellbeing resources ensures that support is accessible and timely. Reducing administrative barriers signals that wellbeing is a priority, not a procedural obligation.

Addressing Personal Challenges: Stigma around Mental Health

One of the most significant barriers to engagement with wellbeing initiatives is the stigma associated with discussing mental health. In policing, where resilience and toughness are often emphasised, acknowledging vulnerabilities can be seen as a sign of weakness.

- **Normalising Conversations**: Campaigns featuring testimonials from officers and staff who have sought help successfully can challenge stigma. For example, a video series titled "We've Been There" could showcase personal stories that normalise seeking support and demonstrate success stories of people receiving the help they needed.
- **Confidentiality and Safety**: Reinforcing the confidential nature of wellbeing services is critical. Leaders must communicate that accessing these services will not impact career progression or reputation.

Embedding Psychological Safety through Communication

Psychological safety – the belief that one can speak up, make mistakes, and share ideas without fear of reprisal – is foundational for creating a supportive environment in policing. Achieving this requires intentional communication practices:

1. Role Modelling: Leaders should model vulnerability and openness by sharing their own challenges and how they have navigated them.
2. Recognition and Gratitude: Small acts of recognition, such as thanking staff for their contributions, create a sense of belonging and value.
3. Encouraging Feedback: Leaders should actively invite feedback in various formats, such as anonymous surveys or one-on-one discussions, to accommodate different comfort levels.

Practical Tips for Creating the Right Environment

- **Build trust and Connection**: Consistent messaging that emphasises shared values and purpose helps build trust. For example, a campaign focused on the unique challenges of policing could create a sense of connection and shared understanding.
- **Focus on Inclusivity**: Communication strategies must ensure all voices are heard, especially those from underrepresented groups. Encouraging diverse perspectives enriches the culture of psychological safety.
- **Celebrate Successes**: Recognising individual and team achievements, no matter how small, reinforces the message that staff contributions are valued.

By embedding these practices into daily interactions and organisational culture, policing organisations can create an environment where communication supports wellbeing, creates trust, and empowers staff at every level.

Case Study: Launching a Mental Health Crisis Line for Policing

Background

The National Police Wellbeing Service (NPWS) recently launched a pioneering 24/7 mental health crisis line designed to address the unique pressures faced by police officers and staff. This service aims to provide immediate, confidential, and expert support to those experiencing a mental health crisis, including suicidal thoughts. Given the high-profile nature of the initiative and the sensitivity of the topic, NPWS placed communication at the core of its planning and execution. The approach combined insight-driven messaging, stakeholder engagement, and a phased rollout strategy to ensure success.

Communication Strategy: Insight-Led and Research-Based

To craft an effective communication campaign, NPWS collaborated with a creative agency and conducted extensive research, gathering insights from focus groups involving police officers, staff, and external stakeholders such as mental health charities. Key insights included:

- **Context Matters**: Understanding the lived experience of policing was critical to tailoring the messaging.
- **Address Stigma**: Communication is needed to confront and reduce the stigma around seeking help for mental health.
- **Confidentiality Assurances**: It was vital to emphasise the independent and confidential nature of the crisis line to alleviate fears of exposure.
- **Perceptions of Suicide**: Messaging sought to dismantle myths, ensuring inclusivity for anyone affected by suicidal thoughts, regardless of cause.

These findings informed the campaign's creative concept, which centred around the human aspect of policing, emphasising that behind the uniform or the role, is a person deserving of care and support.

Creative Execution: Resonating with the Workforce

The campaign was built on four messaging pillars derived from research and behavioural science principles, including social norming and homophily:

1. General Support: Acknowledging the diversity of crises individuals may face and emphasising that help is always available.
2. Immediate Support: Highlighting the toll of stress, fatigue, and trauma in policing while reassuring officers and staff they are not alone.
3. Dedicated to Policing: Stressing the service's confidentiality, independence, and understanding of the specific pressures faced by police professionals.
4. Breaking the Stigma: Normalising mental health challenges and encouraging individuals to seek support without fear of judgement.

The campaign materials featured diverse imagery representing various roles, ranks, genders, and ethnicities within policing. This ensured inclusivity and relatability. The visuals incorporated subtle blue gradients to connect with the policing identity while maintaining the drama of black-and-white photography.

Stakeholder Engagement: Building Support from the Ground Up

Engaging stakeholders was as critical as crafting the campaign. NPWS worked closely with a network of Single Points of Contact (SPOCs) in each pilot force to facilitate local promotion and gather feedback. Pre-launch webinars, briefing notes, and regular communication ensured stakeholders were informed and aligned with the campaign's objectives.

The phased rollout, beginning with seven forces in the North East of England, allowed the NPWS to manage demand effectively while gathering data to refine the service and communications strategy. This incremental approach ensured quality control and laid the groundwork for a future national rollout.

Key Campaign Elements

The communication toolkit provided to pilot forces included:

- **Core Materials**: Posters, leaflets, coasters, key fobs, and digital banners.
- **Key Messages**: Copy emphasising the service's independence, confidentiality, availability, and tailored support for policing.
- **Channels**: Social media, intranet, and physical promotional materials.
- **Measurement**: Metrics such as intranet visits, placement of materials, and anecdotal feedback were collected to evaluate the campaign's reach and impact.

Challenges and Lessons Learned

Launching a service of this magnitude required navigating several challenges:

- **Managing Expectations**: Communicating the phased rollout clearly to avoid misconceptions about availability.
- **Sensitivity**: Ensuring messaging struck the right balance between urgency and empathy.
- **Stakeholder Buy-In**: Securing engagement from local forces through consistent communication and support.

Impact and Future Goals

While the full evaluation of the pilot is pending, the campaign's research-driven and inclusive approach has set a strong foundation for success. By addressing stigma, ensuring confidentiality, and creating trust through clear communication, the initiative aims to save lives and support the mental health of those in policing. The pilot's learnings will inform future phases, with the ultimate goal of expanding the crisis line nationally and reinforcing the commitment to the wellbeing of police officers and staff.

This case study demonstrates how strategic, insight-led communication can drive the success of critical wellbeing interventions, offering valuable lessons for similar initiatives across the public.

Section Three—Engagement Strategies for Sustainable Wellbeing

Creating a sustainable culture of wellbeing requires engagement strategies that go beyond surface-level interventions or one-off campaigns. Sustainable engagement involves embedding wellbeing into the fabric of an organisation, empowering staff, and leveraging innovative and evidence-based methods to ensure long-term impact. This section explores key engagement strategies that enable organisations, especially within high-pressure environments like policing, to create lasting and meaningful wellbeing.

Building Ownership: Co-Creating Wellbeing Initiatives

Engagement begins with ownership. When staff feel they have a stake in shaping wellbeing initiatives, they are more likely to engage with and champion them. Co-creation not only creates a sense of shared responsibility but also ensures that initiatives are tailored to the real needs and lived experiences of the workforce.

- **Empowering Local Champions**: Identifying and training wellbeing champions at every level of the organisation can create a ripple effect. Champions act as relatable peers who promote and model positive practices, bridging gaps between leadership and staff.
- **Collaborative Design Workshops**: Hosting workshops that bring together diverse staff to co-design wellbeing initiatives ensures that programmes resonate with all segments of the workforce.

Using Behavioural Science: Evidence-Based Approaches

Behavioural science offers powerful tools to shape engagement strategies, using insights into human behaviour to encourage participation and build lasting habits. In policing, where stigma and operational pressures can be barriers, concepts like nudge theory and social norming can be transformative.

- **Nudge Theory**: Subtle changes in communication or the environment can significantly influence behaviour. For example, framing wellbeing messages around the idea that "most officers in your unit use this support service" leverages social proof to normalise participation.
- **Social Norming**: Highlighting positive behaviours already prevalent within the organisation helps build momentum for change. Sharing stories of how officers benefited from wellbeing services without negative repercussions reinforces a supportive culture.

- **Gamification**: Introducing elements of competition, rewards, or recognition can make engagement more appealing. Activities such as team-based challenges or points systems for participating in wellbeing initiatives can create healthy competition and camaraderie.

Feedback Loops: Creating Continuous Improvement

Feedback is the cornerstone of engagement. Establishing mechanisms for collecting, analysing, and acting on staff feedback demonstrates that their voices are heard and valued, which in turn builds trust and participation.

- **Two-Way Feedback Channels**: We've talked about this throughout the chapter as it is critical to creating genuine staff engagement. Regular pulse surveys, anonymous suggestion boxes, or digital feedback tools provide platforms for staff to share thoughts openly.
- **Actionable Outcomes**: Feedback should be used to drive visible changes. Sharing updates on how input has influenced decisions builds confidence in the process. For example, regular communications could outline "You said, we did" updates to showcase transparency and accountability.

Creative Engagement Channels: Reaching Diverse Audiences

Traditional communication methods often miss the mark in today's dynamic and diverse workplaces. Creative approaches that resonate with different roles, generations, and preferences can ensure wider engagement and inclusivity.

- **Peer-Led Campaigns**: Involving trusted colleagues in promoting wellbeing initiatives can be more effective than top-down communication. Officers are more likely to respond positively to messages delivered by someone who shares their experiences.
- **Innovative Media**: Use digital storytelling, podcasts, or short videos featuring real staff experiences to humanise wellbeing campaigns.
- **Interactive Approaches**: Gamification, virtual wellbeing fairs, and immersive workshops can create memorable experiences that drive deeper engagement.

Building a Foundation for Sustainable Wellbeing

The ultimate goal of these strategies is to embed wellbeing into the organisational culture, making it a continuous priority rather than a reactive response to crises. Engagement is not a single campaign—it is an ongoing commitment to understanding, supporting, and collaborating with staff to create an environment where they can thrive.

By empowering staff, leveraging behavioural insights, creating feedback, and embracing creativity, policing organisations can ensure that wellbeing is not just a value on paper but a lived reality for every member of the workforce.

Section Four—From Strategy to Practice: Implementing Communication and Engagement Plans

Turning strategy into actionable and impactful communication and engagement plans requires careful planning, tailored approaches, and continuous evaluation. In policing, where the stakes are high and organisational culture is deeply rooted, it is critical to move beyond theoretical frameworks and adopt practical steps that ensure success. This section outlines the key components of implementing communication and engagement plans effectively.

Defining Clear Objectives

A strong foundation for any communication or engagement plan is a set of clear, measurable objectives that align with broader organisational priorities.

- **Link to Strategic Goals**: Wellbeing initiatives should directly support organisational goals such as improving workforce resilience, reducing absenteeism, or enhancing operational performance.
- **SMART Objectives**: Ensure objectives are Specific, Measurable, Achievable, Relevant, and Time-bound. For example, "Increase awareness of the mental health crisis line among frontline officers by 25% within six months."
- **Outcome-Oriented Focus**: Move beyond activity-based objectives (e.g., "Produce five posters") to focus on outcomes (e.g., "Increase utilisation of wellbeing services by 15%").

Tailoring to Organisational Culture

Policing's hierarchical structure and unique challenges require communication approaches that are both practical and culturally sensitive.

- **Understanding Hierarchies**: Acknowledge the role of rank and structure while ensuring messages resonate at all levels. Communication should be clear and inclusive, ensuring that senior leaders, managers, and staff feel equally valued and engaged.
- **Integration into Daily Practices**: Embed wellbeing messages into existing workflows, such as briefings, shift handovers, and team meetings. This makes engagement part of the routine rather than an additional task.
- **Celebrating Policing Values**: Align messages with values like teamwork, service, and resilience, framing wellbeing as essential to fulfilling these principles.

Training and Capacity Building

Empowering staff to communicate and engage effectively is essential to the success of any plan.

- **Leader Training**: Equip leaders with the skills to model empathetic communication, handle sensitive topics, and create psychologically safe environments.

- **Peer Support Programmes**: Train peer advocates or champions to promote initiatives and act as trusted points of contact for their colleagues.
- **Skill Development for All Staff**: Provide regular workshops or e-learning modules on topics such as effective communication, active listening, and giving/receiving feedback.

Leveraging Technology

Technology can amplify messages, enhance reach, and provide real-time insights into engagement.

- **Intranets and Apps**: Use organisational intranets or mobile apps to centralise wellbeing resources, share updates, and allow for anonymous feedback.
- **Social Media for Internal Use**: Use platforms like Microsoft Teams or Slack to facilitate peer-to-peer communication and provide informal spaces for sharing experiences.
- **Digital Campaigns**: Create visually engaging digital content, such as videos or infographics, that can be easily shared across platforms to maximise visibility.
- **Impact Tracking**: Use analytics tools to monitor message reach, engagement levels, and staff participation in initiatives.

Evaluation and Adaptation

Evaluation ensures that communication and engagement plans achieve their intended outcomes and provide actionable insights for improvement.

- Key Performance Indicators (KPIs): Define metrics that align with objectives, such as participation rates, feedback volumes, or shifts in attitudes measured through surveys.
- The OASIS Model: A proven framework for public sector communication planning that includes five stages:
  - Objective: Clearly define the purpose of your campaign.
  - Audience: Identify and understand your target audience.
  - Strategy: Develop a strategic approach to reach the audience effectively.
  - Implementation: Execute your plan using tailored tactics and channels.
  - Scoring/Evaluation: Measure outcomes against objectives to assess success.
  - GCS Evaluation Cycle: Apply the Government Communication Service (GCS) evaluation cycle to refine strategies. This includes three stages:
  - Inputs and Outputs: Assess resources and campaign activities.
  - Outtakes: Evaluate audience reactions, such as awareness or engagement.
  - Outcomes and Impacts: Measure tangible results, such as changes in behaviour or organisational benefits.
  - Feedback Mechanisms: Use staff surveys, focus groups, and informal check-ins to gather qualitative and quantitative insights.

Building for the Long Term

Implementing communication and engagement plans is not a one-time effort but an ongoing process. By defining objectives, adapting strategies to fit the unique culture of policing, equipping staff with necessary skills, leveraging technology, and committing to robust evaluation, organisations can create a sustainable culture of wellbeing.

The ultimate goal is to ensure that wellbeing becomes an integral part of everyday organisational life, with staff at every level feeling heard, valued, and supported.

Right Place, Right Time: Ensuring that you explore and use the widest range of channels available to you, over a period of time, and not relying on "one-time" communications means that you'll likely reach more people. Officers and staff are often time-poor, with many roles not getting the time or space to read or find things on their force intranets, for example—so it's important that multiple channels are used—go to them, don't expect them to come to you.

Section Five—Challenges and Considerations

Effective communication and engagement strategies for wellbeing initiatives face several challenges, particularly within the policing context. Resistance to change, sustaining long-term engagement, and ensuring cultural sensitivity are critical areas that require thoughtful strategies. This section explores these challenges and provides practical approaches to address them, including the important consideration of initiative and survey fatigue.

Resistance to Change: Strategies to Overcome Resistance

Resistance to change is a natural response in many organisations, but it can be particularly pronounced in hierarchical and tradition-bound environments like policing. Resistance may stem from a lack of trust, fear of judgement, or scepticism about the effectiveness of new initiatives.

Causes of Resistance

- **Hierarchical Inertia**: Long-standing chains of command may discourage innovation and input from all levels of staff.
- **Fear of Judgement**: Officers and staff may worry about being perceived as weak or incapable if they openly support or use wellbeing services.
- **Past Experiences**: Ineffective or poorly communicated past initiatives may lead to cynicism and resistance.

Strategies to Overcome Resistance

We've discussed many of these throughout the chapter, but to reiterate, here are some of the key areas to consider:

1. **Empathetic Leadership:** Leaders should openly acknowledge challenges and demonstrate a genuine commitment to wellbeing. By sharing personal stories or actively endorsing initiatives, they build trust and break down barriers.
2. **Transparent Communication:** Clearly explain the rationale, benefits, and processes behind new initiatives. Address concerns such as confidentiality and potential career impacts directly.
3. **Co-Creation of Initiatives:** Involve staff in the design and rollout of wellbeing programmes to create a sense of ownership and collaboration.
4. **Incremental Implementation:** Begin with pilot programmes or phased rollouts to build momentum and demonstrate value without overwhelming the organisation.

Sustaining Engagement: Keeping the Momentum Alive

Long-term engagement can wane without ongoing attention and adaptation. A significant challenge in policing is maintaining enthusiasm and participation in initiatives over time, especially when competing priorities arise.

Causes of Engagement Decline:

- **Fatigue from Initiatives:** Repeatedly introducing new programmes without clear follow-through can lead to disillusionment.
- **Survey Fatigue:** Overuse of surveys and feedback requests can result in diminished responses and reduced quality of insights.
- **Competing Priorities:** Operational demands may overshadow wellbeing efforts, making sustained engagement difficult.

Strategies to Sustain Engagement:

1. **Communicate Progress and Impact:** Regularly share updates on the success of initiatives, such as metrics, personal testimonials, or improvements in team morale. Seeing tangible results can renew enthusiasm.
2. **Dynamic and Refreshed Initiatives:** Revitalise programmes by incorporating new ideas, tools, or approaches to maintain interest. This could include seasonal campaigns or interactive activities.
3. **Thoughtful Use of Surveys:** Minimise survey fatigue by aligning feedback requests with meaningful actions. Use focused, concise surveys and communicate how responses will directly inform decisions.
4. **Integrate Wellbeing into Daily Operations:** Embed wellbeing practices into routine activities, such as team briefings or training, so they become part of the organisational fabric.

Cultural Sensitivity: Adapting Strategies to Policing

The culture of policing is deeply rooted in tradition, camaraderie, and a sense of duty. These qualities offer unique strengths but also pose challenges when implementing wellbeing initiatives.

Why Cultural Sensitivity Matters:

- **Respecting Traditions and Pride in the Job**: New initiatives must align with the ethos of service and the values of honour, resilience, and pride.
- **Recognising Subcultures**: Different roles within policing (e.g., frontline officers, detectives, specialist units, support staff) have distinct experiences and stressors that must be acknowledged.
- **Overcoming Stigma**: In a culture where toughness and self-reliance are highly valued, addressing mental health and wellbeing can be particularly sensitive.

Strategies for Cultural Sensitivity:

1. **Tailored Messaging**: Use language and imagery that reflect the realities of policing life, ensuring messages feel authentic and relatable.
2. **Engage Diverse Voices**: Include representatives from various ranks, roles, and backgrounds in planning and communication efforts. This ensures that strategies resonate across the workforce.
3. **Leverage Existing Networks**: Utilise trusted networks, such as peer support groups or unions, to disseminate messages and encourage participation.
4. **Honouring Values**: Frame wellbeing as essential to sustaining the strength, resilience, and effectiveness required in policing. Emphasise that seeking support is a sign of professionalism, not weakness.

By addressing these challenges with thoughtful, evidence-based strategies, organisations can create a culture where wellbeing initiatives are not just implemented but embraced, enabling staff to thrive both personally and professionally.

Section Six—Conclusion: Building a Culture of Wellbeing through Effective Communication and Engagement

Effective communication and engagement are the cornerstones of creating a sustainable culture of wellbeing in policing. Throughout this chapter, we have explored the significant challenges faced by policing organisations, from the physical and emotional demands of the job to the systemic and cultural barriers that hinder progress. We've also seen how thoughtful, empathetic, and strategically delivered communication can drive meaningful change, create trust, and build a sense of shared ownership in wellbeing initiatives.

Key Takeaways:

1. **Empathy and Trust Are Foundational:** Communication that acknowledges the realities of policing life—its pressures, challenges, and rewards—is essential to building trust. By openly addressing stigma and providing clear, honest messaging about wellbeing services, organisations can create an environment where seeking support is seen as a strength rather than a vulnerability.

2. **Engagement Requires Active Participation:** Engagement goes beyond awareness. It calls for co-creation, consistent feedback loops, and inclusive approaches that empower staff at all levels. Innovative methods, such as leveraging behavioural science or peer-led initiatives, ensure that wellbeing efforts resonate and are embraced.
3. **Sustainability Is Built over Time:** Creating a culture of wellbeing is not a one-off effort but an ongoing process. Integrating wellbeing into daily practices, celebrating progress, and adapting strategies to reflect the needs of the workforce are critical to maintaining momentum. Thoughtful evaluation and responsiveness to feedback further reinforce this commitment.
4. **Cultural Sensitivity Enhances Impact:** Recognising and respecting the unique culture of policing ensures that wellbeing initiatives are relevant and relatable. Tailored messaging, diverse representation, and alignment with core policing values reinforce the idea that wellbeing is not an add-on but integral to professional excellence.
5. **Leadership Is Essential:** Leaders set the tone for organisational culture. Their ability to model openness, encourage dialogue, and visibly support wellbeing initiatives determines the success of these efforts. Leadership must not only endorse initiatives but embody the principles of care, empathy, and resilience.

The Path Forward: Policing is an inherently challenging profession, but it is also one defined by resilience, teamwork, and a deep sense of purpose. By embedding communication and engagement into the heart of wellbeing strategies, organisations can create environments where officers and staff feel valued, supported, and empowered to thrive.

This chapter provides a roadmap for leveraging communication and engagement to transform the wellbeing landscape in policing. By prioritising these elements, organisations can not only enhance individual health and morale but also strengthen the collective capacity to meet the complex demands of policing with professionalism and care. Through sustained effort and a commitment to innovation, the journey towards a healthier, more resilient workforce begins—one conversation, one connection, and one step at a time.

18

COULD WEARABLE HEALTH TECHNOLOGY BE A SOLUTION TO THE ISSUES OF WELLBEING IN THE POLICE SERVICE?[1]

Carol Cox and Andy Rhodes

Introduction

The National Police Wellbeing Service, Oscar Kilo, was established as a national capability in 2018 to support the 43 forces of England and Wales, a workforce in excess of 260,000 staff. To add value, the chosen approach reflects recognised public health principles requiring a disciplined prioritisation process to ensure the national work is scalable, affordable, evidence-based and personalised.

Whilst technology and data insights are used in core policing functions to investigate, prevent and detect crime, less attention has been given to their application in workplace health strategies, and this chapter sets out details of an ambitious vision to harness these new innovations whilst influencing the industry to help improve the health of emergency service personnel.

According to McKinsey's Future of Wellness survey (McKinsey & Company 2024), wearable technology is playing an increasingly significant role in the wellbeing market, reflecting a growing desire for personalised, data-driven health solutions.

Approximately 50% of surveyed consumers have purchased a fitness wearable, with smartwatches being the most prevalent. Emerging devices like biometric rings and continuous glucose monitors are also gaining popularity. Notably, over 75% of respondents expressed openness to using wearable devices in the future.

Consumers are increasingly seeking personalised wellbeing experiences. Around 20% of consumers in the US and UK, and 30% in China, prefer products and services that utilise biometric data for tailored recommendations. Wearables, combined with generative AI, are facilitating this by offering customised workout plans, nutrition advice and sleep optimisation strategies.

The insights from McKinsey's survey highlight a clear direction of travel: Wearable technology is becoming integral to personalised wellbeing solutions. As consumers demand more tailored and scientifically validated health tools, the integration of advanced wearables with AI-driven analytics is poised to redefine the wellness landscape.

DOI: 10.4324/9781003518860-19

A decision was made to explore how wearable technology could be used in UK policing, and previous research into sleep, fatigue and recovery carried out by Oscar Kilo led to this national priority being chosen as the focus of the study.

Why Is Sleep, Fatigue and Recovery a National Policing Priority?

It is recognised that policing across the world is a high-stress occupation; the ordinary business of policing makes extraordinary demands on police officers. In the UK, cuts in police budgets and the reduction in the police workforce have resulted in individual workloads that officers are unable to manage. All of this has exacerbated a challenging situation, and finding ways to ameliorate the pressures on individual officers is a retention issue as much as it is a wellbeing issue.

The need for additional support for police officer wellbeing has never been clearer, as mentioned in recent years, the College of Policing has prioritised the wellbeing, subsequent support and awareness for all the policing family by establishing the Oscar Kilo, the National Police Wellbeing Service, 2018 and the Police Covenant 2022.

Oscar Kilo has created a priority workstream to take forward the sleep fatigue and recovery of police officers. This priority was based upon findings of the importance of sleep, fatigue and the link to shift work from several surveys by several sleep centres across the world (Rajaratnam et al., 2011, Violanti et al., 2017, Graham et al., 2020). These findings identified an acute problem within operational policing roles, particularly where shift working is required. With this robust evidence that a police officer's fatigue, sleep and recovery can be detrimental to health and a hidden operational risk, Oscar Kilo commissioned the research team at Liverpool John Moores' University (LJMU) to begin to investigate innovative wearable health technology (WHT). These studies were the largest of their kind in the world and were designed to establish if police officers engaged with wearable technology to support their wellbeing and if the health data collected identified any trends.

Wearable Health Technology Research (WHT)

Early studies (Jovanov, 2015; Wang, 2017; Liau, 2018) have indicated that WHT specifically in relation to smartwatches and their health benefits in monitoring conditions and promoting wellness. Liau (2018) specifically found that WHT and the regulation of participants' own data improved physical activity, which in turn could improve wellbeing and mental health. Other studies (Yurkiewicz, 2018) focused on specific conditions such as cancer patients and how smartwatches have assisted them in tracking their health with physical activity increasing (79%).

The use of wearable technology to improve health and fitness has in recent years boomed, with the annual growth of such technology estimated at 14.6% by 2030 (Wearable Technology Market Share & Trends Report, 2030). Advancements in the design of wearable technology to monitor health are on the increase, with more companies developing smart rings (Samsung 2024) that offer all the health benefits of watches, such as measuring sleep, heart rate and steps, but with new advanced features such as movement tracking. Globally, many companies are now investing in wearable technology for their employees.

Nonetheless, to date, the examination of the use of WHT in emergency service populations has received little attention, with most studies utilising WHT being conducted in the healthy general population and clinical populations (Germini et al., 2022). Although there have been studies assessing how WHT may be used to promote the health and wellbeing of employees in the workplace (Henning and Van de Ven, 2017) and how the technology may be used to detect issues such as burnout in healthcare professionals (Barac et al., 2024). Recent studies utilising wearable technology on police personnel—such as De Vries et al (2022) and Cox et al (2024)—both do provide some evidence that WHT could provide some benefits to police staff, although small numbers were used.

Early Pilot Studies of WHT on UK Policing

The early studies carried out by LJMU and Oscar Kilo were used to evaluate the use of wearable technology on different groups of police personnel, with a focus on sleep, fatigue and recovery. Due to the limited research evaluating wearable health technology on police officers and staff, the early studies utilised reflective grounded theory (Strauss and Corbin 1998) to allow the researchers to use their "own theoretical sensitivity" to interpret the literature and findings and let the research develop. The first study (Study 1) began with 36 new recruit police officers wearing a fitness band, with further studies (Study 2, n = 40; Study 3, n = 64) utilising police personnel from diverse groups such as firearms officers, counter terrorism, menopausal staff and others (from various police forces across the UK), using different WHT. These early pilot studies were the groundwork for a large STAR-funded longitudinal study with 121 police personnel from Merseyside Police over a period of nine months.

Findings from Early Pilot Studies, with Police Personnel across the UK

Study 1 was designed with two aims in mind: To critically analyse whether new police officers engaged with WHT for their wellbeing and to critically analyse if the health data (sleep, resting heart rate, heart rate variability and recovery) indicated any patterns or trends. The early results from Study 1 identified that before commencing any study with WHT, there was the need to establish trust with participants. During this study, recruit officers with only one year of service appeared socialised into policing and displayed negative aspects of police culture, with a lack of trust of the researchers and the organisation from the onset. This lack of trust was grounded in their questions referring to data retention and storage and how data could be misused for the officer's detriment. Study 1 also revealed evidence of a decrease in some physiological metrics such as heart rate variability (HRV) when the officers were not carrying out shift work, compared to when they were working on a shift. The physiological findings from Study 1 and the unanticipated finding that recruit officers began to talk about their wellbeing with peers led to further studies with different WHT and diverse groups of officers.

Studies 2 and 3 had the same aims in that the researchers were examining relationships between WHT and sleep, fatigue and recovery, but with different technology and different units of officers from forces across the UK. Again, these studies revealed that trust and confidence were important considerations for police personnel, with questions raised such as who had access to their data, storage etc. These studies also revealed that firearms officers recorded shorter periods of sleep (and less sleep overall), had a lower sleep performance and less sleep consistency, but a lower resting heart rate suggesting they were fitter than the mixed personnel group.

Crucially, all these early pilot studies were indicating to the research team that wearable health technology was providing positive results, with police personnel recognising the potential value of biometric data in the context of their future wellbeing.

STAR Longitudinal Study

In July 2024, OK and the research team at LJMU received funding from the STAR fund to develop a longitudinal WHT study with Merseyside Police. This study was designed to address the question, "Can wearable technology and education improve the quality of life of police officers and staff?" Learning from the pilot studies was incorporated into the design of this new study, which included a data protection plan, to ensure the trust and confidence of participants. Over 300 staff were interested in taking part in this study, but due to the limits of numbers of WHT, only 121 places were available. Again, results from this study indicated that WHT was valuable to have and increased health awareness, with improved sleep habits and quality of sleep. Importantly, several health behaviour changes were made by the participants across the study; these included exercise, positive diet changes and sleep adjustments, with most participants indicating that the study had led to positive outcomes. Results from the study not predicted were the links that the participants made with their positive behavioural changes and work outcomes. Results indicated that participants who remained on the study for the full nine months believed their "resilience at work," (60%) "capacity for work," (57%) "ability to handle work stress" (57%) and their "concentration at work" (55%) had all improved during the study. Nearly half stated that the changes were beneficial for their "overall performance at work" (48%). Moreover, many survey respondents were also positive regarding the effect of the behaviour changes on other aspects of work such as their "desire to continue working in a policing environment," (42%) "attendance at work," (38%) "enjoyment at work," (38%) and "enthusiasm for work" (30%). It was also encouraging that over half of respondents (52%) suggested that they were having conversations about wellbeing with colleagues due to the study. Further to this, 43% believed they were less likely to take sickness absence, and 27% suggested they were less likely to leave the police in the future.

At the beginning of the longitudinal study, 58% of participants suggested they had thought about leaving the police due to the impact of the job on their wellbeing. These studies clearly showed OK to the research team at LJMU that innovative solutions are needed to support police wellbeing and that for most police personnel involved in the studies, when tailored correctly, WHT could be an effective solution.

As with all studies, there are limitations, most notably the fact that participants were part of a research study, which can make it difficult for researchers to identify which aspects of the study produced the changes identified, McCambridge et al (2014) termed this "Research Participation Effects" to enable researchers to understand such biases. For the longitudinal study described, a control group was used, and although some behavioural changes were identified for this group, these were not as great as the group with the WHT, which enabled the researchers to have greater confidence in their findings. It is also worth noting that a minority of participants did express negativity towards the WHT and removed it, suggesting WHT is not for every individual.

Police Trust, Confidence and Wellbeing

Police culture and socialisation in early studies was found to be a barrier to participation in studies employing WHT (Cox et al., 2024). Police culture can be enduring and resistant to change (Van Maanen, 1973), as well as "deeply entrenched and persuasive" (Davies and Thomas, 2003). However, of note is the difference between the described pilot studies using WHT, which revealed some aspects of police culture with a *lack of trust of outsiders*, lack of acceptance to change and a refusal by many to wear the technology (Cox et al., 2024), in comparison the STAR longitudinal study, where these issues were not evident.

In contrast to previous studies (Studies 1–3), the STAR study was developed at a time when the research team had a data protection agreement in place and had been engaged with the Occupational Health Department of the police forces, gaining trust with officers. This groundwork completed by LJMU and Oscar Kilo to increase trust and ensure belief in the confidentiality of the research was vital to ameliorate some elements of negative police culture (e.g., lack of trust). Any future initiatives or research concerning the use of WHT with police officers and staff will need to ensure the correct support package concerning data protection and confidentiality is in place as it was for the present study. It is this groundwork which ultimately allowed for successful recruitment and uptake.

In summary, WHT can be utilised as a possible cost-effective solution to wellbeing in the police service, but there must be a full support wrap-around package. This support package must incorporate several identifiable stages, giving the individual responsibility for their wellbeing and enabling the most suitable participants to benefit.

Translating Research into Practice

The STAR study has provided a much-needed evidence base to address workforce challenges in relation to workplace restrictions, absence and retention. Despite the wealth of evidence linking investment in workplace health to productivity, performance, attrition and quality of service, there remains scepticism amongst decision-makers faced with making hard choices with limited funding.

The study has proven that, if the right conditions are in place, police officers and staff will seize the opportunity to use wearable health technology to learn about what works for them, change behaviours and engage with their organisation to shape the way health systems are designed with their needs at the forefront, not as an afterthought.

Adopting a person-centred approach which recognises that there must be a balance between organisational and personal responsibility whilst accepting individuals have a right to data privacy and to make their own choices, enabled rather than coerced by their organisation.

A well-thought-through system where humans and technology operate together with clear boundaries, non-negotiable privacy, ethical practice and therefore high levels of trust presents game-changing opportunities for workplace health globally.

Conclusion and Next Steps – Operation AKESO

Operation AKESO will take the findings of the STAR study and the system which was designed to accompany the wearable technology and deploy it at scale into several proof of concepts across the 43 police forces in England and Wales.

Op AKESO will enable the police service to further refine this innovation opportunity taking into account critical success factors such as cohort selection, cost, peer support and personalised coaching.

Note

1 This work summarises reports from LJMU for OK, corresponding authors for reports Karecha, J., Ward, M., Bannell, D., O'Brien, F., Pajon, L., Baker, J., Yates, J.

References

Barac, M., Scaletty, S., Hassett, L. C., Stillwell, A., Croarkin, P. E., Chauhan, M., Cox, C., Yates, J., O'brien, F., Pajon, L., Farrell, A., Ward, M., Mccabe, P., James, A., & Mcnamara-catalano, I. (2024). Wearable technology: A wellbeing option for serving police officers and staff? A comparison of results of a pilot study with firearms officers and a group of mixed officers and staff. *International Journal of Environmental Research and Public Health*, *21*, 186.

Davies, A., & Thomas, R. (2003). Talking cop: Discourses of change and policing identities. *Public Administration*, *81*, 681–699.

De Vries, H. J., Pennings, H. J., Van Der Schans, C. P., Sanderman, R., Oldenhuis, H. K., & Kamphuis, W. (2022). Wearable-measured sleep and resting heart rate variability as an outcome of and predictor for subjective stress measures: A multiple N-of-1 observational study. *Sensors*, *23*, 332.

Germini, F., Noronha, N., Borg Debono, V., Abraham Philip, B., Pete, D., Navarro, T., Keepanasseril, A., Parpia, S., De Wit, K., & Iorio, A. (2022). Accuracy and acceptability of wrist-wearable activity-tracking devices: Systematic review of the literature. *Journal of Medical Internet Research*, *24*, e30791.

Graham, L., Brown, N., Plater, M., Gracey, S., Legate, N., & Weinstein, N. (2020). *National policing well-being survey 2019: Summary of evidence and insights*. Durham University. Available at: https://oscarkilo.org.uk/app/uploads/2020/06/ISSUED-2019-National-PoliceWell-being-Survey-1.pdf Accessed June 18, 2023.

Henning, A., & Van De Ven, K. (2017). 'Counting your steps': The use of wearable technology to promote employees' health and wellbeing. *Performance Enhancement and Health*, *5*, 123–124.

Jovanov, E. (2015). Preliminary analysis of the use of smartwatches for longitudinal health monitoring. In *Annual International Conference of the IEEE Engineering in Medicine and Biology Society*. IEEE Engineering in Medicine and Biology Society.

Liau, A. K. (2018). A quasi-experimental study of a fitbit-based self-regulation intervention to improve physical activity, well-being, and mental health. *Cyberpsychology, Behavior, and Social Networking*, *21*(11).

McCambridge, J., Witton, J., & Elbourne, D. R. (2014). Systematic review of the Hawthorne effect: New concepts are needed to study research participation effects. *Journal of Clinical Epidemiology*, *67*(3), 267–277. https://doi.org/10.1016/j.jclinepi.2013.08.015

McKinsey & Company (2014). https://www.mckinsey.com/industries/consumer-packaged-goods/our-insights/the-trends-defining-the-1-point-8-trillion-dollar-global-wellness-market-in-2024

Rajaratnam, S. M., Barger, L. K., Lockley, S. W., Shea, S. A., Wang, W., Landrigan, C. P., O'brien, C. S., Qadri, S., Sullivan, J. P., & Cade, B. E. (2011). Sleep disorders, health, and safety in police officers. *JAMA*, *306*, 2567–2578.

Strauss, A., & Corbin, J. (1998). *Basics of qualitative research: Techniques and procedures for developing grounded theory* (2nd ed.). Sage Publications, Inc.

Wang, I. (2017). *Using Smartwatches to improve health and wellness.* [Online] Retrieved December 2, 2024, from http://mason.gmu.edu/~iwang2/Using%20Smartwatches%20to%20Improve%20Health%20and%20Wellness%20Final%20Draft_Isabelle%20Wang.pdf

Van Maanen, J. (1973). Observations on the making of policemen. *Human Organization*, *32*, 407–418.

Violanti, J. M., Charles, L. E., Mccanlies, E., Hartley, T. A., Baughman, P., Andrew, M. E., Fekedulegn, D., Ma, C. C., Mnatsakanova, A., & Burchfiel, C. M. (2017). Police stressors and health: A state-of-the-art review. *Policing: An International Journal of Police Strategies & Management*, *40*, 642–656.

Yurkiewicz I. R., Simon P., Liedtke M., Dahl G., & Dunn T. (2018). Effect of fitbit and iPad wearable technology in health-related quality of life in adolescent and young adult cancer patients. *Journal of Adolescencent and Young Adult Oncology* 7, 579–583. https://doi.org/10.1089/jayao.2018.0022

19

MENTAL HEALTH SUPPORT IN UK POLICING

Tony Parnell

Introduction

UK policing provides a wide range of opportunities with a diverse job role availability. The roles available within policing offer great opportunities and challenges. Those working within the policing environment are offered a high level of support in all areas to enable them to carry out these roles effectively and safely. The impact on physical and psychological wellbeing is central to this support process. The biggest growth in support in recent years has been within psychological support. This is in recognition of the potential for negative mental health responses resulting from carrying out the roles within policing.

In this chapter, I will be discussing the range of psychological support systems available across the UK policing estate. The chapter will outline these psychological support systems, the processes and underlying applications and how they address specific psychological impacts and mental health issues.

When discussing support systems within UK policing, it is important to note that there is a significant difference in the support offered across the 43 home office police forces in the UK. These include a range of occupational health and psychological services systems across the UK police estate. The most common resources include: (1) fully in-house system – where both occupational health and psychological services are provided by in-house staffed departments, who provide all of the services; (2) externally provided services – both occupational health and psychological services – these are usually provided by an EAP (Employer Assistance Programme – an external provider who carries out all of the services agreed in a contracted service plan); (3) a hybrid service where there is a mixture of a limited in-house team and an external provider contracted to carry out limited services. There are also variations on these three systems. Those working within policing in the UK would need to explore what support is available in their workplace.

DOI: 10.4324/9781003518860-20

The areas of psychological support we will address in this chapter are as follows: One-to-One Therapy, Post-Incident Psychological Support, High-Risk Role psychological screening/surveillance and Psychoeducation inputs.

One-to-One Therapy (EMDR/TF-CBT/PCA)

One-to-one therapy is often seen as the main process of therapeutic psychological support. One-to-one therapy relates to the process of a person seeking psychological therapy from a trained and qualified mental health professional; these include: psychologists, psychotherapists, counsellors, CBT therapists and EMDR therapists. As the name suggests, this is characterised by the individual nature of the interaction. A variation on one-to-one therapy is that of group therapy. This is where a group of individuals (usually related in either personal relationships, occupational or role relationships), seek support from a trained mental health therapist/facilitator.

The process of one-to-one therapy is used to address significant psychological issues/symptoms that an individual may be experiencing. The way these issues may be addressed will be determined by an initial review/assessment. This is where the therapist and client discuss the issues experienced along with associated symptoms (if present), and a therapy plan is developed. Depending on the type of therapy that is utilised within the therapy process, this assessment/review may be completed in an initial single or couple of sessions prior to engaging in the therapy process.

There are a number of therapeutic approaches that can be used; these hold a focus on different aspects of the problem/issue to be addressed. This is where there has been a great deal of confusion. When looking for therapy, it can be difficult to know which therapy type could be the most advantageous to address the issue/problem. Understanding what therapies are available within a specific force is essential. The psychological/therapy service within an organisation will be able to identify what types of therapy are offered and what might be useful to address the presenting issue/problem.

When looking at what kinds of therapy approaches are available, it is important to review the most popular/prevalent. These include, but are not an exhaustive or complete list (singular models) – person-centred therapy, cognitive behavioural therapy (CBT), psychodynamic therapy, eye movement desensitisation and reprocessing (EMDR) and also included are variations of core approaches – (combined approaches) – which include integrative therapy, eclectic therapy and pluralistic therapy.

Individual organisations may not have all these approaches available; however, they will certainly have access to the core approaches and possibly more specialist approaches should they be required. The therapists available will utilise one or more of the approaches described and as such will create a therapy plan following discussion with the individual seeking support. This plan can be adapted throughout the therapy process in relation to the developed awareness arising from the therapy.

Achieving a good fit with the therapist and therapy process has been shown to enhance the outcome of therapy. This is why it is important for the individual to be open and clear about what they need when engaging in therapy. Therapists are used to having open and focused conversations about aims and objectives and will not be upset or offended if the individual feels that the therapist or the therapy process is not a good match for them.

In relation to the types of therapy, individuals may access, there are a significant number of differing approaches that can make it difficult to know which would be the best fit for the individual and their issue/problem. An individual may feel that a therapy process which holds a focus on cognition/thinking or one which addresses emotional impact would work better for them.

Researching the type and focus of therapy may be useful, so an individual can choose and have an informed and open conversation about their needs at the referral stage or later with the therapist. Identifying what types of therapy are available within the individual's organisation is a great starting point to develop more information and research that can inform the individual's choice.

One-to-one therapy can be a great resource and can be central to insight and resolution of specific issues that emerge out of daily and work life. In the policing environment, individuals will be exposed to more than the average difficult and sometimes traumatic experiences. One-to-one therapy is provided to address these issues should they emerge. It seems a reasonable assumption that if policing requires individuals to face and confront difficult and traumatic situations as part of their working life, it provides evidence-based and professional support at any point should the person need it. This is why one-to-one therapy is offered within all policing environments in the UK.

To aid decision-making and clarify some key points in the therapy options available, here is a brief summary of three of the main therapies available within the policing environment. Two of these approaches are recommended by the National Institute of Clinical Excellence (NICE, 2018), for the treatment of post-traumatic stress disorder (PTSD). The first of these is EMDR.

EMDR

Eye movement desensitisation and reprocessing (EMDR) is based on the Adaptive Information Processing (AIP) Model. This proposes that most psychological disturbance has its foundations within distressing past events that have not been appropriately processed (Shapiro, 1997).

The model proposes – with severe trauma, an imbalance occurs in the nervous system, causing a block with the unprocessed associated disturbing information encoded neurologically. Eye movements (EM) or other bilateral stimulation facilitate adaptive reprocessing on both a neurological and consequent 'mental change' level. With each set of EMs, the disturbing information moves at an accelerating rate along the neurophysiological pathways. EMDR treatment progresses through memory networks or 'channels', which are accessed through targets or 'nodes'. The precise mechanism by which the AIP model produces these changes is unclear. Shapiro suggests possibilities such as – dual attention focusing, the effects of neuronal bursts and de-conditioning caused by a relaxation response (Shapiro, 1997).

Alternatives to this explanation have been proposed by other researchers who have proposed: 'reverse learning' (Hassard, 1996) and 'an orienting response' (Armstrong & Vaughan, 1996).

EMDR is driven by bilateral brain stimulation, which results from a client tracking the therapist's fingers from side to side (or by sound moving from ear to ear or by tapping the hands left and right), which stimulates brain activity, alternating between the left and the right hemisphere of the brain. Simultaneously, the client reactivates an image, with its accompanying sensory experiences, of a traumatic event, along with the associated distorted negative self-beliefs. The process generates emotions, which are often felt as body sensations during the bilateral stimulation.

The client is instructed to uncritically follow his/her thoughts and associations, which often leads to the retrieval of old memories and rapid insights, accompanied by a systemic letting go of the traumatic event and the symptoms associated with it. After an EMDR therapy process, the person can adjust their belief to integrate an adapted belief such as – the crisis is in the past, or for example, they were not responsible, they are safe now and they can go on with their lives. This results in a person finally letting go and engaging in recovery and healing.

To summarise, EMDR (Shapiro, 1997) helps process the negative images, emotions, beliefs and body sensations associated with experiences that have become stuck; if left untreated, these can develop into a range of mental health problems.

The second NICE-recommended treatment for PTSD is trauma-focused cognitive behavioural therapy (TF-CBT).

TF-CBT

There are a number of well-researched cognitive behavioural therapies used within trauma work: prolonged exposure therapy (PE; Foa, Rothbaum, Riggs & Murdock, 1991), dialectical behaviour therapy (DBT; Becker & Zayfert, 2001), acceptance and commitment therapy (ACT; Hayes et al., 1999) and cognitive therapy (CT) for (PTSD; Beck, 1976; Ehlers & Clark, 2000; Ehlers et al., 2003; Tarrier et al., 1999).

I will briefly address one of the treatment processes, which come under the banner of TF-CBT: cognitive therapy for PTSD developed by Ehlers and Clark (2000).

Ehlers and Clark (2000) identified a key dilemma at the heart of therapeutic work with clients who present with a PTSD diagnosis that anxiety holds a focus on 'future' threat. PTSD holds a focus on memory for a past event. A key issue to overcome in the therapy process is that individuals are processing and/or remembering the trauma and/or its connective events in a way which poses a current threat to self. A significant implication for therapy is that within this approach the aim of therapy is to process the trauma, so it is seen as a time limited, past event which does not necessarily have global implications for the client's future.

This is a treatment model developed for people who become 'stuck' in their recovery, which holds a focus on identifying and reversing 'maintaining factors'. It is proposed that current threat arises as a consequence of excessively negative appraisals of the event and/or its connective events. This is a result of a number of factors: the fact that the trauma happened; the clients' behaviour and response in the event; the initial PTSD symptoms; the perceived response of others – these are often highly idiosyncratic and may reflect shattering or confirmation of previous beliefs.

Current threat arises as a consequence of the nature of trauma memory and unintentional triggering of memory fragments by a wide range of low-level cues along with poor intentional recall which influences the client's appraisals. The client's ability to recall the trauma within PTSD is often inhibited; this is commonly due to parts of memory being disjointed and lacking updating, confusion about the order of events that took place and important details potentially missing from the memory.

Ehlers and Clark (2000) identified the mismatch in memory processes from ordinary function to function expressed within a PTSD response. They identified that ordinary autobiographical memory is characterised by an awareness of remembering; emotion being less strong; details of the memory have context; the memories are rarely spontaneous and if they are spontaneous there is usually a closer specific match of triggers.

This differs when experiencing PTSD symptoms where autobiographical memories are characterised by involuntary re-experiencing of events and memories; a limited awareness of remembering 'nowness'; experiencing of the original emotions (physiology/behaviour); details without context as a result of memory not updated and memories and intrusive thoughts easily and involuntarily triggered from a wide range of triggers, sensory similarity and partial match triggers.

A key treatment strategy within this approach is to reduce the client's symptoms and their ability to control intrusive thoughts and imagery. The process of 'reliving' is fundamental to this therapy and is a central feature of the cognitive therapy approach to PTSD. The treatment component of reliving has three main goals; these are – **Goal 1**: To reduce re-experiencing by elaboration of trauma memory and identification of triggers by use of imaginal reliving, narrative, stimulus identification. **Goal 2**: To modify excessive negative appraisals by engaging directly with appraisals of the trauma and identifying 'hotspots', the use of cognitive therapy strategies to integrate new appraisals into the reliving process, engage with appraisals of related connected events by use of behavioural experiments. **Goal 3**: To drop the 'maintaining behaviours' and develop cognitive strategies that enhance the client's capacity to integrate, understand and update the trauma memories.

To summarise, cognitive therapy for trauma (TF-CBT) is focused on updating trauma memories and helping the client to integrate new information and interpretations of the initial trauma event. This enables the client to reduce trauma symptoms and disarm the sense of 'current threat' that those impacted by a significant trauma experience.

Another therapy widely used within UK policing settings is that of person-centred therapy (PCT). This therapy is not recommended by NICE for the treatment of PTSD; however, it has a wide utility for a range of psychological issues and is a key therapeutic approach offered within most therapy services.

PCT

Person-centred therapy (PCT), also known as client-centred therapy or Rogerian therapy was founded in the 1940s by American psychologist Carl Rogers (1951). The therapy proposed that given the right conditions, a person can reach their full potential and become their true self. He termed this process 'Self-Actualisation'. This actualisation process is seen as innate and accessible to everyone. To achieve self-actualisation, the person-centred therapist would need to offer – (1) **Unconditional Positive Regard**; this is the process of offering acceptance and valuing of the client within the therapy process, (2) **Congruence**; this is the process of the therapist being honest and transparent in how they experience you and your world, (3) **Empathic Understanding**; this is the therapist's effort to accurately perceive and communicate the client's subjective world, feelings and meanings as if it were their own, without adding their own interpretations.

Person-centred therapy holds some core assumptions – it holds a focus on the 'whole' person, holds the quality of the therapeutic relationship at its core and proposes that the quality of the therapeutic relationship between client and therapist is central to the positive outcome of therapy and that the therapy process is informed by practice-based research.

Person-centred therapy holds at its core a non-directive attitude/humanistic approach and sees the client as the person who leads the process, with the therapist taking a facilitator role. This is expressed in a manner where the therapist and client create a facilitative environment where conditions exist to promote growth, challenge and change. In practical terms, person-centred therapy holds a focus on the potential for positive, personal and social change. It holds the view that environmental influences, specifically those impacting relationships with others. These include relationships within therapy and other facilitative relationships. These relationships are seen as influential in whether the person generates a positive or negative self-concept and, by extension, whether they engage in healthy or unhealthy functioning.

To summarise, person-centred therapy holds a focus on the present, exploring current experiences and feelings. The client is seen as the expert in their own problems and difficulties. The therapist is seen as a facilitator, helping the client to become more self-actualising. This is achieved by the use of a non-judgemental approach which leads to the client's self-discovery and understanding, offering greater self-awareness. This awareness can lead to accessing personal resources which initiates personal growth and the ability to address and resolve problems.

Post-Incident Psychological Support

(TRiM/CISM)

One of the key mental health support processes offered within UK Policing is that of post-incident psychological support. There are a number of support systems available. They include, but not exclusive to – Trauma Risk Assessment (TRiM), Critical Incident Stress Management (CISM), Psychological debriefing (Dyregrov) and Emergency Services Trauma Intervention Programme (ESTIP). All of these models approach post-incident support in a similar manner. They hold a focus on helping the participants to engage with the trauma experience in a structured and safe manner. They, of course, differ in their application of this process but hold a general perspective that shares key elements.

To gain an understanding of this process, it is worth looking at a couple of these approaches in a little detail. The first of these is TRiM.

TRiM

Trauma Risk Assessment (TRiM) (Jones et al., 2017) is a peer-ed, evidence-based intervention for assessing and supporting individuals following exposure to traumatic events. This process is designed to help mitigate psychological harm by identifying risk factors and signposting to support. This process is carried out by non-clinical practitioners who are not counsellors or therapists. TRiM practitioners are trained in the process of trauma risk assessment by attending a formal training course which holds a focuses on the impact of trauma events on individuals and offering confidentiality, guidance and support.

TRiM was originally developed in the 1990s by the UK military – the Royal Marines. This development came as a result of observations following the Falklands conflict. It replaced a less successful single session model that was previously employed. The model is based on an 'active monitoring' principle. This principle was identified by the National Institute of Clinical Excellence (NICE, 2018) in its guidance for the management of post-traumatic stress disorder.

TRiM has a risk assessment matrix at its core; this is designed to identify individuals and groups/teams who may be at risk of developing mental health issues as a result of exposure to traumatic events. This risk assessment categorises individuals into risk levels from low to high. This is based on their likelihood of developing stress-related issues. The risk level can aid in prioritising support and intervention to those who are at higher risk.

TRiM practitioners are trained in listening skills, empathy and how to recognise trauma-related symptoms and impacts in peers. The process is a peer-to-peer interaction, and it is common for colleagues to help each other following a traumatic event by developing a supportive and resilient workplace environment. The aim of TRiM is to address trauma early and prevent long-lasting psychological impacts.

Another post-incident intervention process offering a different perspective on post-incident support that is worth looking at in a little detail is CISM.

CISM

Critical Incident Stress Management (CISM) (Everly & Mitchell, 1999) was developed during the 1970s and then was widely applied in the 1980s to police, firefighters and emergency medical responders and other emergency personnel. The health and human services commission established the Texas CISM Network in 1992 to assist emergency response workers who had experienced or survived a critical incident. CISM has been refined and developed since the early introduction of the model.

CISM is a multicomponent structured system of education, prevention and support for those exposed to traumatic events. It is not a therapy intervention and confidentiality is central to the process. There are a range of elements within the model which include pre-incident preparedness, immediate crisis intervention methods (defusing and critical incident stress debriefing) and post-incident follow-up and referral. The key aim for the process is to normalise the individual's experienced psychological, physiological and emotional trauma reactions and offer psychoeducation. The wider education elements are offered to help individuals understand that their stress responses are normal reactions to abnormal events.

There are a number of elements within the CISM process: pre-crisis education, disaster demobilisations and pre-deployment briefing sessions for large groups, defusing, debriefing, crisis management briefing, Critical incident adjustment support and follow-up and referral mechanisms for further assessment and therapy.

Two of the most utilised group-focused elements are (1) defusing; this is a short intervention with a small group/team that is designed to take place shortly after the crisis event (usually 4–12 hours following the event). The defusing sessions usually take around 30–40 mins to complete with the group.

And (2) debriefing – Critical Incident Stress Debriefing (CISD); these sessions are active and supportive interventions carried out by trained facilitators to support groups/team members during the period of distress resulting from a critical/traumatic incident and designed to build on the group/team's resistance to traumatic stressors. These usually take place a number of days following the critical incident. The psychological debrief is structured into a 1–3-hour session (depending on the size of the group). The debriefing format follows a seven-stage process that engages the group in discussion with the focus of the traumatic event and the personal impact it has had. It also employs a significant level of psychoeducation input; this is to normalise the trauma responses and create space for the participants to explore, in safety, the experience. This process is facilitated by CISM practitioners who are trained within a formal structured training programme.

To summarise, CISM offers a comprehensive process of psychological support that facilitates individuals and groups to cope with the psychological impact of traumatic and critical events. It has utility in environments where repeated exposure to critical and traumatic events makes up the working environment, such as policing and other emergency response professions. The primary goal of CISM is to reduce stress/trauma symptoms and prevent the development of long-term psychological disorders like PTSD. The process of normalising symptoms resulting from traumatic exposure and promoting emotional recovery by means of psychoeducation is central to the CISM process.

High-Risk Role Psychological Surveillance/Screening

One of the significant methods of identifying and addressing potential mental health issues is the development of psychological screening/surveillance. UK policing has incorporated a process of psychological screening and surveillance; this is to monitor officers' mental health and identify those at higher risk of psychological distress due to the roles they carry out. Oscar Kilo and the National Police Wellbeing Service (NPWS) have created the Psychological Risk Management (PRM) programme (CoP, 2022). This is a proactive support process that aims to identify and support those who may be at risk of psychological impact.

Different police forces across the UK have varying applications of this process; however, most have identified those officers and staff who work directly within 'high-risk roles' within the organisation as being the focus of this screening and surveillance process. The College of Policing (CoP) identified a core list of 'high-risk roles' within policing, which has been used by most forces as the baseline for the identification of high-risk roles within their organisations. These are as follows:

- Counter Terrorism
- Crime Scene Investigation
- Dedicated Source Unit
- Digital Forensic Teams

- Disaster Victim Identification
- Family Liaison Officer – Crime
- Family Liaison Officer – Traffic
- Firearms
- Force Collision Investigation Unit
- Hostage and Crisis Negotiators
- Internet Child Abuse Teams
- Offender Management
- Paedophile Online Investigation Unit
- Serious Collision Investigation
- Violent and Sex Offender Register

Although the College of Policing (2022) have identified these key high-risk roles within policing, some forces have extended this list to incorporate other teams/departments that they have within their own force. This is done to take into account roles that, due to the size of the force or range of specific specialisms, are not represented on the CoP list.

The process of risk assessment/surveillance follows five main phases: role risk assessment, assessment, reviewing, reporting and further intervention. The process of psychological surveillance is a joint endeavour between NPWS and an appointed assessment supplier – Noreen Tehrani Associates Psychological Screening Ltd (NTAPS). The Force Management Team and Force Occupational Health (OH) Service are also central to this process.

To summarise the psychological surveillance process, the identified individual (within a high-risk role) completes an online battery of psychometric and questionnaire-based forms. These can be completed over a period of time, saved and returned to at a later date before submission. This was constructed to accommodate time restrictions within the roles of the participants and to reduce stress during the completion process.

Once submitted (by secure link), the provider runs an assessment analysis protocol and generates an individual bespoke report for each participant. This report is sent (by secure link) to the force OH Team. The report will have one of three outcomes: (1) no follow-up required, (2) requiring a structured interview (SI) and (3) requiring a psychological assessment (PA). These reports will be reviewed by the OH clinician, and follow-ups arranged where required.

This process has been in place with a number of police forces nationwide for a number of years and has identified that an average of around 15% of those completing the psychological surveillance process are referred for follow-up (either SI or PA). When follow-up is completed, referral to psychological support (therapy) or other support options is available. This has contributed to access to support for a number of individuals at an early stage and resulted in a reduced impact of potential mental health problems.

Psychoeducation Inputs

Bespoke Inputs Range of Topics

Another area of mental health psychological support that is offered in some police forces in the UK is that of bespoke psychoeducation inputs. These take a variety of formats and are dependent on the resources and facilities available within the OH or wellbeing departments. For those organisations that provide this service, these inputs can be created in collaboration with the department or team requiring the support. Common input subjects requested are: trauma, bereavement/loss, anxiety, workplace stress, menopause, mindfulness, relaxation techniques, suicide/self-harm, etc. Any subject that the mental health team within the OH department has knowledge or experience in providing. This is easier to offer if the OH department has access to psychological therapists or counsellors, who will have experience of working with most mental health issues as part of their therapy role and will usually be able to create a bespoke input to meet the needs of the requesting team.

Summary

In this chapter, I have discussed a range of psychological support systems available across the UK policing estate. The chapter has outlined these psychological support systems and how they address specific psychological impacts and mental health issues.

When discussing support systems within UK Policing, it is important to note that there is a significant difference in the support offered across the 43 home office police forces in the UK. These differences have a direct impact on the type and range of support systems that will be available within different forces in the UK.

All mental health support systems within the policing estate are designed to offer an evidence-based psychological support process. Whether the specific force offers a fully in-house system – where both occupational health and psychological services are provided by in-house staffed departments, who provide all of the services or externally provided services – both occupational health and psychological services – these are usually provided by an Employer Assistance Programme (EAP) or a hybrid service where there is a mixture of a limited in-house team and an external provider contracted to carry out limited services. All are focused on providing services and support to individuals and teams in response to mental health needs. Resilience development, post-incident support and general psychological support are all available to support those who work within the policing environment. These services are designed to be focused on the needs of a workforce consistently exposed to high-level stressors and have developed interventions to counterbalance these impacts. Given the diversity of mental health support offered across the UK policing environment, it would be useful for those who work within policing, in any role, to explore what support is available in your workplace.

References

Armstrong, M. S., & Vaughan, K. (1996). An orienting response model of eye movement desensitization. *Journal of Behavioral Therapy and Experimental Psychiatry*, *27*(1), 21–32.

Beck, A. T. (1976). *Cognitive therapy and the emotional disorders*. International Universities Press.

Becker, C. B., & Zayfert, C. (2001). Integrating DBT-based techniques and concepts to facilitate exposure treatment for PTSD. *Cognitive and Behavioral Practice*, *8*(2), 107–122.

Ehlers, A., & Clark, D. M. (2000). A cognitive model of post traumatic stress disorder. *Behaviour Research and Therapy*, *38*, 319–345.

Ehlers, A., & Clark, D. M., Hackman, A., McManus, F., Fennell, M., Herbert, C., & Mayou, R. (2003). A randomized control trial of cognitive therapy, a self. *General Psychiatry*, *60*(10), 1024–1032.

Everly, G. S., & Mitchell, J. T. (1999). *Critical Incident Stress Management- CISM – A new era and standard of care in crisis intervention.* (2nd ed.). Chevron Publishing.

Foa, E., Rothbaum, B. O., Riggs, D. S., & Murdock, T. B. (1991). Treatment of posttraumatic stress disorder in rape victims: A comparison between cognitive-behavioral procedures and counseling. *Journal of Consulting & Clinical Psychology*, *59*(5), 715–723.

Hassard, A. (1996). Reverse learning and the physiological basis of eye movement desensitization. *Medical Hypotheses*, *47*(1), 277–282.

Hayes, S. C., Strosahi, K. D., & Wilson, K. G. (1999). *Acceptance and commitment therapy: An experiential approach to behavior change.* Guilford Press.

Hesketh, I., Tehrani, N., & Harrison, J. (2017). *'Psychological Risk Management: Introduction & Guidance.'* College of Policing Ltd. Available at: https://assets.college.police.uk/s3fs-public/2021-02/psychological-risk-management.pdf Accessed November 19, 2025.

Jones, N., Burdett, H., Green, K., & Greenberg, N. (2017). Trauma risk Management (TRiM): Promoting help seeking for mental health problems among combat-exposed UK military personnel. *Psychiatry*, *80*(3), 236–251.

National Institute of Clinical Evidence (NICE). (2018). Post-traumatic stress disorder: NICE Guideline, NG116, Pub – Dec 05, 2018.

Rogers, C. (1951). *Client-centred therapy: Its current practice, implications and theory.* London: Constable.

Shapiro, F., & Forrest, M. S (1997). *EMDR The breakthrough "eye movement" therapy for overcoming anxiety, stress, and trauma.* Brunner- Routledge.

Tarrier, N., Sommerfield, C., Pilgrim, H., & Humphreys, L. (1999). Cognitive therapy or imaginal exposure in the treatment of post-traumatic stress disorder: Twelve month follow-up. *British Journal of Psychiatry*, *175*, 571–575.

20

MOVING FORWARD

Considering the Future of Police Mental Health and Wellbeing in the UK

Emma Williams and Sarah-Jane Lennie

Introduction

After nearly two decades of focus, discussion and research, mental health and wellbeing among British police officers and staff shows little improvement. Juxtaposed with the persistent and challenging issues related to police recruitment, retention, presenteeism, long-term sickness and a growth in demand, the evidence suggests a growing mental health crisis within British policing.

Despite increased awareness through the development and work of the National Police Wellbeing Service (NPWS), a national survey on police wellbeing and a volume of academic research, police wellbeing is still not prioritised enough in conversations about workforce planning, prevention, productivity or efficiency at a senior level. Nor is it considered in equal balance to physical ill health in policing or publicly debated in the media to the same extent as it is about other public services such as those that work in the National Health Service.

The authors feel that raising the profile of this crisis and further recognition is urgently required especially as police officers are at considerable risk of experiencing health inequalities when it comes to mental wellbeing. Indeed, their vocation alone puts them at risk of concerning health inequalities. The consequences of this ignorance are evident not only within the service – through rising issues with retention, recruitment and sickness absence – but also in the communities officers serve. Without a healthy and present workforce, can chief officers and commissioners realistically expect to meet operational demand or deliver the professional, compassionate police service the public expects? Furthermore, what might these factors mean for victim engagement, legitimacy and trust in the police?

In 2019, we saw a two-million-pound grant awarded to Oscar Kilo as the face of the NPWS (College of Policing, 2025). The work they have driven forward is vast and includes peer support training, a recently launched crisis line for officers, a bereavement service for families of officers and staff, wellbeing vans, OK9 welfare dogs, a national

DOI: 10.4324/9781003518860-21

wellbeing survey and much more. In 2018, the Front-Line Review was published (Home Office, 2018), and in 2019, the Home Secretary announced the Police Covenant, which pledges to those who serve or have served as police officers that 'they and their families are not disadvantaged as a result of that commitment and seeks to mitigate the impact that has on day-to-day life' (Home Office, 2021).

However, what we still see a gap in is evidence-based preventative work that can help to reduce the escalation of stress into burnout as it builds and accumulates. The last published Police National Wellbeing Survey (2022/23) showed that the average score for depression across the sample (15% of the workforce) was 5.31, and though this is reported to have improved from 2019, a reduction from 5.76 to 5.31 for police officers is not the success we should be shouting about. This is particularly pertinent when considered in the context of moderately high symptoms of anxiety at 6.31 for officers (moderate at 5.74 for police staff), high levels of fatigue (5.01 for officers and 4.51 for staff) and low levels of emotional energy (3.13 for officers and 3.89 for staff). This, coupled with a low sense of both perceived value and organisational and leadership support, indicates that police wellbeing is essentially in a critical state. Indeed, research from Brewin et al. (2022) showed combined results of PTSD and CPTSD at 20.6% across a national sample (international average of 14.2). That is, 1 in 4 of police officers or staff experiences PTSD or complex PTSD. The latest absence figures show that in the financial year 2024–25, over 17,700 officers across the UK were signed off work due to stress, depression, anxiety or PTSD (Sweeting & Bennie, 2025).

So, given we know, repeatedly, that there is a problem, is all this 'acknowledgement of the problem' merely window dressing? There is a significant gulf between the rhetoric espoused by the service and the reality of those on the front line (Lennie, 2019; Bikos, 2021; Foley et al., 2022). This is a critical issue when you consider the research from Charman and Bennett (2022) who demonstrate the link between psychological ill-health and voluntary resignations and that of Operation Soteria which found a connection between wellbeing and victim dissociation (Sondhi et al., 2025).

Too often we see articles lauding the benefits of some recent wellbeing intervention which only seek to airbrush the reality of police mental health for the officers on the ground. We believe that such portrayals can be damaging – not only to individual officers who are struggling with their mental health and read about these initiatives, but also to any potential work going forward that may address the true structural and endemic issues that exist as a barrier to true support and help seeking.

What We Know

Within this wealth of research into police mental health and wellbeing, we are seeing strong and consistent themes. Although there are some areas that remain under-examined (particularly a focus on diversity and intersectionality), there is much we do know. Despite an increase in dialogue around wellbeing, there is still a stigma around speaking out about mental health, and there is a distinct disconnect between the rhetoric and strategic intent often espoused by chief officers and the reality of those on the ground (Lennie, 2019; Foley et al., 2022). Despite being told that wellbeing is being taken seriously both locally and nationally, research continues to tell us that the implied message, delivered through process and policy, contributes to silencing and the stigmatisation of help seeking (Lennie, 2019; Edwards & Kotera, 2021). We continue to hear narratives about those seeking support experiencing a punitive response where officers are removed from their role and team, leading to social isolation; or placing someone on an action plan when they return to work after being off sick with depression – preventing them from entering promotion processes. It appears that the risk of speaking out involves a reduction in the ability to build social capital and credibility which exacerbates the issues even further.

Police culture often requires officers to suppress their authentic emotions, with officers and staff feeling that any emotional expression is perceived as a weakness and career limiting (Parkes et al., 2018; Edwards & Kotera, 2021). This leads to dissociative behaviour and emotional numbing by officers as they attempt to compartmentalise emotions and normal responses to traumatic stress, experienced as part of the operational role and often because of organisational stressors and processes (Lennie, 2019; Williams et al., 2022). This is clearly a barrier to help seeking and reflects a climate of distrust with colleagues and supervisors (Bell & Eski, 2016; Edwards & Kotera, 2021). Consider the work of Davies (2022) and the evidence about depersonalisation, emotional numbness and dissociation as forms of coping. Is it not naive to think that such maladaptive coping won't potentially lead to poor decision-making and misconduct outcomes? This has grave implications for public trust and police legitimacy.

There are clearly pockets of work going on around the country, often hard fought for by people who desperately want to see change for the better, but these are often independent, lack wider organisational support or cultural integration and are rarely evaluated, leading to an almost ritual de-funding of interventions. These decisions are worsened during times of budget cuts as wellbeing and its connectivity to police efficiencies and productivity are not recognised, and it seems that wellbeing initiatives can be the first to go. This not only removes the much-needed services but also sends a clear message to officers and staff as to how valued their mental health and wellbeing needs are. The impact of this on internal trustworthiness is not only damaging but also is a message that promotes further silencing.

We need to start thinking about wellbeing and good mental health through business models and as being connected to effectiveness and efficiency. If the service wishes to improve service delivery to the public, reduce investigation times, meet operational demand and be cost-effective, it needs to improve on the factors linked to productivity driven by an unhealthy workforce. There needs to be reduced presenteeism and staff absence, and a drive to both attract talent and retain staff. This means looking after officers and staff and genuinely understanding what it means to be healthy and well at work. In Charman and Bennett's research (2022, p. 170), they found that the greatest factor that might make officers consider returning to the service after voluntary resignation was improvements in welfare. This mirrors research looking at the role of compassion as a competitive advantage within business – perhaps something the police service should consider (Meechan, 2018; Paakkanen et al., 2024).

Prevention as an Opportunity

The research completed for Operation Soteria[1] showed clear stages of burnout amongst officers who investigate rape and sexual offences. We know that burnout is prevalent, but what this work concluded was that the profile of the workforce and stages of burnout differ. Using categories defined by Maslach, the research found that 39% of the sample were considered effective, around one-quarter (26%) ineffective or overextended (24%), and just over one in ten classified as disengaged or burnt out. The increased chances of becoming disengaged and burnt out were associated with several factors, including long-term, unaddressed stress, organisational and voluntary pressures to work despite being ill and being mid-career. Dissociation towards victims also worsened as officers became more burnt out. This is clear evidence of a significant need to identify symptoms of these stages of burnout and subsequent treatment pathways that prevent this build-up. The Soteria research further concluded that the organisational learning environment is a protective factor for burnout as is the value of credible and effective organisational health policies. The need to allow for and to validate officers' experiences of wellbeing at an earlier stage is illustrated in this work. Subsequently, we need to move towards a place which puts prevention at the heart of wellbeing strategies rather than responding to it when it might be too late. Alongside this, evaluations and understanding what works and for whom is critical. The new national wellbeing survey needs to be used more strategically to track national and local progress and help facilitate the measures required to track change. There needs to be accountability and governance over police wellbeing nationally as we move forward with police reform. Without a healthy workforce who are willing to advocate for their service by being empowered and supported, reform will fail.

Progress

The recently published Blue Light Wellbeing Framework and Wellbeing Strategy are positive starts to change. What local forces need is to become more willing to have difficult conversations with their staff about welfare and allow for those uncomfortable conversations and reflections to become the norm. Goodwill initiatives which go some way to legitimising senior teams' willingness to 'do something' are often not seen as salient by the front line as the core issues remain unquestioned. What Casey (2023) called 'initiativitis' is common but often such activities remain detached from proposed outcomes, are not evaluated effectively through good metrics and the underlying barriers to cultural change are not considered in the strategic planning. Wider centralised governance structures are required to hold leadership to account for staff wellbeing so that the workforce health needs are considered when new policies, structures and procedures are implemented. It needs to become embedded in business as usual. Policing is excellent at setting targets and defining expected charge rates but when it comes to those who are expected to deliver this, the progress is at best limited.

Planning Ahead

Developing a theory of change for the national wellbeing space which more coherently articulates where we are, what our desired outcomes for the future are and how we might measure and track progress would be beneficial. This needs to consider the barriers that inhibit real transformative change in this area of policing. These factors are often ignored as new activities are rolled out. Issues such as stigma to report wellbeing, cultural resistance, funding, competing priorities, demand and inconsistent delivery plans need to be considered and recognised when wellbeing plans are developed. Perhaps recognising some short-, medium- and long-term outcomes which start by ensuring that workforce wellbeing is a recognised priority in reform programmes, in policy development and in efficiency and business planning would raise the profile of the vital nature of this crisis in policing.

The Police Wellbeing Academic Reference group, which is attended by academics, local practitioners and more central portfolio leads, has started to consider these aspects in their planning. A theory of change to drive this work forward is a starting point – the next step is to put this into action.

Note

1 Operation Soteria was a Home Office-funded project exploring the investigation of rape and serious sexual offending.

References

Bell, S., & Eski, Y. (2016). 'Break a leg—it's all in the mind': police officers' attitudes towards colleagues with mental health issues. *Policing*, *10*(2), 95–101.

Bikos, L. J. (2021). "It's all window dressing:" Canadian police officers' perceptions of mental health stigma in their workplace. *Policing: An International Journal*, *44*(1), 63–76.

Brewin, C. R., Miller, J. K., & Burchell, B. (2022). Estimating the total prevalence of PTSD among the UK police force: Formal comment on Stevelink et al. (2020). *PLOS ONE*, *17*(5), e0268621. https://doi.org/10.1371/journal.pone.0268621

Casey, L. (2023). *Baroness Casey review, Final report: An independent review into the standards of behaviour and internal culture of the Metropolitan Police Service*. Metropolitant Police Service.

Charman, S., & Bennett, S. (2022). Voluntary resignations from the police service: The impact of organisational and occupational stressors on organisational commitment. *Policing and Society*, *32*(2), 159–178.

College of Policing. (2025). *Blue Light wellbeing framework*. Retrieved May 14, 2025, from Available at: https://www.oscarkilo.org.uk/blue-light-wellbeing-framework-blwf Accessed December 10, 2025.

Davies, L. E., Brooks, M., & Braithwaite, E. C. (2022). Compassion fatigue, compassion satisfaction, and burnout, and their associations with anxiety and depression in UK police officers: A mixed method analysis. *The Police Journal*, *96*(3), 509–529.

Edwards, A. M., & Kotera, Y. (2021). Mental health in the UK police force: A qualitative investigation into the stigma with mental illness. *International Journal of Mental Health and Addiction*, *19*(4), 1116–1134.

Foley, J., Hassett, A., & Williams, E. (2022). 'Getting on with the job': A systematised literature review of secondary trauma and Post-Traumatic Stress Disorder (PTSD) in policing within the United Kingdom (UK). *The Police Journal*, *95*(1), 224–252.

Home Office. (2018). *The Front Line review: Recommendation report*. The National Archives. Retrieved May 14, 2025, from https://www.gov.uk/government/publications/front-line-policing-review

Home Office. (2021). Response to the consultation on a Police Covenenant for England and Wales. Retrieved May 26, 2025, from GOV.UK. https://www.gov.uk/government/consultations/police-covenant-for-england-and-wales/outcome/response-to-the-consultation-on-a-police-covenant-for-england-and-wales-accessible-version

Lennie, S. J. (2019). *Emotional (in) authenticity: The psychological impact of emotional labour on the police officers of England and Wales* (Doctoral dissertation, Manchester Metropolitan University).

Meechan, F. (2018). *The compassion at work Toolkit*. The National Forum for Health and Wellbeing at work. Retrieved June 1, 2025, from https://www.researchgate.net/publication/322404395_Compassion_at_Work_Toolkit?enrichId=rgreq-f6432fe3d13b7ae6b605ad613c34c18f-XXX&enrichSource=Y292ZXJQYWdlOzMyMjQwNDM5NTtBUzo2MjUwMTY3OTg0NDU1NjhAMTUyNjAyNzAyNTI2Mw%3D%3D&el=1_x_2&_esc=publicationCoverPdf

Paakkanen, M., Martela, F., & Pessi, A. B. (2024). Battling the barriers to compassion in organizations. *Australian Journal of Management*, *50*(3), 836–875.

Parkes, R., Graham-Kevan, N., & Bryce, J. (2018). You don't see the world through the same eyes any more: The impact of sexual offending work on police staff. *The Police Journal: Theory, Practice and Principles*, *92*(4), 316–338.

Sweeting, C., & Bennie, M. (2025). Number of UK officers signed off due to depression and anxiety passes 17,700. *Police Oracle*.

Sondhi, A., Harding, R., & Williams, E. (2025). Segmenting the Rape and Serious Sexual Offence (RASSO) investigator workforce: Implications for wellbeing and burnout. *Police Practice and Research*, *26*(3), 312–324.

Williams, E., Norman, J., Ward, R., & Harding, R. (2022). Linking professionalism, learning and wellbeing in the context of rape investigation: Early findings from Project Bluestone. *International Criminology*, *2*(3), 262–275.

INDEX

Note: Page numbers in **bold** indicate tables, while page numbers in *italics* indicate figures.

For Product Safety Concerns and Information please contact our
EU representative GPSR@taylorandfrancis.com Taylor & Francis
Verlag GmbH, Kaufingerstraße 24, 80331 München, Germany